To
DANIELLA,
ALL THE VERY,
BEST TO YOU,
K B
(WILLIAM B MATSON)

To Daniella
Crazy Horse Grandson
Floyd Clown Sr.

CRAZY
HORSE

CRAZY HORSE

HORSE

The

Lakota
Warrior's
Life & Legacy

THE EDWARD CLOWN FAMILY

as told to

WILLIAM B. MATSON

GIBBS SMITH
TO ENRICH AND INSPIRE HUMANKIND

First Edition
20 19   11 10
Text © 2016 The Edward Clown Family and William B. Matson
Photographs © 2016 as noted throughout the book

Published by
Gibbs Smith
P.O. Box 667
Layton, Utah 84041

1.800.835.4993 orders
www.gibbs-smith.com

Designed by Renee Bond
Printed and bound in the United States

Gibbs Smith books are printed on either recycled, 100% post-consumer waste, FSC-certified
papers or on paper produced from sustainable PEFC-certified forest/controlled wood source.
Learn more at www.pefc.org.

Library of Congress Cataloging-in-Publication Data
Names: Edward Clown Family, authors. | Matson, William B., author.
Title: Crazy Horse : the Lakota warrior's life & legacy : the Edward Clown family / as told to
William B. Matson.
Other titles: Edward Clown family | Lakota warrior's life and legacy, the Edward Clown family
Description: First edition. | Layton, Utah : Gibbs Smith, [2016].
Identifiers: LCCN 2015028841 | ISBN 9781423641230 (alk. paper)
Subjects: LCSH: Crazy Horse, approximately 1842-1877. | Lakota Indians—History. | Crazy
Horse, approximately 1842-1877—Family. | Clown, Edward, 1908-1987—Family. | Lakota
Indians—Biography.
Classification: LCC E99.O3 E48 2016 | DDC 978.004/9752440092 [B] —dc23
LC record available at https://lccn.loc.gov/2015028841

This book is dedicated to all of the Crazy
Horse family members who left before us,
and to the ones who are still here today.

It is also dedicated to William's
father, Emerson N. Matson.

Contents

Foreword

It is rare when a Lakota family is willing to share their family's oral history in detail, even more so when the family is that of the great Lakota leader, Crazy Horse. Crazy Horse was one of the most revered leaders the Lakota ever had. Brave by example, he always put his people first, and they loved him for it. He led his people against the invasion of George Armstrong Custer and the 7th Cavalry, one of the most modern, well-trained, and equipped armies in the United States arsenal in 1876, at the Battle of Little Bighorn, and routed them. It still stands as the greatest defeat of the US military on American soil of all time. Crazy Horse also led his people in victories over the best US military leaders of their day, like General George Crook at the Battle of the Rosebud and Captain William Fetterman at the Fetterman Fight at Fort Phil Kearny.

When the US Army finally did convince Crazy Horse to turn himself in, he did so because he had obtained a promise from the army that his people could continue to roam the sacred Black Hills as they always had. He considered his surrender a small sacrifice compared to what his people's continued presence in the Black Hills meant to them. When he discovered that the promises were all a ruse, he rose up for all to see and fought to be free once again, and was killed doing so. Today Crazy Horse stands as a man who sacrificed himself to maintain the Lakota way of life for his people. He is a shining light for many Lakota who live in the darkness of reservation life.

Edward Clown was the son of Crazy Horse's sister (half-sister by blood—same father, different mother), Iron Cedar. Iron Cedar was raised in the same tipi as Crazy Horse and lived her life among his closest family members. Floyd Clown was raised by Edward Clown and his wife, Amy Talks. Doug War Eagle and Don Red Thunder were raised by another of Edward's sons, Blaine Clown. They all refer to Crazy Horse as their grandfather.

In the Lakota culture, "grandfather" is a term of respect. For actual family members, it is an honoring or sign of reverence for male family members who came before them. In traditional European terms, Floyd, Doug, and Don would actually be considered grandnephews to the famous warrior. However, in the Lakota culture they are grandsons.

A relative in the Lakota culture is precious. And in the time of Crazy Horse, sharing a campsite, visiting relatives in other camps, and going out of the way to greet relatives after they were away for a period of time was done quite frequently. As groups of Lakota surrendered to the army, counting the relatives greeting surrendering Lakota outside the soldier fort and then joining as part of the surrendering group was probable. It also afforded those same relatives a chance to cash in on the extra blankets and rations afforded surrendering Lakota by the US government.

So many books on Crazy Horse are drawn from sources other than those of family members. They are quite often drawn from sources that stress regimented beliefs about indigenous cultures, and people promoting specific agendas. As an example, the use of census and ration and surrender records, although having its purpose, can at times be misleading. It was quite possible that many Lakota were counted more than once, and in more than one place. The language barrier also led to inaccurate information being logged into the formal records, as well as soldiers filling out paperwork with their own assumptions or faulty data. And those historians who maintain that the Lakota people fell in line and willingly gave their information like sheep obviously have never lived among them.

Government documents and notations from the army, tales from missionaries, and stories from contemporary journalists and scholars all have found their way into what has become the accepted historical record about Crazy Horse. The Clown family members felt the need to put their stories into print because so many historians and authors had written what they knew to be inaccurate books about Crazy Horse and other members of their family. They decided it was time to clarify who Crazy Horse was, who their family was, and what they know. The value of what they share here is priceless.

Spending an unlimited amount of time with the Clown family members was an honor and unbelievably enlightening. I saw and heard them in unguarded moments. I saw them angry, I saw them laugh. I saw them cry. I have seen them forgive. I asked obscure questions. Floyd Clown, Doug War Eagle, and Don Red Thunder were gracious and generous enough to answer. They supervised and had the final approval on this manuscript and would only allow it to be published if it remained unchanged. Now that the manuscript is finally in print, you can be assured that it is identical to the one they approved.

Since this is the family's story, it is written from their point of view or in the first person. It would have been disrespectful to write it differently than the way they told it. While they recounted their oral history, they would re-enact their relatives at times by reciting specific lines in a different tone of voice, as though they were speaking as that relative. These lines were repeated word for word as though they were quotes, and they were the same if I asked to hear the story again at a later date. Thus these lines are in quotations throughout the book as a service to the reader.

What happens behind a wall of a home or tipi is normally just that family's business. Private. But today, members of the Edward Clown family have been generous enough to share their family's story as passed down by Iron Cedar. The family has chosen to give this story to the world, albeit under a strict monitoring of my pen to insure that their story remains true to the story their ancestors told. To stay true to the life that Crazy Horse and his family lived.

CHAPTER ONE

We Will Remain Lakota

T he history of North America did not begin with Leif Erikson or Christopher Columbus. Nor did it begin with the Spanish explorers or the Pilgrims. It began with our Native nations. North America had thriving and prosperous nations from the Pacific to the Atlantic Oceans long before the Europeans figured out that the American continents even existed.

The Lakota, Dakota, and Nakota Nation was and is one of these Native nations. Our family is one of the families that make up this nation. We are members of the Crazy Horse family.

We do not like the fact that our history has been painted incorrectly by other cultures. After all, would the United States accept the French or Chinese version of American History? Absolutely not. You would get an identical rejection from the Chinese or French in accepting the American version of their history. So why must our people continue to be defined by other cultures? This is one of the reasons that we need to tell our own history.

Our history was not written down. Instead, it was passed from adult family members to our children. We hope that by putting our oral history in print, we will help our children, grandchildren, and unborn to know it, and at the same time, help other cultures to see us for who we are.

Other cultures call us Native American. This is not what we call ourselves. We are Lakota, Dakota, and Nakota. Native American is the federal government's term used to identify us for accounting purposes. We were already here. We did not wait for Columbus to arrive so we could be "American."

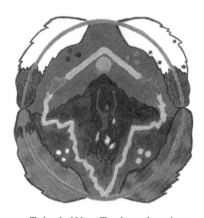

Tashunke Witco Tiwahe trademark. Everything bearing this trademark means that the material has been approved by the Crazy Horse Family. Created by Kyle Clown of the Edward Clown family.

The other cultures that try to define us say our ancestors migrated from Asia to North America. We wish to correct that belief by saying we are native to North America.

Our ancestors' remains are spread all across North America. Their remains are what grow the grass and vegetation that feed and sustain all who live on North American soil. This is why our people and the North American continent are as one.

Our language has always been a spoken one. It had never been written down prior to the early 1900s when American clergymen devised a way to write our words down. They made many mistakes because they were raised in another culture and brought their own cultural baggage and language into the equation.

These other cultures even named us wrong. They called our nation the Great Sioux Nation. The name Sioux was given to us by the early French traders. It was a shortened version of the word *nadouessioux*, which is taken from the Ojibwa Tribe's word *nadouessiouak*, meaning "speaker of foreign tongue." The Ojibwa were an enemy tribe. Many of us have protested being called Sioux, but these other cultures do not listen much.

Lakota, Dakota, and Nakota people speak the same language, but with three different dialects revolving around the sounds made by the letters *l, d,* and *n*. The Lakota group uses the sound of the letter *l* in their speech at the expense of *d* and *n* letters. The Dakota group uses the sound of *d* to replace the sound of *l* and *n* letters, and the Nakota group uses the sound of *n* in place of the sounds of the other two letters. Our Lakota, Dakota, and Nakota names all mean the same thing in English—a word best translated as "ally."

The Crazy Horse family, our family, is Lakota.

We believe that the four-legged, the winged, the insects, the fish, the grass, the trees, the two-legged, and everything else are all here to live in their own way without restraints. They are all equal to each other. We do not believe that one species has the right to dominate all others. We all have the same mother. Our mother is Earth. She is who we owe our lives to.

The spiritual center of our people's world are our sacred Black Hills. The Black Hills are located mostly in what today is western South Dakota. Most of our family's dead are buried there.

Our family has been around for as long as anyone can remember. We carry our legend stories and oral history in our minds and in our hearts. We know legend stories from long ago. Legend stories that took place before our warriors wore eagle feathers in their hair.

One legend story that was passed on to us from our elders tells of the Great Flood. It goes like this:

There was a time long ago when heavy rains exploded from the sky and our Mother the Earth became a sea of water. Our people ran to our sacred Black Hills for refuge because our Black Hills were the birthplace of our people and our first home. Our people were told by the Creator to enter into a cave within our Black Hills to save themselves from drowning.

However, there was one woman who was curious and wanted to stay on the surface. No one could believe that she could be so foolish. The elders begged her to join them in the cave, but she said no because she wanted to watch what was happening. The heavy rain was without end. When the waters rose to a certain point, the Creator sealed off our cave so that we would stay dry. In the process, it locked the woman out.

With the cave sealed, our people lived underground and waited for the flood waters to subside. We were thankful to the Creator for giving us a dry place to stay and survive.

Meanwhile, the woman who had stayed outside had to climb higher to avoid being drowned. Upon reaching the highest point in our Black Hills, the woman began to cry. The flood waters had risen so high that there was no place for her to go and she saw that she was about to drown. She regretted that she had turned a deaf ear to our elders and began to resign herself to dying. Then an eagle swooped down and grabbed her. He held her above the water for a long time.

Finally, the rain stopped and the waters slowly receded to their preflood levels. As they did, the eagle set the woman back on our Earth. Once she was firmly on the ground, she began thanking him for saving her life. Before she had finished her thank-you, the eagle had turned into a young warrior. The young warrior looked no different than other young warriors except for the fact that he now wore an eagle feather in his hair.

Back in the cave, our people were not aware that the flood waters had receded. They stayed inside the cave waiting for a sign to come out. They did not know what that sign would be.

During this time the animals had resumed living their normal lives aboveground. One animal, the wolf, knew where our people were located and how to reach them from the surface. He knew by our people's scent where the cave had reopened to the outside. Inktomi, otherwise known as the spider or trickster, was aware that the wolf knew our people's whereabouts.

Inktomi asked the wolf to take him to our people's cave. When the wolf said he wanted to stay on the surface, Inktomi tricked him by telling the wolf that if he took him into the cave, in return he would show him how to increase his food catches. So the wolf agreed.

As the wolf headed toward the cave, Inktomi hopped on his back and the wolf took him into the cave where our people stayed. Once Inktomi met our people, he tricked them into abandoning the safe confines of their cave and had the wolf lead them back to the surface.

The first of our people to emerge on the earth's surface was named Tokah. Once all our people were on the surface, they marveled at how the vegetation and trees had grown in such wonderful abundance. They saw that all of creation was waiting for them to resume living. After they saw that a good life awaited them, they remembered that Tokah was the one who had been brave enough to be the first of our two-leggeds to step onto the surface. They thanked him and Tokah is remembered in our prayers to this very day.

Finally our people and the woman who had been foolish reunited, and the woman never questioned our elders ever again for the rest of her life.

Legend stories, like the story of the Great Flood, teach us lessons. Lessons we can pass on to our youth.

We also have another kind of story, the stories about our past. It is our oral history, and it teaches us the truth about our people, our ancestors, and ourselves. It teaches us who we are. Our oral history has been passed down from one generation to the next since our people's beginning. It is the way of our people. It is how we define ourselves.

In order for others to understand our oral history, it is important to understand our people's spiritual journey, because we are a spiritual people. Our spirituality is integrated into every move we make and every breath we take. Our spirituality is embedded in what we call Nature's Law.

Nature's Law is a law that exists among the animals. Every animal put on our mother the Earth has its own way including us, the two-leggeds. We are all part of our mother the Earth, and we must remember that our mother the Earth was not created just for us, but for all living things. We must live in harmony with all creation and live our lives with truth and honesty. By allowing all things to live in their own way, we will live as the Creator intended us to.

Our people did this for a long time.

However, after a while our people drifted away from following Nature's Law. We began to make our own rules. Soon we did not know truth and honesty anymore. We became selfish and lost the capacity to understand how to live with respect on our mother the Earth and nearly starved to death. We suffered.

One of the four-leggeds, the buffalo, saw this and took pity on us. He made us his relative. He gave his body to us so we could make our tipis, keep our bellies full, and clothe ourselves so we would stay warm during the cold winter months. He reintroduced the wisdom of sharing. He sacrificed himself so we could survive. We came to look at him as our brother.

This went on for a long time. Our people flourished, our bellies were full, and our world was a happy place once again. Nature's Law had reentered our hearts.

Time passed and we found that somehow we had not learned from the first time and had drifted away from Nature's Law. Once again we lost our way. We forgot about truth and honesty. We again thought of ourselves first and became stingy, threatening our own survival. So our brother the buffalo came to us again, this time as a beautiful woman.

It happened one summer day when two of our young scouts were hunting for game. They happened to spot a white buffalo calf walking toward them. To their amazement the white buffalo calf turned into a beautiful woman. She was dressed in white buckskins with a bundle tied to her back.

The first scout lusted for her. "I want this woman for my own pleasure," he said. "I want to have my way with her."

The second scout did not see her that way. "I would not do that if I were you," he warned. "I believe she is sacred."

The first scout did not listen and reached out to grab her in a lustful manner. As he did, a thick black dust cloud encompassed him. When the dust cloud lifted, all that was left of the first scout was dust.

The second scout knelt and prayed for the first scout. Seeing him pray for his friend, the sacred woman knew that his heart was good. So she chose him to take a message to our people.

"Go tell your people I am coming to see them in four days. I am coming to renew their lives with a sacred bundle. Tell them to form a circle to celebrate this renewal of life, just as the seasons do when they rotate from spring to summer to fall to winter and then back around to spring."

The second scout agreed to do this and hurried to tell our people.

On the morning of the fourth day, our people sat in a circle and waited for the sacred woman to arrive. Soon a white buffalo calf appeared walking toward them. All at once, a whirlwind swirled and the white buffalo calf once again turned into the sacred woman. The sacred woman was called the White Buffalo Calf Pipe Woman.

She told our people that she had brought a gift. She then opened the bundle that had been tied to her back and presented it to our people. It was the Sacred Buffalo Calf Pipe.

Our people marveled.

The bowl of the pipe was made of red stone. The stone represented our mother the Earth. The red of the stone represented the blood of our people that had walked here before us. The stem of the pipe was made of wood and represented all things growing on our Earth. It reminded us of Nature's Law.

The White Buffalo Calf Pipe Woman lit the pipe. As our people watched her, she held the pipe to the sky, then to our mother the Earth, and then to each of the four cardinal directions: east, north, west, and south. She told our people that when they smoked the pipe and prayed, the smoke would carry their prayers to the Creator. Since the Creator is everywhere, the smoke will reach the Creator in all ways and the Creator will listen.

"This is the pipe of truth and honesty," she told them. She handed them the pipe and told them to make sure each generation knows of its power and existence and to make sure it is kept safe. Our people thanked her with all their hearts.

As she got up to leave, she told them that someday she would come back and the sign that she had returned would be the birth of a white buffalo calf. As she walked away, the whirlwind swirled once again and she changed back into a white buffalo calf. Then she disappeared.

We were sorry to see her go and still keep a look out for a white buffalo calf to be born any day.

Today our people have many personal pipes, but there is only one Sacred Buffalo Calf Pipe which is kept safe by our Sacred Buffalo Calf Pipe Keeper, who today resides in the community of Greengrass on the Cheyenne River Reservation in South Dakota.

As time went on, the buffalo continued to stay sacred to us. Our grandparents would follow the buffalo wherever they went so that we could eat and live. Because the buffalo were nomadic, our grandparents became nomadic too. We would still be nomadic today had we not been forced to live on reservations by those cultures who claim to know what's best for us.

In our earlier days, we hunted the buffalo by wearing wolf skins and sneaking up to a herd and killing a buffalo with our bow.

We would also stampede them over cliffs, which we called buffalo jumps. Quite often this required the participation of nearly our entire village. We would line up on either side of a buffalo herd and wave our blankets and hides at them, spooking them into a stampede, which resulted with them charging over the buffalo jump to their death. If we were successful, we had plenty of meat.

We would store this meat by cutting it into thin strips and hanging it out in the sun to dry. Drying it would help keep it from spoiling for long periods of time. Much of the dried meat we ground up by beating it into little pieces with rocks and then mixing in berries and the buffalo's kidney fat to make a treat we called *wasna*. It tastes really good.

Our earliest grandparents used dogs to pull their travois and help carry their belongings from place to place whenever they followed the buffalo. Around the year 1700, the Creator allowed our people to obtain horses descended from those abandoned by Spanish explorers.

The horse changed how we lived. It meant the days of waiting for the buffalo to approach a cliff so we could stampede them with blankets was gone. The horse allowed us to travel about seventy miles on an average day. With that kind of range we could hunt the buffalo wherever we found them because a horse could run as fast as a buffalo, which is about 35 miles per hour. This allowed us to be more frugal in our hunts because now we killed just enough to fill our needs rather than the feast-or-famine approach of stampeding a herd over a buffalo jump whenever the opportunity finally presented itself.

The horse became so important that much of our lives soon revolved around them. In fact, by the time a toddler took his first steps we put him on a horse so that when that same toddler grew into a warrior, his ability to maneuver his horse during the hunt or in battle was second to none. Not even the European invaders very best cavalry came close in comparison. Only when the European invaders killed off our brother the buffalo and caused us to starve did we submit to their demands to live on their tiny islands that they call reservations. We accepted their food in exchange for moving onto these reservations. Our children had to eat. Once they had us there, they took our horses away so they could keep us penned up.

For well over a century these European invaders have used their religion, their money, and the power of their government to try to convince us that living in our Lakota ways is not so good.

However they failed to take our minds away, and so today many of us still have our red Lakota heart. We are still Lakota in the spirit of our grandparents. We have remained spiritual people.

And a spiritual people are never beaten.

CHAPTER TWO

Walks With Sacred Buffalo

O ur knowledge of our family tree was given to us by our family elders.
In understanding any Lakota family tree there are two things that can make it complicated for those who are not familiar with our culture. First, it was not uncommon for a Lakota warrior to have multiple women living as his spouses in the same tipi. Secondly, Lakota men and women changed their names to mark or celebrate important occasions.

We cross-checked our family tree and verified as much of our oral history as we could against government records such as probates, censuses, allotments, rations, and surrender records. The probates were the most important records because only immediate family members can obtain them and they are legal documents that can be used in government courts to determine someone's heirs. The rest of the census, allotment, surrender, and ration records are also useful in following our story, but certainly not as reliable as our oral history. We included many of these government records in the back of this book.

Our oral history has been much maligned by other cultures for many years. These other cultures do not believe that our oral history is the truth because most of them did not grow up in families with strong oral traditions. These other cultures teach their children that when they tell somebody something orally, that by the time it passes through several ears and lips, the story will become different from the original story. We believe this is told to emphasize that the written word is a better way. It is a way of saying that their cultural ways are superior. However, when we look at their written word we quite often wonder why they think it is so much better. If they believe in it so fervently, why do they need lawyers and spin doctors to give oral arguments as to the true meanings of their written words when they have something important to present?

If you speak from your heart, then your words are true and do not change with the shifting winds.

Many of our Lakota people still have the habit of repeating our stories over and over to our young so they will remember them in the right way. The right way is not just letters and words, but the feelings that go with them. We carry our oral history in our hearts. Our oral history has served our people for as many winters as there are blades of grass on the prairie. It is sacred to us.

Unfortunately, during our more recent history some of our people were taken from their parents at a young age by missionaries to attend faraway English-speaking schools, thus losing their chance to learn our oral history at a young age. Our family was fortunate because we were able to raise our own children in our Lakota way. Our children's minds were not poisoned by allowing outsiders to define us or our history.

These other cultures also criticize our people's oral history because sometimes when it is told by different families, the different histories do not totally match. We think these other cultures should look into the mirror. None of their history books are the same, and when they are, they end up suing each other for plagiarism. Our people's history is rich and diverse. Each family has its own story to tell.

To us *Tashunke Witko*, or Crazy Horse, as his name is loosely translated into English, is not only a very spiritual name, but it is our *tiwahe*, or family, name.

The Crazy Horse name was passed from generation to generation. Our Lakota names do not include suffixes like "Junior" or "Senior," so it can be confusing. In this book, we will tell about three generations of head men named Crazy Horse. The youngest of the three Crazy Horses is the one that most people outside of our family know about. He was preceded by a grandfather and father who also carried the same name.

Our first family member to carry the Tashunke Witko name was born in the western part of the Black Hills, where our winter camp was located, in the late 1760s. He was a member of the Minnikojou band of our Lakota people. Our winter camp at that time was located near Hot Springs, South Dakota.

Many outsiders mispronounce our band name *Minni-KO-jou* as *Mini-CON-jou*. Listening to them pronounce it is one way we quietly recognize the difference between those who have spent time among us and those who learned about us through the library. When we say it, the 'n' is silent. So for the sake of this book, we will spell it the same way that we say it among ourselves.

Our Minnikojou band's ways were not always the same as other Lakota bands, just as our family's ways were not always the same as other families. Yet we all understood that we were one nation, and that's all that mattered.

As a young man, our first Tashunke Witko, or Crazy Horse, was fearless when it came to protecting our family, our people, and our camp. During the time he was a warrior, there were seventeen council fires in our band. Each council fire had a head man. Our first Crazy Horse was the head of our family and council fire at a young age. Our family was not a large one at that time, at least not like it is now.

He also was known as a shirtwearer.

Shirtwearer was the title given to those who were appointed to make sure our helpless ones did not go hungry, that our people were protected, and that our Sacred Buffalo Calf Pipe was safeguarded. Our shirtwearers were chosen by a group of our spiritual elders. These spiritual elders would pray, participate in a Sundance, and then make the sacred shirts our shirtwearers would wear. They would bring the sacred shirts to our Sacred Calf Pipe Keeper, who would bless them. After four days of fasting and praying, one of our spiritual elders would announce to our people who our shirtwearers would be. Our Sacred Calf Pipe Keeper would give our newly appointed shirtwearers their shirts, and our people would celebrate.

Our first Crazy Horse was always competing to exceed our other warriors and head men's exploits in both battle and hunting. He had a friendly rivalry with another of our head men and fellow shirtwearer, Black Buffalo. They loved to compete at something we called "counting coup."

Counting coup is touching an enemy with your hand or a special stick and escaping unharmed. It was more prestigious to humiliate an enemy by touching him without consequence than to kill him. Risk of injury or death must be present for it to count as a coup. Our people battled many enemies, including the Shoshoni, Omaha, Arikara, Mandan, Hidatsa, Crow, Assiniboine, Pawnee, Gros Ventre, Piegan, Ojibawa, Sauk-Fox, Ute, Nez Perce, and Winnebago tribes. When a coup was counted, the warrior making it earned an extra feather to wear in his hair or cut an extra notch in his coup stick.

Our first Crazy Horse was of medium build and stood around five feet nine inches tall. When he went to protect our camp, he painted his face with a red lightning bolt. The lightning bolt started at the corner of his eye, extended out to his cheek, and then angled back to the corner of his mouth. From the corner of his mouth, it was drawn down and away to the outer bottom edge of his chin. These lightning bolts were painted on both sides of his face. He decorated his forehead with three yellow *was-u* markings, or hail stones, resembling yellow dots equally spaced in a horizontal row.

A *was-u* is brought by the *wakiyans*. A wakiyan is a thunder being, and it brings the storms along with the thunder and lightning from the west. It can produce rain, wind, hail stones, and snow. It is a powerful being in our culture.

As our first Crazy Horse got older, he found a woman that made him happy, and so they married and had a son sometime around 1810. His wife died shortly after his son's birth, leaving him as the child's lone parent. As the surviving parent, he gave up being a warrior and paid greater attention to his parental side. He did the best he could. He also spent time listening to our elders so he could learn the spiritual ways of our people in more depth.

At fifteen years old, our first Crazy Horse's son counted coup and killed an enemy warrior. It happened while he was returning from a hunting trip. Our hunter's horses were tired and thirsty. One of our elders took them to the river to quench their thirst. A Shoshoni warrior was waiting on a hill among the shadows, watching him. When our elder seemed to be all alone, the Shoshoni warrior rushed him with hopes of stealing the horses and counting coup on him. Once the Shoshoni reached him, he did more than count coup. He killed our elder with his war club.

The Shoshoni was in the process of taking souvenirs off our dead elder when our first Crazy Horse's son saw him. His whole body reeled in shock. The Shoshone warrior had killed and was now robbing someone he knew—someone he respected. So he attacked. He hit the Shoshoni with his war club and knocked him into the water. He then hopped off his horse and pushed the Shoshoni's head under the water with all his might until the Shoshoni's body went limp and he drowned.

The son of our first Crazy Horse rode back into our camp, his entire body was shaking with adrenaline. Upon returning and telling his father, his father calmed him and told him that his actions had made him proud. Our first Crazy Horse then pondered what should be done to recognize his son's brave act in the best way.

He decided to give his son a new name to recognize his new stature as a warrior. However, before he did that, he decided it was important to have his son *hemblecha,* or vision quest, as it is called by other cultures, so that he would know what direction to take in his life and what medicines the Creator wanted him to gather so he could protect himself and our people. The new name required new responsibilities. His son enthusiastically agreed, so he took him to a prairie dog town near a river located west of what is today Hot Springs, South Dakota. He set him out among the prairie dogs with a pipe and a buffalo skull altar to pray.

In our hemblecha, we pray directly to the Creator while fasting. If our prayer comes from our heart, we will receive a vision of what we're supposed to do in our lifetime. We will be told how we're supposed to walk on our Mother the Earth while we're here. And once we are told, we are supposed to follow that vision, because we know that every step during our time on our Mother the Earth is sacred.

Just prior to his son's hemblecha, our first Crazy Horse built a sweat lodge in order to hold a purification ceremony. The ceremony was done to put his son's spirit where it was supposed to be—with the Creator.

Our sweat lodges are made of eight chokecherry, willow, or cedar branches with one end of each branch embedded into the ground and the other end bent over and tied to the other branches to form a domed structure. In the center of the sweat lodge, a small pit is dug into the ground. The structure is covered by buffalo or bear hides, with a place that can be pulled back and used as a door to enter and exit. About three feet outside of the entrance, a mound of dirt is built from the soil taken from the small pit in the center of the sweat lodge. This mound is an altar to the Creator. It is where we plant our staffs and place our sacred pipes. The altar symbolizes the highest point so that the Creator can better hear our prayers.

Outside the sweat lodge, a fire is built and rocks are heated to a fiery glow.

After crawling inside the sweat lodge, our first Crazy Horse and his son sat around the empty pit. All living things are represented inside the sweat lodge, including fire, water, earth, and air. The rocks, which represent the earth, were taken from the fire and brought into the sweat lodge in the claws of a deer antler. The rocks were dropped in the pit as they were brought over from the fire. Then the sweat lodge was sealed up and water was poured over the rocks to make steam, which is the Creator's air. They breathed this air in.

Once the purification ceremony started, our grandfathers from the other side, our Mother the Earth, and our Creator entered and prayed with him. Crazy Horse's son prayed for the animals, the trees, creation, and everything that grows, because they are all like a medicine that has a purpose, which is why the Creator allows them to carry life. He prayed for all people because each person also has a purpose. It is why our heart breathes and why we can draw life from the air. He prayed with Nature's Law beating in his heart.

During his son's hemblecha, our first Crazy Horse and an elder named Old Man Poor Buffalo sang for him while the prairie dogs brought him his medicine from the west and north. This medicine, a root, came from out of the ground. The prairie dogs laid his new medicine upon his buffalo skull altar. His vision told him that if he marked or painted himself, then nothing would harm him.

His markings would be a yellow lightning bolt like his father's, except only down one side of his face. It was painted from his right eye out to his right cheek, then back down to the right-hand corner of his mouth, and finally down to the outer right-hand corner of his chin. He would also carry the three hailstone markings on his forehead like his father, except they would be red.

Once his son had finished his hemblecha, he smoked the pipe. Then our first Crazy Horse took him back to our camp to feed and nourish him. Our first Crazy Horse then held a naming ceremony, where he gave his son a spotted eagle feather to tie onto a buffalo bone, which in turn was tied into his hair. The quill of the feather was painted red. During the ceremony, he passed his own name, Crazy Horse, on to his son and gave himself a new name, Walks With Sacred Buffalo.

Our new Crazy Horse spent the next few days searching for and collecting medicines that the Creator had told him about in his vision that would help protect our people, protect himself, and heal our people's ailments.

In about 1829, Walks With Sacred Buffalo caught one of the diseases brought to North America by those who had come from Europe. He passed away a short time later to the other side. His son, who now carried our family name of Crazy Horse, was nineteen winters old at the time.

During his lifetime, Walks With Sacred Buffalo made an important friend and ally who would eventually become the father of the woman who would give birth to his first grandchild and a leader of our Nation.

CHAPTER THREE

Black Buffalo

W alks With Sacred Buffalo's friend and amiable rival, Black Buffalo, was born where the Muddy and Good Rivers meet around 1760. Today the Muddy River is known in other cultures as the Missouri River. We called it the Muddy River because it is often muddy. The Good River has been renamed by the Americans, and now they call it the Cheyenne River. We called it the Good River because its water was so clear and tasted very good. Like Walks With Sacred Buffalo, Black Buffalo was a member of our Minnikojou band. He stood around 6 feet 4 inches tall and had a husky build. He carried a buffalo horn attached to a rawhide rope. It was his most treasured personal possession and always hung at his side. He is best known outside our Lakota world as the head man that the American explorers Meriwether Lewis and William Clark had a run-in with on the Bad River in 1804.

Prior to his confrontation with Lewis and Clark, Black Buffalo had proven himself to be a brave and honorable warrior and head man. He had taken White Cow, who later took the name Iron Cane, as his wife. White Cow was a good woman who wanted nothing more than to be a good mother. Together they had a son named One Horn around 1794.

As Black Buffalo aged into his forties, he began to assume the role of a traditional elder and spent much of his time showing our young men how to become good warriors and spiritual beings. Our young men had come to respect him very deeply.

During his lifetime, Black Buffalo had earned three eagle feathers to wear in his hair. He earned his first one by participating in our Lakota spiritual ceremonies, a second feather represented his role as our family's head man, and the third denoted that he was a shirtwearer.

In late summer of 1804, White Cow gave birth to his second son, Lone Horn. It had been about a decade in between the birth of this first child and his second. Joy consumed his heart. It was during this time of great happiness that our people summoned him. Our scouts had spotted Lewis and Clark's ship sailing up the Muddy River.

At first our scouts thought Lewis and Clark were French traders, but upon closer observation, they realized Lewis and Clark were a type of people that they had never seen before. They also told Black Buffalo that a group of Santee warriors was following the boat.

The Santees were a band that belonged to the Nakota branch of our nation. They were led by the head man Medicine Buffalo and his son, Tokahongar. Tokahongar roughly translated into English means First One Seen. Tokahongar had been nicknamed "The Partisan" by French traders.

Medicine Buffalo and about two hundred of his warriors had been stalking Lewis and Clark's boat for several days. Their stalking had made the Americans leery of spending time on shore, which was exactly what the Santees wanted. They hoped to keep the Americans sailing until they got to the mouth of the Bad River, where they could confront them on a more favorable terrain because the waters where the Muddy and Bad Rivers met were rough and difficult to navigate.

Medicine Buffalo and his Santees roamed the east side of the Muddy River while Black Buffalo and his Minnikojou roamed the west side. Seldom did they roam as one unit. After a brief council meeting, these two bands decided they would confront the invaders together.

On the evening of September 23, 1804, three of our young scouts swam out to Lewis and Clark's keelboat and invited them to parlay with our head men at the mouth of the Bad River. Both Black Buffalo's Minnikojou band and Medicine Buffalo's Santee band were camped there. The Americans agreed.

The next day, the Americans sailed to the appointed meeting place and caught sight of our Lakota and Nakota men but stayed on their vessel for a reason we did not know.

The following morning, September 25, Lewis and Clark landed on our shore. They were met by Black Buffalo, Medicine Buffalo, and Tokahongar, along with about fifty of our warriors. However, the meeting lacked a reliable interpreter for the Americans because they said they had left their Sioux interpreter downriver to promote peace between another of our Nakota bands and the Omaha tribe. So the Americans relied on a Frenchman named Pierre, who only understood a smattering of our Lakota language. Medicine Buffalo's son Tokahongar knew some French. So between his crude French and Pierre's awful Lakota, they did their best to communicate for us. Unfortunately, it created a real problem for both sides to comprehend exactly what was being said.

It wasn't long before Black Buffalo's young men realized that Medicine Buffalo's young men were scheming to acquire as many supplies as they could from the Americans. Not to be outdone, Black Buffalo's young men began planning to accrue more from the Americans than Medicine Buffalo's warriors. It became a friendly competition, which our warriors are prone to engage in. Lewis and Clark, sensing the escalating aggressiveness of our two bands to secure more and more of their supplies, became defensive, and our meeting became tense.

Black Buffalo, who was still feeling good about the birth of his second son, saw that Lewis and Clark were well armed with very modern weapons and wanted to keep his wife and newborn safe. He worried that if his young men pushed Lewis and Clark too far, the Americans would begin supplying their enemies with these modern weapons or, worse, use them to attack our village. He chose to try to work out a diplomatic solution that would be agreeable to all three groups.

After a while, all parties agreed to move the meeting onto Lewis and Clark's keelboat.

Once on the boat, Black Buffalo's Minnikojou and Medicine Buffalo's Santee negotiated hard and believed that they had come to an agreement where they would both receive an equally large portion of the American's supplies. However, Lewis and Clark must have understood the talks differently, or maybe they were just being slippery. In any event, they gave our head men a drink of whiskey to celebrate whatever they were thinking, ushered our head warriors into a pirogue, and then took our two warrior contingents back to shore.

After landing, Black Buffalo, Medicine Buffalo, and Tokahongar stepped out of the pirogue. They fully expected Lewis and Clark to do the same. However, when the Americans began to head back to their keelboat as though our business was finished, we were all surprised. Three of our young warriors immediately grabbed Lewis and Clark's bowline to prevent their boat from leaving. Our bands wanted the supplies we thought the Americans had agreed to give us. Being held against their will made the Americans angry. Clark yelled at us angrily. Tokahongar returned his anger in kind. The Americans readied their guns. It was at this point that Black Buffalo grabbed the bowline and ordered our warriors away.

Clark treated Black Buffalo's action as an attempt to promote a personal showdown between the two. Clark prepared to do battle. Seeing that Clark was not thinking rationally, Black Buffalo defused his anger by asking if our women and children could come see their vessel.

This was one of the rare moments in these talks that Clark accurately deciphered what Black Buffalo was asking. The request seemed to have caught him off guard and he calmed. He decided to allow Black Buffalo to re-board the keelboat and ride with him to our village, where our women and children were located.

Our Lakota and Nakota watched in awe as Black Buffalo and two of our warriors rode in the keelboat with Lewis and Clark up the river. This was very brave as we were not sure that Lewis and Clark were trustworthy.

Anchoring the boat about one hundred yards from the riverbank where our village was located, Lewis accompanied Black Buffalo into our camp. Once among our people, Black Buffalo asked the Americans to stay for a feast. Lewis, seeing nothing but goodwill, agreed, and Clark joined him in our camp later that afternoon. The feast seemed to impress the Americans greatly, and they countered with some gifts of their own, including coffee. The festivities went into the night.

Meanwhile, Tokahongar and a few of the Santee young men decided they wanted to sleep on the keelboat. They wanted those back in our village to know that they were just as brave as Black Buffalo. Feeling good from the festivities, the Americans agreed.

The following morning, Black Buffalo and a large gathering of our warriors congregated on the riverbank. Black Buffalo asked and was granted his request to re-board the keelboat for another ride up the river. He was seated in the cabin this time. Meanwhile, Tokahongar, the Santee young men, and some of our Lakota young men began to be ushered off the boat by the crew. This made Tokahongar angry. He felt slighted by the Americans and wanted to prove to our people that he was Black Buffalo's equal. He too wanted to ride up the river.

While our warriors watched, Tokahongar showed his outrage and hurled threats at the Americans, so Lewis tossed a tobacco carrot in his direction to shut him up. The tobacco pacified his anger because now he had been given something that Black Buffalo had not. It was a tangible gift he could hold in his hand long after Lewis and Clark had gone. In addition, the fact that he had to fight to get it made it even more impressive. It was as if he had counted coup. This caused Black Buffalo's young men to hunger for the same. The competitiveness in them came to the forefront. Now they wanted their head man, Black Buffalo, to receive the same tribute, to count the same coup in these negotiations.

As the crew prepared to cast off the bowline, a few of our Lakota young men grabbed the line to stop them. Clark, seemingly still in the dark as to what was taking place, became agitated by our actions and complained to Black Buffalo. Black Buffalo rushed onto the deck to survey the situation. After talking to our young men, he turned to Lewis and told him that our warriors were holding the cable in lieu of another tobacco carrot. This seemed to incense Lewis and Clark.

It was the end of September, and we surmised that the Americans were worried about being caught without shelter in the rapidly approaching frigid winter weather that can strike in the plains as early as October. They probably felt the need to get upstream so they could find a place to shield themselves from our mercilessly freezing north winds. Why else would they be in such a hurry?

We also knew they had planned a long trip and might be a little stingy with their supplies, including their tobacco. However, we did not foresee them being so stingy as to tell our head man, Black Buffalo, that there would be no more gifts and summarily order him off the ship.

We believe the Americans underestimated our warriors' respect for Black Buffalo.

Upon observing their stinginess, our Lakota young men became more determined than ever and continued to cling to the line. Seeing that his actions had only made matters worse, Clark ordered his men to prepare their weapons for battle. Our Lakota young men responded by aiming their bows at his ship from the riverbank.

The Americans shouted threats at our people, but still our young men would not budge. They were resolved that the Americans pay tribute to their head man. Black Buffalo countered the American's anger with a bit of his own and asked the Americans what kind of people they were when they were willing to die for a single carrot of tobacco. Lewis suddenly seemed to understand the foolishness of their stand and tossed a tobacco carrot in Black Buffalo's direction.

With that, Black Buffalo jerked the line out from our warriors' hands and allowed the ship to leave. As the ship left, our young men asked Black Buffalo if he wanted them to pursue it. He told them that the tobacco they had received was enough. He was just happy that nobody had died that day and wished to keep it that way.

Grey Horn Butte, also known as Devil's Tower by non-Lakotas. Photo by Bill Matson.

We found the American tobacco was different than ours. We normally filled our pipes with the inner bark of the willow tree, which we called 'chanshasha.' Chanshasha was our true tobacco. However, Black Buffalo came to enjoy the American tobacco, and over the years, he obtained it whenever the opportunity presented itself.

Sometime after the Lewis and Clark affair, Black Buffalo married his second wife, Good Voice Woman. Between her and White Cow, they would bear him four more children, starting around 1810 when White Cow gave birth to his first daughter, Good Looking Woman. The following year, 1811, Good Voice Woman delivered a son to Black Buffalo named Makuhu, or Buffalo Breast Bone, but most historical references refer to him as Hump. White Cow followed that by delivering Black Buffalo two more daughters. In about 1814, she gave birth to Rattling Blanket Woman, and the following year, 1815, she had his last child, who was named Looks At It.

That same year, while camping near a place we call Grey Horn Butte, known to other cultures as Devil's Tower, Black Buffalo received word that he was invited to St. Louis to participate in discussions on a new treaty with the Americans. However, he became too sick to attend, so he sent his twenty-one-year-old son One Horn in his place. He told One Horn to be sure to bring him back some American tobacco and coffee.

After his son left, his health worsened. Our people asked our Sacred Calf Pipe Keeper, who was with them at the time, what to do in order to help Black Buffalo regain his health. Our Sacred Calf Pipe Keeper suggested a Sundance ceremony. He said if we used a live tree in the ceremony to call for his survival, then his spirit might stay. Normally, a cottonwood tree is cut down and brought to the Sundance arena, but by moving the arena to the site of a live tree, we thought that through its roots we could reach inside our

Mother the Earth and make our prayers heard by our Creator in additional ways. So we held a Sundance to keep his spirit with our people. It was held on the banks of the north fork of the Good River, which today is referred to as the Belle Fouche River.

Our Sundance is a way of praying to the Creator. Our prayers are supposed to ask the Creator to maintain the health and survival of our people. The cottonwood tree represents Creation. Everything that lives on our Mother the Earth, including the grass, the trees, and the flowers, looks up at the sun. It is something that the two-leggeds need to do as well, because the sun is the Creator's light and the source of many visions.

Our Sundancers danced around the tree while looking at the sun with a prayer. However, despite our prayers, the sickness ate away Black Buffalo's body and his internal organs began shutting down.

During his final days, Black Buffalo would still load his pipe and smoke. He loved the taste of American tobacco. His fondness for it may have contributed to his sickness. The sickness overwhelmed him in the spring of 1816.

As he lay dying in his tipi, Black Buffalo told his family that he had done the best he could for the Sacred Buffalo Calf Pipe Woman, for his family, and for our people. He told Good Looking Woman and Hump that he was sad that he would not be there to see them grow up. He also regretted that he would not see his baby girls, Rattling Blanket Woman and Looks At It, grow into young women. However, he told them that his heart would always reach out to them from the other side.

Black Buffalo gave his second eldest son, Lone Horn, the horn that he carried at his side. It was a horn from a black buffalo that he had used for all his medicines. He had been carrying it as a result of a vision he had received during a hemblecha in his younger days.

As he gave his horn to Lone Horn, Black Buffalo said, "You have this from me to get yourself strong and ready. You carry a part of me." Lone Horn accepted the horn, and it never left his side for the rest of his life.

Black Buffalo's last act was to give his son One Horn our family's most important possession, our sacred bundle, which carried our family's sacred pipe. Now it was his eldest son One Horn's turn to assume our family's leadership role. He told One Horn to keep our family strong. One Horn assured him that he would.

CHAPTER FOUR

Passing the Sacred Bundle

One Horn was around twenty-two years old when he inherited our family's leadership role. As a warrior and hunter, he was without fear. During hunts he would impress us all by running alongside a buffalo herd, picking out a buffalo, and driving an arrow through its heart. In the mid-1820s, One Horn took a wife, and together they had a son around 1825. His name was Spotted Elk. They cherished every move their young boy made. Family was everything.

One Horn's village normally numbered about six hundred families during this period of time. Around the summer of 1832, One Horn and his wife had a second son.

Left to right: Spotted Elk, Lone Horn, Lone Horn's wife and child, Lone Horn, and Has Sacred Horn, Oglala interpreter, drawn by George Catlin. Identities shown in ceremony to the Edward Clown family. Courtesy Edward Clown family.

It made him very happy, and for the rest of that summer, One Horn spent as much time in our village as he could to be near his newborn son. It was during that time that we saw a thunder boat for the first time. It was sailing up the Muddy River and making a great deal of noise. Other cultures called it a steamship. We could hear it for miles. It scared away the game. The very sight of it was mesmerizing. It stopped near us, and a visitor named George Catlin got out and asked to stay with us. We found him both amusing and harmless. And so we accepted him.

Catlin was an energetic American painter who had journeyed from the east in

One Horn, painted by George Catlin, circa 1832.
Print courtesy of Edward Clown family.

hopes of painting our tribal members. Intrigued by our exuberant guest, One Horn invited him to his tipi. His sisters were already at his tipi visiting. It was windy and One Horn's hair was blowing wildly. His blowing locks covered his face so much that it was hard to tell him from any of his siblings at a distance. Catlin asked One Horn if he could paint him. One Horn agreed and tied up his thick dark-brown hair to pose for the painting.

Catlin painted and drew many pictures that summer. We enjoyed him a great deal. Our tribal members honored Catlin with a Lakota name that meant "Medicine Painter" in English. Catlin left our village later that summer to return to his people in the east.

In about 1833 while One Horn was away on a hunt, an Arikara war party attacked our village and killed his wife and infant son. He was devastated. Luckily his eldest son, Spotted Elk, survived.

One Horn was never the same after that.

The following year, One Horn went on a buffalo hunt in the Stronghold area along with his brother Lone Horn and a few other warriors. The Stronghold area was normally the location of our fall camp because of the abundance of buffalo that migrated there as colder weather approached. For us, fall was the time to secure plenty of buffalo meat to store for the winter. The Stronghold, or Slim Buttes as other cultures call it, is

Southern Slim Buttes, also known as the Stronghold. Photo by Bill Matson.

located in the northern Black Hills near the northwest corner of what is now the state of South Dakota.

One Horn had always been known for his daring ways during buffalo hunts. One of those ways was to ride up on a buffalo while on horseback, jump off his horse, grab the buffalo by the horns with one hand, and then take his knife with the other hand and slit its throat. His younger brother Lone Horn had seen him do this and was determined that he would do it too.

As a buffalo herd came into sight, Lone Horn broke for one of the buffaloes and tried jumping on it as he had seen his brother do. However things did not go so well, and Lone Horn landed wrong, breaking his leg. Luckily the Creator smiled on him, because a buffalo can easily kill a two-legged when angered. The buffalo spared him and kept running. Our warriors who had accompanied them helped Lone Horn back to camp. One Horn decided to stay out and chase down one more buffalo. He told our warriors he would join them later.

When the day was nearly done, our warriors noticed that One Horn had not shown up at our camp, so they went back to the place where they had left him. As they fanned out to find him, one of our warriors saw an ominous sight. It was a buffalo with bloodied horns. As he followed the buffalo's bloody trail to its origin, our warrior found One Horn's horse standing over its dying rider. Word of his condition quickly spread, and our warriors hurried to bring him back to our village. Once they brought him back to his tipi, his brother Lone Horn, even with his broken leg, struggled to be by his side. As One Horn lay dying, he gave his brother our family's most treasured possession, the sacred bundle.

Touch the Cloud. Courtesy Edward Clown family.

"Keep our family safe and strong," he said.

"I will," vowed Lone Horn.

One Horn died that night. His surviving son, Spotted Elk, was taken in by Lone Horn and his wives. They raised him as if he were their own.

Lone Horn had seven wives, but he found that four of his wives could not have children, so he gave them back to their families. He kept his wives that were fertile. His fertile wives were all daughters of the warrior Red Leaf. Their names were Stands On Ground, Wind, and Stiff Leg. Red Leaf was the younger brother of a Minnikojou head man named Yellow Leaf.

Stands On Ground, who had a second Lakota name, Little Old Woman, was the eldest and first of his wives to get pregnant. She gave Lone Horn a boy named Touch The Cloud around 1839. As an adult, Touch The Cloud grew to be incredibly tall, hence the name.

Wind became pregnant shortly afterwards and gave him his second child, a daughter named Four Horses. The following winter, Stands On Ground became pregnant again and gave birth to another son, named Frog, about 1843.

Stiff Leg, being the youngest, spent most of her time tending to Lone Horn's adopted son, Spotted Elk, and taking care of their campsite while her sisters were limited by their pregnancies. This made Stiff Leg jealous that her older sisters had children of their own and she did not, so she ran away. Her disappearance upset Lone Horn.

As a result, Lone Horn went to visit his mother, White Cow, and threw himself down in her tipi with a fit of anguish and told her Stiff Leg had run away to the north.

White Cow told him, "Your wives are her sisters. Take your oldest wife and go after her. If you want her, you have to go get her."

So Lone Horn gathered up Stands On Ground and they went after Stiff Leg. When they caught up with her, she told them she had left him because she wanted a child of her own. Lone Horn told her that if she came back he would get her pregnant, so she agreed to return. About two months later, she became pregnant with Lone Horn's second daughter, Her Iron Cane.

Stiff Leg gave birth to Lone Horn's third daughter, named Plenty Clothes, a short time later.

Stands On Ground had two more children. They were a boy named Standing Elk, born around 1855, and a girl, born about 1862, named Two White Cows who later married and became Ida Crow.

Stiff Leg's final child was a boy named Talks About Him, born approximately 1850. Things were good for Lone Horn. The Creator had blessed him with a family he could be proud of.

*　　*　　*　　*　　*

We are direct descendants of Talks About Him. When Talks About Him grew up, he took White Weasel as his wife, and together they had a daughter named Ellen Talks. Talks About Him then took a second wife, named Otter Woman, around 1873. Otter Woman was the daughter of Cheyenne head man Dull Knife. He had two daughters with the same Otter Woman name, and the one that Talks About Him took was the younger of the two.

White Weasel did not want to share her tipi with a Cheyenne, so she separated from Talks About Him. She took their daughter, Ellen Talks, with her.

Otter Woman had four children with Talks About Him: Yellow Leaf, who in later life became known as George Talks; Takes the Horses, who in later life became known as Charley Talks; Red Leaf, who in later life became known as Peter Talks; and a daughter named Book Agnes Talks. She got the name "Book" because she carried the bible. Red Leaf and Yellow Leaf were named after Stiff Leg's father and uncle.

*　　*　　*　　*　　*

Lone Horn had more to worry about than just his immediate family. As head of our family, he had three sisters to watch over until they were matched with a man.

CHAPTER FIVE

A New Life

When Walks With Sacred Buffalo died in 1829, his son, our second warrior to be given the name Crazy Horse, found solace with his friends. Foremost among them was Black Buffalo's youngest son, Hump. Hump had grown into a powerfully built man like his father, and he, too, stood about six feet four inches tall. Crazy Horse and Hump were inseparable and continuously went on hunts, pony-stealing raids, and war parties together.

During the summer solstice of 1838, our second Crazy Horse was chosen as a shirtwearer. A shirtwearer's sacred duty was to protect our people, especially the elderly, women, and children, in all ways. Normally shirtwearers were chosen by our spiritual elders to wear the shirts for either four or seven years, and sometimes even their entire lives. The visions our spiritual elders received in their ceremonies determined the length of time. Our second Crazy Horse was told he would be a shirtwearer for seven years.

About this time, our second Crazy Horse began to notice Hump's second youngest sister, Rattling Blanket Woman. Around 1839 Rattling Blanket Woman's elder sister, Good Looking Woman, married a prominent warrior from the Oohenonpa band. The Oohenonpa, or Two Kettles band, was another band of our Lakota Nation. This made Rattling Blanket Woman next in line to be claimed by a man.

Rattling Blanket Woman had a smooth, light complexion and long sandy-brown hair. Crazy Horse, who had a dark complexion with black hair, would visit her with a buffalo robe in hand and ask her elder brother, Lone Horn, if he could talk with her. Once Lone Horn consented, they would meet outside the tipi, and he would bring her under his robe to keep their conversations from being overheard. He told her how wonderful she was and how he could not imagine being happy in a tipi without her. Her giggle and blush gave her feelings away. She really wanted to be the woman in his tipi, and she told him so. Knowing that their love was mutual, Crazy Horse set out to make Rattling Blanket Woman his wife.

When asking a Lakota family for the hand of one of their women, it is customary to offer horses to the head of the family. So Crazy Horse put on his best outfit and gathered up his tiny herd of three horses and led them over to Lone Horn's tipi. Upon entering Lone Horn's tipi, Lone Horn summoned the elder women of his family and made them part of the group that Crazy Horse had to win over. They feasted and told stories, and then came the moment of truth. Crazy Horse asked them if they would consent for Rattling Blanket Woman to be his wife. The tipi went silent, and all eyes turned to Lone Horn.

"What do you have to offer?" Lone Horn asked.

Crazy Horse tore back the tipi cover and revealed three horses. He smiled broadly. Lone Horn and the women peeked out, and the women's faces dropped in disappointment. Lone Horn saw their disappointment and turned to his sister's suitor.

"It's not enough," he said.

Crazy Horse's smile disappeared into stunned shock.

"She is better than that," Lone Horn asserted firmly. Crazy Horse exited the tipi, picked up the lead rope on his horses, and slowly trod back to his empty tipi.

He felt hurt and embarrassed. He had been told that what he had to offer for the love of his life wasn't good enough. At first he was depressed, but then he thought, "What does Rattling Blanket Woman think? Has she mislead me? Am I being tested?" There was only one way to find out.

He grabbed his courting robe and decided to pay her another visit. When he showed up at her tipi, her relatives were both surprised and pleased to see him. They liked his determination to continue to pursue her after what had happened. It said something about his character and devotion to her, and they allowed him to see her again.

Once they were both underneath his robe, he asked her if she still wanted to marry him. She told him she did. Then he asked her what it would take for her brother and the elder women to consent to their union. She told him that she didn't know, but that she would talk to them and ask them to accept his three horses as enough. They both knew they were meant to be together, and now she was going to try to remove the last obstacle. They went back to their respective tipis that night dreaming that she would succeed.

The next morning, her pleas to her family were met with understanding eyes and quiet mouths.

Later that day, Crazy Horse brought his three horses over once again and met with Lone Horn and the women. But once again, they turned him down.

He went back to his tipi distraught and tore into his belongings to find all the hides and parfleches that he owned so he could add them to his three-horse offer. Once he was able to stockpile these added belongings, he marched back over to ask her family for her hand one more time. One more time they said no.

Befuddled by his continued rejection, Crazy Horse turned to his best friend, Hump, and asked for help. Crazy Horse figured that Hump, being one of Rattling Blanket Woman's brothers, could find out what the family wanted.

"I talked to my mother and she told me that they want eight horses. There are four of our women that want horses, and they want two apiece," Hump reported.

"Eight horses? I don't have eight horses," a desperate Crazy Horse replied. He thought for a moment and came up with a plan.

"I'll steal some horses from our enemies."

"When?" asked Hump.

"The next good day."

"I'm going with you. I can think of no better man than you to become my brother."

They exchanged a heartfelt smile and readied themselves for the next good day that they could go on a raid together and bring back some horses.

The day of the raid came, and the sky was gray. A wind blew a steady cadence, causing the cottonwood leaves to rattle.

A group of about thirty Crow warriors had just finished a buffalo hunt and were in the process of carving up the meat. The Crows seemed to be in high spirits.

Crazy Horse and Hump watched from the crest of a knoll.

"I see many horses," smiled Crazy Horse.

"And many Crow," Hump smiled back.

"Some of the horses have loads of meat on them. Do you think that's enough to please your family?"

"It pleases me."

The two friends, or kolas, as they referred to each other in our Lakota language, crawled through the grass back to their horses. Once they mounted, they rode whooping and yelping towards the Crow hunting party, catching them by surprise. The Crow warriors nearest their horses mounted to meet them. Crazy Horse and Hump turned their horses around, and the Crow gave chase over the rolling plains, through heavily wooded gullies, and finally into a creek.

It wasn't long before Crazy Horse and Hump had eluded their pursuers long enough to circle back to the horses the Crow had left behind with one of their youngsters. Among these horses was a group of sixteen near the outer perimeter of the herd. Four of these horses were loaded with meat and hides. They cut these horses from the herd before the youngster noticed and herded them back to our village.

Once inside our village, Crazy Horse and Hump escorted the horses to Lone Horn's tipi. As they did, Rattling Blanket Woman spotted them, and her heart burst with joy. Our people emerged from their tipis. The men whooped and the women trilled.

Lone Horn and the women greeted Crazy Horse warmly and could no longer refuse him. Their previously quiet mouths now chattered excitedly. They had a feast with the meat he had brought back on some of the captured horses. Rattling Blanket Woman became his wife that fall.

Life was good.

In 1840, our women gathered at Crazy Horse's tipi during the spring, when our wakiyans, or lightning and thunder beings, come. Rattling Blanket Woman was about to have Crazy Horse's baby.

She had had her contractions, and now her pain was blinding. It was as though a rawhide rope had been put around her waist and was tightening with each new moment. Our women wiped her sweat with warm water, held her hand, and gave her encouragement. As was our tradition, the men stayed away, including the baby's father. But his heart was at her side. He could think of nothing else.

Finally the baby arrived without a whimper. The women cut his umbilical cord and tied it with a deerskin strap. They cleaned the newborn with warm water and sweetgrass and wiped him down in bear grease. After wrapping the baby in a deerskin, they handed him to Rattling Blanket Woman. Suddenly her pain was a distant memory as she held her newborn child, a boy. As he lay in her arms, his memory of his previous world faded, and his senses were flooded with her scent. She would be his life during his infancy, and he would be hers.

His father, Crazy Horse, was summoned. It was a proud time for the new parents. They named their child *Ca-oha,* which means "Among The Trees" or "In The Wilderness." To them he was a part of all creation, which made him sacred. They gave him the nickname Curley.

Young Ca-oha had smooth, light skin and sandy-brown hair like his mother. He had dark-brown eyes, and during the summer months, his hair would quite often become a lighter brown. His mother would dote on him, and as was the case with most Lakota children, she would allow him to learn by doing things himself without interfering. In that way, he was also able to learn from Creation directly.

Being a father gave Crazy Horse the best feeling he had ever known. Rattling Blanket Woman wanted to enhance that feeling and give him a second child. So they attempted to conceive again. They attempted for the next four years. After awhile, Rattling Blanket Woman started feeling frustrated over their lack of success.

During the spring of 1844, Crazy Horse was leading some of our young warriors on a buffalo hunt in the northern Black Hills. It was the time of year when the buffalo herds begin to migrate towards the east. While searching for buffalo, he heard the sounds of battle coming from a nearby valley and led our warriors to investigate.

When they arrived, they saw about sixty Crow warriors attacking a Lakota village at a seasonal creek called Iron Cedar Creek, located near what is today the South Dakota and Wyoming border on the ridges northwest of Interstate 90.

Iron Cedar Creek got its name from the petrified wood in the forest that surrounds the creek. The Crow had come to steal horses, supplies, and whatever else they could get. The Lakota village would not give them up without a fight.

Crazy Horse led our warriors into the village and chased the attacking Crow all the way back into what are now the hills of Wyoming.

Once the Crow had been chased away, Crazy Horse and our warriors returned and were thanked by the village's head man, Corn, or *Wagmeza* as he was known in Lakota. Corn, born around 1798, was very sad because he had lost both his wife Iron Between Eyes and his brother Little Hawk during the battle. They buried them both near Iron Cedar Creek.

Corn was a proud man and made sure to show his gratitude to Crazy Horse and our warriors for helping to save the rest of his family. He fed them and told them where he had last seen the buffalo herds. He then asked them to stay for a giveaway.

A giveaway is part of our cultural tradition. It happens when we have either something to celebrate or when we lose someone dear. When we lose someone dear, our traditional cultural ways tell us to give away everything that we own and start over.

In this case, Corn had lost his wife and brother. So Corn offered his two eldest daughters to Crazy Horse to take as his wives. The two daughters were Iron Between Horns, who was about twenty winters old at the time, and Kills Enemy, who was around eighteen winters. He had a third daughter, Red Leggins, who was about fifteen winters old. He had not included her in the giveaway. However, Red Leggins asked him if she could be included because she wanted to stay with her sisters. Corn agreed and offered all three to Crazy Horse.

Corn was still suffering from a previous loss at the time. Not only had he lost his wife and brother in the raid, but he had

Corn, painted by George Catlin, circa 1832.
Print courtesy of Edward Clown family.

recently lost his eldest son, Bull Head, who was only twenty-six winters old when he passed away earlier that year.

Bull Head's death happened after he had been having dreams that beckoned him west near a sacred rock called "The Rock Belonging to the Black Tail Deer" in what is now known as southwestern Montana. The Cheyenne knew this rock as Deer Medicine Rock, which is what most other cultures call it today. Four medicine men accompanied him there to help him on a hemblecha. While Bull Head was on a hill, crying for his vision, the medicine men left to find medicines.

When the Creator showed Bull Head his vision, it was not good. The vision told him that his family and our people would be wiped out by the soldiers and government of the European invaders, who we called *Wascius*, coming from the east. Wascius means "fat gatherer" in our Lakota language, as in only taking the best or fat of the land for themselves and leaving the scraps for the rest of us. Their name described how they behaved. He did not want his vision to come true, so he asked the Creator to take him to the other side in exchange for letting his family and our people live. The Creator heard his prayer and took him.

When the medicine men returned to bring Bull Head back from his vision, they found him dead. The Creator had already prepared him for burial.

One of the medicine men was a member of the Minnikojou's Lame Deer family and wondered why this had happened. It was at this point that a black-tail deer came and

Bull Head's
Grave

Drawing of Bullhead's grave made by local Rosebud County artist E. W. Gollings in 1902. A felled tree from a storm scattered the rocks years later. Courtesy of Jack Bailey's family collection.

communicated to him that this area was to be a future spiritual haven for our people. The black-tail deer told him that a sandstone rock west of Bull Head's hemblecha site had been marked by a bolt of lightning and the rock now possessed the medicine to foretell our future. No one knew how to put this medicine to use and learn our future until the summer solstice of 1876.

Having lost his son, wife, and brother in such a short span of time, plus knowing he must now take care of his brother Little Hawk's suddenly fatherless family, as is our Lakota custom, Corn felt overwhelmed. He decided his girls would have a better chance at happiness with Crazy Horse. So they became part of the give away.

Crazy Horse thought about Corn's proposal long and hard and decided to accept the three girls and bring them back to our village along the White Earth River, which runs through what is today the Pine Ridge Reservation in South Dakota. It is known to other cultures as the White River.

Corn took the wife of his deceased brother into his tipi along with her three daughters and her one-year-old son, who was now given his father's name of Little Hawk, to take care of them. (Little Hawk's eldest daughter grew up to take a man named John Two Moons of the Cheyenne tribe, and she became known as Elizabeth Two Moons, while his middle daughter, Plays With Earth Woman, grew up to marry Patches The Robe. We do not know the third daughter's name.)

When Rattling Blanket Woman saw Crazy Horse lead Corn's daughters into their tipi, she was stunned. She thought because she had been unable to conceive since she gave birth to Ca-oha that she had now become expendable.

Corn's daughters showed they were anxious to prove their worth. They took over all the women's chores at Crazy Horse's tipi, including keeping the fire going and even taking care of Ca-oha. Although the daughters still regarded Rattling Blanket Woman as

Crazy Horse's first wife and the elder woman in the tipi, in Rattling Blanket Woman's mind it wasn't enough.

One night she disappeared.

Once we discovered her gone, Crazy Horse and the rest of our camp went looking for her. On the second night of her disappearance, one of our men looked up into one of the trees along the White Earth River and saw her. She had hung herself. We took a deep breath and cut her down.

In his sorrow, Crazy Horse cut his long hair off with a knife and tied it with sinew. He put it with her so a piece of him could accompany her to the other side. Then we performed a quick burial. An *enochmaya* is what they call it in Lakota, which translates as a "hiding." Just certain family members were allowed to prepare her, and we buried her immediately into the ground without putting her up on a scaffold first. Crazy Horse did not fully understand why she had done this and was at a loss to explain it to anyone, including his son.

Ca-oha did not understand death. He was too full of life, and it was his mother, Rattling Blanket Woman, that had given it to him. Now she was gone. We tried to keep Ca-oha away from her grave, but he knew where she was and would not be denied. It broke Crazy Horse's heart to watch him, and he did not know how he could make his son's world right ever again.

A grieving Crazy Horse gave up his shirtwearer status to spend more time with his son and the Creator. His new wives had yet to experience raising a child and were mystified as to how to help Ca-oha get over the loss of his mother in a way Ca-oha would understand and accept. With the loss of his first true love, Crazy Horse decided to start his life all over again in a spiritual way. He would spend the next four years experiencing our hemblecha and Sundance all over again. During that time, he could not be with any of his wives.

Good Looking Woman, upon hearing of her sister's death, left her Oohenonpa husband and hastily rode to Crazy Horse's camp.

"Where did you put my sister?" she asked.

They showed her the place on the hill where she had been buried. Once she realized that her sister was really dead, she cried a long time. Good Looking Woman's life had not been good with her husband. She had failed to conceive any children in their five years together, and he was not happy about it. She had suffered from one of the white man's diseases when she was younger, and it had left her barren, but she did not know it at the time. In hopes of having a child, she and her husband had gone to a medicine man in order to doctor her into a fertile state. However, it wasn't long before the medicine man found that she would be forever barren, and he told her the bad news. Knowing this and knowing how disappointed her husband was, she left him. Yet deep down inside she had not given up on being a mother, and she knew Ca-oha would need someone special.

"I want to be one of your women," she told Crazy Horse with tears glistening. "I want to replace my younger sister so I can take care of her boy."

Crazy Horse heard her. He saw how much it meant to her, but he had no desire to take another wife. With Corn's daughters, he had all he wanted. But he saw the wisdom in her offer to raise his son. Ca-oha would have many questions about his mother—questions that an elder sister that grew up in the same tipi as his mother could answer. They would be answers that would bring his mother to life and not remind Ca-oha of her death. He looked at her with his heart.

"Help him grow. It will be good to have you here."

And so she stayed.

Good Looking Woman felt a new life enter into her heart, and she took charge of our family tipis. Corn's daughters treated her as their elder and listened to her.

Good Looking Woman stood around five feet six inches tall and had light skin and dark sandy-brown hair, with a build similar to her sister, Rattling Blanket Woman. She had a vast knowledge of medicines and other remedies that had helped other family members heal from many different sicknesses and wounds. It was her dream to be a mother, and although her sister's death was the worst possible way to become one, she gave herself to Ca-oha and never looked back. Ca-oha ended up calling her "mother," and she called him "son."

Good Looking Woman's youngest sister, Looks At It, who had their father's huskier build, was the tallest of Black Buffalo's daughters. She also helped mother Ca-oha. Looks At It had a strong spirit and was able to take care of herself even in the most difficult circumstances. She had her own tipi, her own travois, and was an excellent hunter.

Previously, Looks At It had married a man named Stands Up For Him shortly after Rattling Blanket Woman had married Crazy Horse. Looks At It and Stands Up For Him had a son whom they had lost to a disease the European invaders had brought to our land called whooping cough. They buried him in what is today the Slim Buttes area.

Once they lost their boy, Stands Up For Him tried to take her south to be with his family and away from ours. She refused to go, and when he tried to force her, she left him with bruises. After that, we gave her a new name—They Are Afraid Of Her—and she came back to stay with our family for the rest of her life.

Both Good Looking Woman and They Are Afraid Of Her spent a great deal of time helping little Ca-oha heal. Both of these women had beautiful hearts.

CHAPTER SIX

The Coming of the Americans

Ca-oha spent much of his childhood learning to live with nature. They Are Afraid Of Her helped him to do this by teaching him to shoot straight and true with a toy bow that fired arrows with hide balls filled with buffalo hair on their tips. Learning this skill would serve our people well whenever our stomachs growled for food. He spent hours and hours in the woods learning the language of the animals. He would sit still and watch the deer wander close. When the deer caught his scent, it knew that his heart was good, and it would tell him how to observe their body language so he could recognize if any danger was near. He learned to watch the birds and to learn of changes in the weather. When he wasn't with nature, he was listening to Good Looking Woman tell him our family history day after day so he would know who he was and where he came from. He was raised to be a good Lakota.

Corn, along with his entire family, had now come to live with Crazy Horse's family, and Ca-oha's favorite playmate and best friend was Corn's nephew and adopted son, Little Hawk. They called each other brothers and learned many of our ways together under the skins of our family's tipis.

Around 1847 Crazy Horse completed his spiritual rebirth after losing Rattling Blanket Woman. This meant he could now be with Corn's daughters. Since Red Leggins was now old enough to join her sisters as one of Crazy Horse's wives, they decided to announce their marriage to our entire village.

Corn, as the father of all the wives, called together all our men and told them the story of how his daughters had become Crazy Horse's wives. Then our women served buffalo meat to all in attendance.

In a related ceremony, Little Hawk's widow, who was Corn's new wife, announced to all our family's women that Iron Between Horns, Kills Enemy, and Red Leggins were now the wives of Crazy Horse. Each of his wives was given a buffalo robe that was painted with Crazy Horse's colors on the part of the robe that sat on their shoulders. His colors were red and yellow, the same as his face paint colors.

We are direct descendants of this second Crazy Horse and Red Leggins.

As a boy, Crazy Horse had grown up without brothers and sisters, and he vowed that Ca-oha would not suffer the same fate. So the following year, Crazy Horse and his youngest wife, Red Leggins, had their first daughter, Shell Blanket.

Shell Blanket brought a new joy and excitement to our family. She got her name from a gift Iron Between Horns gave her youngest sister—a blanket with snail shells tied onto it. It had belonged to their mother, Iron Between Eyes. Red Leggins used the blanket to wrap her daughter in, and the rattle of the shells gave the newborn her identity.

Nine year old Ca-oha reveled in the fact that he had a sister of his own, which pleased Crazy Horse immensely. Being nine winters older and realizing his connection to her, Ca-oha felt a sense of responsibility that he had never known before: the responsibility of preserving and protecting our way of life for those who came after him.

At about the same time, there were ominous signs coming from the east. As Ca-oha grew up, he saw more and more of the European invaders encroaching on our people's hunting grounds. Those hunting grounds were central to our way of life. At first it was a trickle, but around 1849 they began to come in greater numbers, riding in their covered wagons on their way west to gather up the shiny metal that they called gold.

As he entered his tenth winter of life, Ca-oha had graduated from killing small game like rabbits and chipmunks to killing deer and elk. While doing this, he had learned to stalk his prey without making a sound. He had also learned to cut his kill's meat up in order to keep it compact so he could bring it back to our camp and share it. These skills had been developed under the watchful eye of his aunt They Are Afraid Of Her. Ca-oha loved to see the proud smiles that erupted from our family's faces when he rode in with fresh meat.

They Are Afraid Of Her had also taught him the value of living in harmony with our Mother the Earth. In addition, he had learned our basic Lakota belief that we belong to the earth and that the earth does not belong to us. While Good Looking Woman had taken over as the mother of his heart, They Are Afraid Of Her had taken over as the mother of his spirit.

That same year, 1849, all three of Crazy Horse's wives bore him children. Red Leggins gave birth to a child they referred to as their Sacred Girl. She was stillborn. They buried her near our family's Bear Creek campsite, which is located seven miles east of what today is Dupree, South Dakota. Iron Between Horns had his second child that year, a son named High Horse. Later that same year, Kills Enemy had twins that died shortly after birth. Losing Sacred Girl and the twins was hard on them, so our family concentrated on the positive and doted over little High Horse to make him strong. It was the way of our family and our people.

The following year, Red Leggins gave birth to a son named Combing. Combing got his name from his thick head of hair that he constantly had to keep brushed or combed back from covering his face.

As our family grew, so too did the influx of the European invaders on their way west. It was a mystery to us why the European invaders liked the shiny metal so much. Anyone could see that it was too soft to have any practical use. However, that didn't seem to matter to them, and to make matters worse, they would kill our buffalo and other game

Oregon Trail wagon wheel ruts still remain today in the sandstone located
near Guernsey, Wyoming. Photo by Bill Matson.

that we depended on for food when they passed through our hunting grounds. They
would leave their garbage along the roads they used. Their wagon wheels cut deep scars
into our Mother the Earth that have not yet totally healed to this very day. Our people
were not pleased by this and demanded that the European invaders, or Americans, as
they called themselves, repair the damages.

The Americans called their nation the United States. Their nation was mostly made
up of the European invaders, or what we referred to as the white people.

In 1851 the United States government decided to do something about our complaints. They asked our people, along with many other Native tribes, some of them our
enemies, to a meeting at a soldier fort called Fort Laramie. This fort was located where
the Swimming Bird River, now renamed the Laramie River, joined the north fork of
the Shell River, now renamed the North Platte River, in what is today southeastern
Wyoming. The Americans promised us gifts if we would attend.

Crazy Horse did not attend the Fort Laramie meeting. He did not understand why
our people should have to touch a pen to the white man's paper saying where we lived.
He already knew where we lived and figured anything that came out of it would be han-
dled by our elders. Besides, he was still glowing from the birth of his third son, Combing.
Making sure his growing family was fed and protected was more important to him than
meeting with the white people. Furthermore, he knew his brother-in-law Lone Horn was
going, so he deferred our family's interests to him.

Attending the Fort Laramie meeting with Lone Horn were around ten thousand
other Natives from various tribes, including our tribe. These Natives brought along their
horses, which were said to have numbered about thirty thousand. In fact, there were
so many horses, the grass around Fort Laramie was not plentiful enough to feed them.

Unfortunately the American government took so long to organize the meeting that some of our horse's ribs began to show. Finally, the government officials moved the meeting to a new place called Horse Creek, which is situated on what is now the border between Nebraska and Wyoming, so our horses would have something to graze on.

Once the meeting started, the US government asked all the tribes to stop fighting with each other because they wanted to keep things safe for their people to cross over our lands. We agreed to this only because we did not trust that they would give us our presents otherwise. They also agreed to give us more gifts every year for fifty years if we would leave the American immigrants alone when they traveled over our lands.

The government had one other unusual request. They wanted only one of our head men to speak for all our people. We had never heard of such a thing. We had head men that spoke for their families but never a head man that spoke for all the families at once. We wondered how this new head man could know what was in all our minds. It was a US government dream that made no sense. If one of our people had a good point or disagreed, they had the right to go their separate way. It was one of the beauties of being Lakota. We would not choose one, so the government chose one for us. They chose a warrior called Conquering Bear.

Conquering Bear was not happy to be in such an impossible position, but he said he would try his best. So we finally got our presents, and we all went our separate ways and planned to meet back at Fort Laramie every year at about the time the chokecherries ripened to pick up our annual gifts.

When the chokecherries ripened the following year, our people returned to Fort Laramie. We found that the government did not have our gifts ready. Needless to say, our relationship was off to a rocky start. After a bit of a wait, the gifts finally arrived. We accepted them and went our separate ways. We did not like the fact that they were late but we were happy the Americans had kept their word.

That summer and fall were kind to us, and there was plenty of game. Our people had many smiles to go with their full bellies. As fall turned into winter, we began to huddle inside our tipis to stay warm. That winter was extremely cold.

During that winter, a hungry and desperate Nez Perce elder and what was left of his ravaged family came to Lone Horn's camp carrying a Lakota sacred pipe. He had been given the sacred pipe by a Lakota warrior who had roamed further north. The Nez Perce elder told Lone Horn that the young men in his family had been wiped out by enemies and all that was left of his family were the women, children, and elderly. He asked if they could take shelter in our village until they regained their strength. Lone Horn saw how weak and hungry the elder and his family were and took pity on them, even though we had a history of fighting the Nez Perce. In fact, our relationship with the Nez Perce was such that had the elder not shown us his sacred Lakota pipe, he would have been killed.

Our family spent a lot of time with this Nez Perce family. We talked to them through sign language and occasional words that we picked up from listening to them. Young Ca-oha spent time with them as well when his father and the rest of our family spent part of our winter in Lone Horn's camp, which was located at Black Horse Butte.

Ca-oha would visit their tipi to learn how these people lived and prayed. He began to respect these people, and in turn, they liked him too. Among the Nez Perce family's possessions was a bright, beautiful, and thick red blanket. It caught everyone's eye.

The Nez Perce family stayed for two moons, and when spring finally arrived, they thanked Lone Horn for his generosity and rewarded him with the red blanket—the one that all our people wished they could have. Lone Horn accepted their gift and passed it to his sister Good Looking Woman. A good blanket like that one was always prized by our women. Having it pleased Good Looking Woman, and she stored it away in a leather pouch. She wanted to keep it looking nice for a special occasion. It stayed in the leather pouch for many years.

As spring turned to summer, the time to collect our gifts at Fort Laramie came upon our people once again. One of our head men, Little Brave, took the lead and brought our Minnikojou band to Fort Laramie. Neither Crazy Horse nor any of our family accompanied him, but what happened that summer would affect our entire tribe and set the table for a war that would last nearly a quarter of a century.

Once again our gifts from the government were late and some of our people became bored waiting.

Near Fort Laramie, the American soldiers operated a barge, or large raft, that was attached to a rope that ferried their people and military supplies back and forth across the Shell River. During our wait for our gifts, a few of our Minnikojou warriors became curious and wondered how the barge worked. It looked like fun. So while it was not in use, these Minnikojou warriors boarded it and set sail to cross to the other side. They found their first river crossing on a barge exhilarating and wanted to do it again, but a group of soldiers stopped them, took control of the ferry, and shooed them away.

However, our Minnikojou warriors did not stay away for long. They had had too much fun, and now it was in their blood. So a few hours later, our warriors returned and took the barge into the middle of the river once again. Once more the soldiers took the ferry boat back, causing our warriors to become agitated. As the soldiers were pulling themselves on the barge by the rope back across the river, one of our warriors fired a musket shot that splashed in the water near them. It scared the soldiers, and they decided to report what had happened to their head man at Fort Laramie, whose name was Garrett.

We were familiar with Garrett because, over the past two years, Garrett had spoken to us about complaints he had received about our people from the immigrants crossing our homeland. We had never attacked or hurt anyone, but they complained nonetheless. So in his mind, he must have thought that the musket firing was some kind of escalation, and if he were to ignore it, he would be condoning some kind of violence towards his men. Our people knew that wasn't the case, so our people went about their lives unconcerned. Late that afternoon, Garrett sent one of his most trusted soldiers, Fleming, and some of his men to try to seize the Minnikojou who had fired the shot.

Just before sunset, Fleming and his soldiers left for our Lakota camp. Once he arrived, he discovered nearly all our warriors were gone. They had gone on a hunt earlier that afternoon and had not yet returned. So Fleming decided to march into our camp and demand we surrender the warrior who had fired the shot. We could not believe Fleming had done such a silly thing. We had never ridden into his fort and demanded one of his soldiers. So we ignored his demand and asked him to leave. He then instructed our entire camp to lay down our arms and surrender.

At first we thought he was joking. However, once we saw that he was serious, some of the warriors that had stayed behind decided to give him a taste of our weapons by firing in his general direction. A skirmish broke out. The result was that two of our people were killed, and Fleming ended up saving his men by capturing two of our people and using them as bargaining chips. When we saw he had hostages, we held our fire. He brought the hostages back to his fort, where they were later released back to us.

When our hunting party returned and heard what had happened, it left all of us with bad feelings towards the soldiers. It was something that we would not soon forget, and most of us left the area immediately.

Only our Lakota brothers who had learned to depend on the government for hand-outs stayed to collect the gifts. These Lakota brothers continued to stay near Fort Laramie that winter. They were commonly referred to as Loafers because they were too lazy to hunt. When they were together in a group, these lazy people were referred to as the Loafer band. Unfortunately the Loafer band would become the face of our people to the Americans. They told the Americans what they wanted to hear in order to maintain a steady supply of coffee and molasses and, in the process, compromised our identity and the true wishes of our people. Our people continue to pay for their indiscretions today.

CHAPTER SEVEN

War Begins in Earnest

The chokecherries had ripened late during the summer of 1854. During an oven-like heat spell in August, our people came to pick up our annual annuities or "presents" once again at Fort Laramie. We hoped that by arriving later in the summer we would not have to waste so much time waiting for our gifts. However, our gifts still had not arrived even though we came late, and the soldiers had no answers for when we would get them. It created an added anxiety and hardship for our people. There was not much in the way of game left around the fort anymore, and sending out a sizable hunting party was out of the question after what had happened the previous year.

During our long wait, an immigrant wagon train passed our village. As they passed, one of their cows got loose from their herd and ran into our village. The whites from the wagons watched as the cow became spooked upon entering our main camp and knocked over our tipis and cooking pots. While this out-of-control cow caused a great deal of havoc within our village, the people from the wagons seemed to be frozen in the belief that our people were out to hurt them. Not one of them approached our people to ask for their cow back or compensate us for the damages it was causing. Had they asked, our people would have been more than happy to allow them to take their troublesome cow back. But instead, their wagon train continued on to Fort Laramie, leaving their cow to continue to do damage in our village.

Watching their departure, a Minnikojou warrior named High Forehead decided to take matters into his own hands and shot the cow dead. He then butchered it, cooked it, and shared it with other members of our camp so they could quash their hunger pangs. The cow was skinny, and the meat did not smell or taste as good as our buffalo meat.

Conquering Bear, who was still acting as the liaison between the soldiers and our people, worried about how the soldiers would react if they heard our people had killed one of the white people's animals. Our people thought he worried too much, because the immigrants had not even asked for it back.

However, he knew that the white people were sensitive about their possessions, and because they had appointed him as our "head chief," he knew he would be their main target if we ever had any misunderstandings. So he sent some of his young boys north to our family's Kettle Butte campsite to ask Crazy Horse and our family to join him at the main camp in case we had to fight the soldiers. Crazy Horse took it seriously because he knew the Americans had proven themselves to be unpredictable. Besides, he liked Conquering Bear. By 1854 our family camp, with the addition of Corn's people and many from Black Buffalo's family, had grown considerably. Our Kettle Butte camp was a little over twenty miles, or a two-hour ride away, from Conquering Bear's camp.

Conquering Bear indeed had good reason to worry, because when the wagons reached Fort Laramie, we heard that the immigrants had complained to the fort's newly appointed head man, Fleming. They even asked him to help get their cow back from our people's bellies.

Fleming was the same soldier who had led his men into our village the year before and killed two of our people. We knew he was the kind of person that would probably do it again. Mindful of this fact, Conquering Bear paid a visit to Fleming at Fort Laramie during the late afternoon. He went to try to stop any bad feelings that may have existed over the cow by offering to negotiate a peaceful solution.

When he learned that the immigrants were upset over the cow, Conquering Bear offered several horses from his own personal herd to pay for the cow. However, the soldiers seemed to be more intent on teaching us a lesson than making things right. So Conquering Bear returned to our camp a worried man. After learning what was going on, our people began to worry too.

Late that night, Crazy Horse and our family's band arrived and camped a few hundred yards from the main camp in a stand of trees.

The next morning Ca-oha, Little Hawk, and two other boys from our family lead their horses to the river to water them. Crazy Horse sent six-year-old High Horse with them and instructed Ca-oha to keep an eye on his younger brother.

After a while, the boys began playing a game where they would attempt to count coup on each other with a chokecherry stick while riding their horses. To please his father, Ca-oha rode double with his little brother during the contest so that he could keep an eye on him. Although it made maneuvering his horse a little more awkward, he accepted the challenge and was doing quite well in their fantasy battle.

Late that day, the Fort Laramie head man, Fleming, sent one of his best men, Grattan, and twenty-nine of his soldiers riding in a wagon to our main village to seize High Forehead for killing the cow. They brought two cannons to show that they meant business. They also brought an interpreter named Auguste, whom none of us liked. Auguste was a drunkard.

One of our most revered and peaceful head men, Old Man Afraid Of His Horses, rode out to Grattan and tried talking him out of entering our village. Grattan had no ears for him. Grattan obviously knew the story of how Fleming had entered our village the year before and had left unscathed. We knew that story too, so we readied ourselves.

Ca-oha and the rest of the boys watched from a hill as Grattan and his men rode into our village and set up their cannons pointing in our direction. Conquering Bear, a holy man who did not carry a weapon, hurried out to talk to Grattan. Conquering Bear hoped to keep the peace and tried defusing the situation as best he could. Grattan told him if he wanted peace, then he must surrender the warrior who had shot the cow. But they both had a problem, the interpreter was drunk and spent more time screaming insults at us than interpreting for his leader. We hated him.

During this time, some of Crazy Horse's warriors were keeping a wary eye on the soldiers from distance. Finally, Grattan said something to his soldiers, and they began to prepare for a fight. We girded ourselves.

A shot was fired, followed by several more. The cannons fired a round of grapeshot that mortally wounded Conquering Bear. The scene turned hellish.

Ca-oha covered little High Horse's eyes to keep him from seeing Conquering Bear's grisly blood-soaked body. He told Little Hawk and the rest of the boys to take High Horse and their horses back to the river and tell his father what was happening. The boys rode off in a hurry. Ca-oha decided to stay and figure out a way to help in the fighting. He was determined to embrace a warrior's role and help fight to maintain our way of life.

Crazy Horse was already aware of what was happening and had lead our warriors up a slough, hidden by chokecherry and buck brush that ran through our village. Within moments of the first shots, our warriors came at the soldiers from every direction. The soldiers panicked and began trying to run along the slough for cover. At that point, Crazy Horse and his band of warriors erupted out of the slough and cut them off. The soldiers had no place to go and were completely wiped out.

Seeing the soldiers being decimated, Ca-oha's desire to become involved outweighed his own safety. He charged into the fray on his horse with his bow ready for action. When Crazy Horse saw him, he stopped him immediately.

"What are you doing? Where's High Horse and the horses?" he asked Ca-oha angrily.

Hearing his father's anger, Ca-oha became guilt ridden and sheepishly told him that he thought them to be safe.

"High Horse is still young and helpless! You are supposed to protect him!" his father admonished. "Our helpless ones are who we live for!"

As Ca-oha rode back through our village, he saw that the soldiers had indeed killed some of our children. Seeing them drove home his father's words. From that point to the end of his life, he would make sure our helpless ones were safe before he would charge into battle.

He also passed by Conquering Bear's bloody body being laid upon a hide. He was still alive and Ca-oha, seeing the gaping holes in his body, could not see how that was possible. Conquering Bear finally passed to the other side not long afterwards.

Once Ca-oha arrived at our family's tipi, he was relieved to be reunited with Little Hawk, High Horse, and the other boys. He was overjoyed to know that they were unhurt.

After the fight, we moved our camp back into the Black Hills to put some distance between ourselves and the soldiers.

The fight with Grattan was the fight that started our war with the white people that would last for the next twenty-three years—and the sad thing is, it all started over a scrawny cow.

CHAPTER EIGHT

The Hemblecha

Ca-oha was having bad dreams. He kept seeing the image of Conquering Bear's gruesome body. The elders from the other side had entered his dreams to remind him that the soldiers could do these bad things. They told Ca-oha that he needed to stay vigilant and learn to protect our people.

When Ca-oha told his father about these dreams, his father knew what had to be done. He told Ca-oha that he needed to come with him and pray. So they took off with a small contingent of medicine men and set up camp near what is today Sylvan Lake in South Dakota. Crazy Horse decided that he and his son would hemblecha on the Spirit Wall, which is located on a line between the lake and a mountain known in our language as *Paha Tokah,* or First Hill. The Americans call this mountain Harney Peak. The Spirit Wall is a long ridge that features steep rock cliffs. The forest around the Spirit Wall was thick in those days.

Crazy Horse needed two hemblecha sites, one for his son and another where he could see his son and still hemblecha himself. Once he led his son towards the Spirit Wall, he found it difficult to find a good place to hemblecha because the sunlight was blocked by trees. An animal helper, the red-tailed hawk, saw their problem. He flew above them to get their attention, and once he had it, he led them to a good place. Ca-oha was able to find a spot where a beam of sunlight would shine on him in the morning, and Crazy Horse found a spot nearer to Paha Tokah where he could watch his son while he fasted and prayed with his sacred pipe. Ca-oha did not yet have a pipe.

During his hemblecha, Ca-oha prayed for the Buffalo Calf Pipe Woman, our people who had passed to the other side, our people who were still walking the earth, and our family. Hearing him, the Creator knew he was worthy of a vision and gave him one.

Ca-oha's vision was revealed through the clouds and it showed that he would be a protector of our people. The Creator instructed him to pay careful attention to the teachings of his father and his uncle Hump so that he would learn to be a great warrior.

When a Lakota man desires to attain our spiritual ways, he must hemblecha once a year for four years. A hemblecha normally lasted four days. While Ca-oha was occupied with learning our spiritual ways, a terrible thing happened to our people about a full day's ride to the south.

The soldiers made no secret of the fact that they were angry that Grattan and his men had been wiped out. They wanted revenge, so they sent a soldier chief named Harney and about six hundred soldiers to punish our people. In September of 1855, the soldiers found one of our villages that wished only to live in peace. The village head man was Little Thunder, whose camp was located along Blue Water Creek near what is today Ash Hollow State Park in Nebraska. Since they only intended to live a peaceful life, Little Thunder's village thought the soldiers would honor their peaceful intentions, and they saw no need to run from them until it was too late. The soldiers brutally attacked the village, killing the elderly, the women, and the children. Neither Crazy Horse nor Ca-oha were there, but word of the massacre spread quickly throughout our Nation. When word reached Ca-oha, his desire to become a warrior that would protect all our people swelled like never before from within his heart.

In 1856, his father and Red Leggins were blessed with another son named Bear Pipe. The wonderful event gave Ca-oha another reason to focus on making himself into a good warrior. He wanted to become a good example for his new baby brother. Family still came first.

The year 1858 was the fourth and final year of Ca-oha's journey to complete his quest in becoming a full spiritual warrior and the last year of his hemblecha. As his father prayed and fasted from his accustomed hemblecha spot on the Spirit Wall, he happened to glance over at his son. He saw Ca-oha sitting cross legged, still in the midst of his hemblecha, talking to an elder who was standing on his south side. Crazy Horse became alarmed that anyone would stop and talk to his son during something as sacred as a hemblecha, and once he finished his prayer, he walked over to investigate. Once again the red-tailed hawk led Crazy Horse through the sea of trees to his son's site. On his way, Crazy Horse happened to catch a glimpse of Ca-oha through an opening in the trees. He saw Ca-oha talking to the beautiful but sacred Buffalo Nation Woman.

Suddenly, the red-tailed hawk screeched overhead. Crazy Horse looked up to see why the hawk was screeching and when his gaze returned to where the beautiful but sacred Buffalo Nation Woman had been, she was no longer there.

Upon reaching his son, Crazy Horse noticed that he was crying and holding a sacred council pipe. Crazy Horse wondered how the pipe got there. From bowl to stem, the pipe measured thirty-four inches. The exact length is known because the pipe still exists in our family's current sacred bundle. The pipe's pipestone bowl was wrapped in a candy-striped manner with a strip of flattened silver. The coiled silver represented the fact that he was to be the people's protector, and he would shield them from harm.

When Crazy Horse asked his son about the sacred Buffalo Nation Woman, Ca-oha told his father she had brought him the sacred council pipe and had told him that the pipe had a spirit inside it that would protect him. He also showed his father something that a white owl had brought him during his hemblecha. It was a medicine made of a small stone resembling a grayish-colored crystal rock. This rock medicine from the White Owl Nation had the ability to prolong his life. If he used the medicine, the white owl told him that he would not be hurt by enemy arrows or bullets. It was something he would keep in his sacred bundle and only use when going into battle. He was to carry it in a little hide pouch and tie it to his rifle, bow, war club, or whatever weapon he planned to use that day.

The Creator showed Ca-oha how he was to make himself look as a warrior when it came time to protect our people, and at the same time be protected himself. He was told to wear two red-tailed hawk feathers in his hair out of respect for the red-tailed hawk that led him to his sacred hemblecha site. He was also told to draw a red lightning bolt from the middle of his forehead to the outer edge of his left eye, then zag down to the left-hand side of the bottom of his nose and back out to the edge of his mouth, and finally, back to the bottom center part of his chin. He was to dip three of his fingers in a special white paint and then dab his body with them on his most vulnerable areas, leaving behind three white spots each time. When the white paint hardened, the Creator told him it would make his body hard just like hailstones so that bullets and arrows could not penetrate.

In addition, Ca-oha had been taken to the west, where the wakiyans, or thunder beings, live, during his hemblecha. There he had been given his sacred council pipe by the sacred Buffalo Nation Woman.

He had also been taken to the south. In our Lakota way, the only time we go to the south is when we die. It is the time when our bodies are put up on a scaffold and then, four days later, put into the ground. However, in Ca-oha's case, our ancestors brought him back alive. They gave him the knowledge of where all our family members were buried and asked him to protect their bodies from desecration by any invaders. They had also taught him a song. The song said that he had been taken to the south and brought back, and then they took him to the west and brought him back. Today it is known as our "Tashunke Witko Song," and it is occasionally heard at our gatherings.

Ca-oha carried his sacred council pipe for the rest of his life. When he wasn't using it for prayer, he would disconnect the bowl from the stem so he could release the spirits that it called back over to the other side. Conversely, when he prayed, he would reconnect the bowl and stem to call the elders from the other side so they could help him with his prayer. When followed, our traditional spiritual ways have always allowed us to communicate to those who have already passed to the other side. It is one of the blessings of being Lakota.

When word got out to our people that Ca-oha had gone to the south and had been given a medicine to protect our people, our elders and warriors looked at him in a different way.

CHAPTER NINE

The Name is Passed

During the fall of 1858, our family camped along the Shifting Sands River in what is today northeastern Wyoming. The Americans now call this river the Powder River.

A short distance from our camp, a young Lakota mother, who had her young son with her, was cleaning buffalo meat in the river. A Shoshoni war party appeared from a stand of trees near the river and spotted her. One of the Shoshoni warriors broke from his war party and attacked her. He beat her to death with his war club. However, before he killed her, the mother yelled to her son to run away. When the Shoshoni warrior was satisfied that the mother was dead, he turned his attention to her fleeing son.

Ca-oha was training a newly acquired brown-and-white paint horse that he had named *Wakiyan* near the river. He was utilizing a long chokecherry branch to maintain the horse's attention and obedience when he heard the mother's screams. He looked in her direction and saw the Shoshoni warrior kill her. When the Shoshoni started after her young son, he sprang into action.

With the Shoshoni closing in fast on the boy, Ca-oha rode up behind him and took the Shoshoni out with his war club. After making sure he was dead, Ca-oha looked around and noticed the rest of the Shoshoni war party watching him from the trees. His immediate thought was that our camp needed to be protected. So he instructed the boy to go back to our camp to warn them and get help.

Having seen one of their own go down, and unsure if Ca-oha was part of a larger group, the war party turned tail and rode away. Ca-oha chased them and was able to get close enough to count coup and whip some of the Shoshoni on slower mounts with the tip of his chokecherry branch.

Once the Shoshoni reached their war party's camp, Ca-oha rode high up on a ridge and stopped. Seeing he was not going to enter their camp, and finally realizing that he was by himself, the Shoshoni became brave and charged him. Ca-oha turned and galloped away. As they chased him over the ridge, a group of our warriors, which had been hastily assembled after learning of the Shoshoni war party from the young boy, greeted the Shoshoni with a vengeance. Our warriors ended up surrounding the Shoshoni and wiping them out. Ca-oha is said to have taken down three of them that day.

When Ca-oha returned and told his father what had happened, his father knew that his son had now achieved the status of a full battle-tested warrior. It made Crazy Horse think back to the time when he had become a warrior and what his father, Walks With Sacred Buffalo, had done for him.

He knew his son would need a new name. So the proud father gathered his son and called all our people to the center of our village. As our people congregated, he planted his staff in the ground and our village went silent. Ca-oha stood quietly as his father spoke.

"Ca-oha, my son, from this day on, you will go by the name of *Tashunke Witko*. And I will take a new name that shall be taken from the simplest thing that has been shown to me. I shall carry the name *Waglula*."

Waglula, roughly translated to English, means Worm. Upon hearing this, our men whooped and our women trilled in celebration. It was a good day for our family. Our sacred name of Crazy Horse had once again been passed to a new generation. Ca-oha now carried the sacred name of Crazy Horse.

Our people already knew he was a great protector. However, the additional recognition of being chosen to carry our family's sacred name of Crazy Horse had given him a greater status among our people and a greater feeling of personal responsibility. He was determined to honor the name.

When he went to defend our people, he made it a point to remember our elderly and bring them back the belongings of enemy warriors that he killed, because those belongings, like buffalo robes and moccasins, would quite often be of use to them.

When he captured horses in a raid, he would give them to a family in need. He brought meat back from his hunts to the elderly widows who had no warriors to depend on. He would spend time teaching our children our Lakota ways, and our people came to love him.

During an overcast day in 1860, Crazy Horse had been out hunting elk in an area west of what is today Deadwood, South Dakota. He was carrying a pistol that his father had given to him in a leather bag.

His hunt had been successful, and he was leading a horse packed

Tashunke Witko, drawn by a migrant artist from a description by his sister Iron Cedar. Once she saw the finished drawing, she cried tears over the resemblance. Courtesy Edward Clown family.

with elk meat along a heavily wooded ridge back to our camp when he came across a party of about nine Crow. The Crow spotted him, and two of them immediately charged up the hill to try to kill him. However, by the time he was able to fire his bow and kill them both, the remaining Crow had surrounded his position. He decided to lie low in the wooded area and wait.

The Crow were anxious to flush him out, and one of them crawled behind a large rock that was uncomfortably close to Crazy Horse's position. Spotting him, Crazy Horse pulled his father's pistol out from its leather bag and fired at the Crow, who had unwittingly left both his legs exposed. The bullet pierced both legs, and the Crow dragged himself down the hill where his fellow Crow could pull him to safety.

The standoff continued all afternoon. Crazy Horse had very few bullets for his pistol, so he fired at the Crow just often enough to let them know he was still there and still dangerous. As the sun began to set, Crazy Horse ate a piece of dried meat he was carrying to gain some additional energy and then used the cover of darkness to escape the encirclement with his pack horse full of elk meat still in tow. Once he was beyond them, he looked back and saw that they had not detected his escape.

After Crazy Horse returned to our camp, he rounded up some of our warriors. Then he led them out to fight the Crow. However, the Crow were no longer there. All that was left were the blood traces of those he had taken out. There was general disappointment among our warriors that the Crow had left. However, upon seeing the site, our warriors marveled at how Crazy Horse had beaten the long odds and lived to tell about it.

* * * * *

Around 1862, a tragic event took place to the east that had another strong impact on our attitudes towards the white people.

Our people to the east, namely the Dakota living in what is today south central Minnesota, had been trying to adapt to the white man ways. They wore white people's clothes, attended white people's churches, and tried to learn farming, but still they ended up depending on government annuities to keep from starving.

Prior to 1862, the white traders in the area had extended the Dakota people credit until the annuities arrived, and then they would get reimbursed out of the Dakota's annuities prior to the Dakota receiving them, quite often for much more than what had been loaned. When the Dakota realized what a big portion the traders were deducting from their annuities, they did not like it. Finally, in 1862, the Dakota demanded that this practice stop. When it did, the traders stopped extending credit.

Thus, when the annuities of 1862 were late once again, there was no credit to buy any food to tide the Dakota's hunger over until the payment arrived. So, many of the Dakota begged to regain their credit so they could buy food. The traders seemed determined to teach the Dakota a lesson and bluntly turned them down. In fact, one trader was heard to say, "If they are hungry, let them eat grass."

Hungry and desperate, the Dakota rose up and killed some of the traders so they could gain access to their provisions and procure food for their families to keep them from starving. Frightened, the traders called for the soldiers to protect them, and when the soldiers came, they took many of the Dakota into custody. Of those in custody, the US government's head man, Abraham Lincoln, told the soldiers to hang thirty-eight. It was the most people the Americans claim to have ever hung at once in the history of their people. When Crazy Horse and our people heard about this from the survivors who had fled to our camps, it made them angry.

To make matters worse, shiny metal had been found once again, this time in the northern Rocky Mountains. Unfortunately, the quickest way the whites could reach this new discovery was by traveling through our best hunting grounds, which they did without asking. Their incursions were getting to be too hard to stomach. Their arrogance had to stop.

During our next summer solstice gathering, our head men made a decision to protect our people from these advancing white people. With this decision in place, Crazy Horse led raids against soldier patrols and soldier supply wagons in order to capture rifles and gun powder: our warriors would be able to use the same deadly weapons on the white people that they used on us and push them from our hunting grounds.

Around 1863, Waglula and Red Leggins had another boy, named Makah, which translated into English means Earth. Waglula was following through on his desire to make sure his children had plenty of siblings. Crazy Horse took time off from his raiding to congratulate them. He was happy to have another new brother to love and defend, but the defense of our Nation continued to call him. So after a brief reunion, he returned to his raids.

Black Buffalo's youngest son, Hump, who was now in his fifties, still participated on many of our war parties. He never grew tired of the fight. Normally, our warriors stopped riding with war parties when they reached their forties. At that age they would take on the role of an advisor or an elder to our people. However, Hump had too much energy for that. As long as his heart felt young, he would continue do as he pleased.

When he wasn't fighting, Hump could quite often be found visiting with the

Makah, also known as Peter Wolf in later life.
Photo courtesy of Edward Clown family.

Cheyenne people. He really liked their women and had married five of them. He had fathered three sons with them, Little Crow, Hump Two, and High Back Bone, along with a daughter, Two Cows. However, one of his wives had been killed by the Shoshoni in a raid, and he never forgave them for what they had done.

Through Hump's women and other Cheyenne who had married into our people, our family became quite familiar with their ways, and they became familiar with ours. The Cheyenne, who roamed an area mostly south of ours, had also become increasingly concerned about the white people's invasion. With both our tribes wanting to keep our hunting grounds for ourselves, we had a common goal that brought our two people together. However, not all of the Cheyenne wanted to fight the Americans. There were bands within the Cheyenne Nation that wanted to coexist. The Cheyenne head man Black Kettle's band was one of them.

In the fall of 1864, white settlers in what today is Colorado fired a cannon at an approaching group of peaceful Cheyenne waving a white flag. This made the Cheyenne quite angry. Later some of the white settlers spread the word that they thought the Cheyenne were another tribe and that it was just a mistake. But still they showed no remorse for what they had done. This further infuriated the Cheyenne. The Cheyenne returned the favor by attacking wagon trains and ranches all throughout the Colorado Territory. In response, the Colorado Territory's head man, who went by the name of Governor Evans, asked a white holy man named Reverend Chivington to lead some soldiers out to fight the Cheyenne. Governor Evans offered $25 for each Cheyenne scalp that the soldiers brought to him. At the time, we did not understand what $25 was or the value of paper money. But the soldiers did.

Black Kettle was aware of all that was going on. He wanted to keep his people safe, so he surrendered to the soldiers. He requested to camp where his people would not be mistaken for any of those wanting to fight the whites. The soldiers gave him a place to camp, where they said he would be safe, and also gave him a colorful piece of cloth they called an American flag to fly over his village in case other soldiers came by so he could show them that he was a friend.

However, Reverend Chivington and his soldiers ignored Black Kettle's American flag, along with his people's claims of peace, and brutally attacked his village. Chivington and his soldiers butchered the elderly, women, and children in a heinous act of barbarism. The atrocities reached the point where many of his soldiers kept dead Cheyenne body parts as souvenirs.

When word reached our camp, Hump's women became distraught, which later smoldered into a white-hot anger that their relatives and people had been mutilated so extensively. It made all of us angry and sick. It was an event our people could not ignore, and if there were any lingering doubts about the cruelty of the soldiers after the Blue Water massacre, the attack on Black Kettle's helpless village answered those doubts. When the Cheyenne came to us and asked for help in their fight against the soldiers, we could not help but agree. We were hard and fast allies from that point forward.

However, before we could join them, some impatient Cheyenne warriors had already vented their rage on a soldier fort called Camp Rankin. Camp Rankin guarded a white settlement named Julesburg on the banks of the south fork of the Shell River. They killed several soldiers.

When our warriors finally arrived, they joined the Cheyenne for an attack on the Julesburg settlement. Together they burned the town to the ground. However, our family stayed up north because Waglula and Red Leggins had just brought another son, named Comes Home Last, into the world, and our family wanted to enjoy the newborn. In our Lakota way, our children are sacred and always come first, even during difficult times.

Following our summer solstice gathering in 1865, Crazy Horse joined the fighting to the south and rode with a group of our warriors to the Shell River area to help the Cheyenne push the whites out. The whites had built a wagon road going west that they called the Oregon Trail, and they had built soldier forts along that route. One of their smaller forts sat on the banks of the north fork of the Shell River and overlooked a great wooden bridge they had built to drive their wagons across the river.

We thought if we could take this fort out, then we could take the bridge down too. The wagons would then have a hard time crossing into our hunting grounds. It would also be a good place for us to capture additional guns.

At the south end of the bridge was the fort that the military called the Platte Bridge Station. It housed the soldiers that were supposed to chase us away from their road if we got too close. Along this wagon road the soldiers had built a long string of wooden poles with noisy, or singing, wires attached, which they called their telegraph. The singing wires were how the soldiers talked to each other over long distances. A singing drum, or telegraph relay, resided inside the Platte River Station. The telegraph poles were planted permanently into the ground, and that was something we had not agreed upon in any of our treaties.

Around July 26, 1865, our scouts told us that there were some supply wagons heading towards the fort from the west. A few hours before the wagons were to arrive, a group of about twenty soldiers rode out of the fort. We knew they were sending these soldiers to meet and escort the wagons back because we had seen them do it before. Along their route to the wagons, they spotted two of our warriors about a quarter mile in front of them cutting the telegraph wires. We planned for them to see it. It was a decoying tactic.

A decoying tactic usually consisted of a handful of warriors or human decoys whose job it was to lure the enemy into an ambush by getting them to believe our warriors would be an easy kill. If our decoys were successful, the soldiers quite often never lived to see the sunset.

Although Crazy Horse was not one of the two warriors cutting the wires that day, he was a participant in the ambush that we and our Cheyenne allies were about to spring on the soldiers.

Upon seeing the soldiers, our two decoys quickly slid down the telegraph poles and hopped on their horses. When the soldiers hesitated to follow, our two decoys pretended that their horses had become lame. Seeing this, the soldiers thought they would indeed be easy pickings and stormed after them. Our decoys rode away at half speed.

After the soldiers chased them a short distance, our decoys led them over a rise. Waiting on the other side was a large group of our Lakota warriors mixed in with our Cheyenne allies. When we sprang the ambush, the soldiers panicked. They turned around and began riding for their lives back to their fort. We raced to cut them off and were able to kill five of them, including their leader, and wound several others before the soldiers ducked back into their fort for safety. With the patrol licking their wounds in the fort, we could now wait for the supply wagons without worrying much about their soldiers riding to the rescue.

Late that afternoon, the wagons showed up.

Upon the wagons' appearance, the soldiers in the fort were indeed too frightened to come help, so they decided to let us have the wagons. All they did was fire a cannon to warn the wagons that we were coming, but it did no good.

There were three wagons with about twenty white men. It did not take long for our warriors to overwhelm them, killing all but three of their men, who somehow made it to the fort. Once the fighting was done, our warriors pushed their wagons into a dried-up creek area and emptied them of all their weapons and shells. Our warriors then set the wagons on fire and watched them burn. It gave us great satisfaction. Our Cheyenne allies went to work on the wagon train's dead. It was payback for Sand Creek.

Unfortunately, our victory did nothing to solve our problem with the white man's encroachment upon our food sources. The white people seemed to be finding new ways to enter our hunting grounds. Farther north, small groups of white people were continuing to travel through our hunting grounds and kill our buffalo on their way to get some of the shiny metal that had been reported in the Rocky Mountains. These small parties began to grow into large wagon trains.

We stopped the first of these larger northbound groups of wagons that tried crossing through our lands. We told them that this was our hunting area and to please leave. But their wagons continued to invade and cross through our hunting area, scaring the game away and scarring the earth to the point that it created a new trail that the white people called the Bozeman Trail. Soon their wagon trains numbered around one hundred fifty wagons in each group.

We had now come to the realization that the whites had no ears. We hated that we had to fight these people who were now bringing their families with them. Killing women and children was not our way, so we scaled back our attacks to see if there was another solution.

In Waglula's younger days, he and a Lakota friend named Black Dog would go on raids and hunts together with an older, much respected warrior named Lone Man. Now those days were long past. Lone Man had passed to the other side. However, Lone Man's lineage lived on. Lone Man's daughter, Blue Day Woman, had married Black Dog. They had a son together named He Dog. As a teenager, He Dog had sometimes joined Waglula and his father as a horse holder on a few of their forays.

Lone Man also had a son named Red Cloud.

When Black Dog came to visit Waglula late that summer, his brother-in-law Red Cloud accompanied him. Seeing Red Cloud instantly brought back happy memories of his old friend Lone Man to Waglula.

Lone Man's family camp was normally located around what is today Mobridge, South Dakota. He had had many friends among our Minnikojou band, even though he hailed from a different Lakota band called the Cut Heads. The Cut Head band got their name from a time when some of their warriors brought back the heads of our enemies to camp.

Lone Man had even known Waglula's father, Walks With Sacred Buffalo, and father-in-law, Black Buffalo, from long-past buffalo hunts. Waglula's family and Lone Man's family often camped in the same camps during these fall hunts. Lone Man's son, Red Cloud, was about eleven years younger than Waglula and was still very young when his father got lost in the whiskey bottle and died from too much of it.

After his father's death, Red Cloud was taken by his mother, Walks As She Thinks, to live with her brother, Smoke. Smoke was the head man of the Loafers and spent a great deal of time trading with the whites. Red Cloud watched and learned the art of negotiating and surviving among the whites from his uncle.

Red Cloud grew into a fierce warrior, and around 1841 he killed another Lakota head man named Bull Bear in a dispute between two families. However, Waglula did not judge him on that, he only saw him as the son of an old friend.

Red Cloud was now an *akicita* head man for a band led by Conquering Bear's son, who had taken his father's name of Conquering Bear. Conquering Bear's son spent much of his time as an intermediary between our people and the soldiers at Fort Laramie, just like his father had. (*Akicita* in the Lakota language roughly means "police" in English.) Waglula knew that Red Cloud observed soldier movements around Fort Laramie every day and asked him if he could supply this useful information to his son, Crazy Horse.

Red Cloud had inherited his father's warrior mind and had also learned the white ways from his uncle, Smoke. He had many skills. However, Red Cloud was also a polarizing figure among our people. Many of our young warriors wouldn't even talk to him because of the Bull Bear incident. Red Cloud was smart enough to know that those who avoided him would listen to his words if they came through the mouth of a respected warrior like Crazy Horse.

Red Cloud had the mind of a politician. Waglula set up a meeting for Red Cloud to meet his son. When Red Cloud and Crazy Horse finally met at our family's camp, Red Cloud advocated attacking any and all whites that entered our hunting grounds. It was exactly what Crazy Horse was thinking too. Red Cloud looked to capitalize.

CHAPTER TEN

Fighting for Our
Hunting Grounds

The wagon trains of the gold seekers were no match for Crazy Horse and our warriors in a fight. So the gold seekers cried to their government, and their government listened. They sent soldiers to defend these gold seekers even though they knew they were in the wrong.

During the summer of 1865, their soldiers invaded our prime hunting grounds near the Shifting Sands River to try to push us out. They failed. We gave them a hard time and then disappeared into places where they could not find us.

While on this invasion, the soldiers came across the Arapaho head man Black Bear's village on the Beaver Tail River near what is today Ranchester, Wyoming. In our Lakota way, we see a beaver tail as looking similar to a tongue. We believe a misinterpretation by the Americans is responsible for its present name of Tongue River.

Since the Arapahos were friends of ours, the soldiers decided to attack their village and left many of their women and children dead. After the attack, the soldiers went ahead and built a fort along their Bozeman Trail; they called it Fort Connor after their head man, General Connor.

Following the soldiers' savage attack, the Arapahos went from being our friends to becoming active allies with us and the Cheyenne in our fight to push the soldiers from our hunting grounds. With all three of our tribes fighting together, our raids became more frequent, and we finally forced the government to come to their senses. They sent word that they wanted to talk peace with us at Fort Laramie the following spring. With that piece of news, we felt our efforts had finally become successful.

Red Cloud, who we knew to be a good speaker, took up the role as our main negotiator at the talks. We expected him to set the government straight and get them to abandon their new fort so we could continue to live in our traditional ways.

However, once Red Cloud arrived at the fort in the spring of 1866, he found out that the US government wanted to trade presents from "The Great White Father in

Washington" (this is what the white people liked to call their head chief) in exchange for keeping their new road and building additional forts along it. We couldn't believe our ears. We did not understand what they were thinking.

Our Mother the Earth is our mother. How could we trade away our mother? How could we sell our food source? Our grandparents' bones? Our children's future? What kind of people would that make us? Our Mother the Earth belongs to all Creation and all Creation belongs to her, including us.

We became even more alarmed when Red Cloud actually began to think their proposal over. Red Cloud told the Americans that he had been the one who was leading our warriors against their soldiers even though we knew it to be untrue. So the Americans began to treat him like a more important head man than he actually was, and he liked it. He liked it so much that he considered doing things he shouldn't have. It made Crazy Horse think twice about how committed Red Cloud was to maintaining our Lakota ways.

While Red Cloud was considering his reply to the Americans, a big group of about one thousand soldiers arrived at the fort. When one of our people at the peace talks asked why they were there, the soldiers' head man said they were on their way to build forts on the new road.

When word got back to Red Cloud, he was stunned. He found that he wasn't as important as he thought he was. It made him angry. He railed against the fact that "The Great White Father" had shown him presents in exchange for selling the road and then ordered his soldiers to steal the road before Red Cloud had a chance to tell him yes or no. With his pride wounded, Red Cloud stormed out of the talks.

While all this was happening, our summer solstice was taking place. During this annual celebration, Crazy Horse was appointed one of our shirtwearers. His grandfathers had been shirtwearers, as had his father, and now it was his turn. It meant a great deal to him, and he was proud to accept the role and prove his worth. Waglula's heart swelled with pride when he heard one of our elders call his son's name to bestow this great honor on him.

Not long afterwards, while our family was staying at Iron Cedar Creek, Red Leggins delivered Waglula his last child, a daughter named Iron Cedar. She was named for the family camping area that now held the graves of Red Leggin's mother and uncle.

Once again the addition of a new life in Waglula's tipi gave our family's happiness a boost. They feasted. Iron Cedar would eventually become our paternal great grandmother. She was the one who passed much of our oral history to our grandparents, who later passed it to us.

While our ancestors enjoyed little Iron Cedar, messengers interrupted our bliss with news that the soldiers were building new forts in our hunting grounds. It made us mad.

During the winter, our people normally camped at our winter camp in the Black Hills. It was a camp located along Eagle Head Creek, which is today called French Creek, in what is present day Custer State Park in South Dakota. The camp is nestled in a valley that runs near the edge of our Black Hills. The many hills that surround this valley help shield us from the icy winter winds. There is also a spring that yields water that never freezes in the winter.

However, 1866 was not a normal year. The soldiers had built three forts that fall. They had rebuilt Fort Connor into Fort Reno, and had built Fort C. F. Smith and Fort Phil Kearny from scratch. We knew we could not let these forts take root in our hunting grounds, so we stayed that winter to force them out.

Red Cloud wanted to lead the fight. However, he had listened to the Americans when they asked to buy the new road that belonged to all our people, not just to him. As a result, Crazy Horse and many of the rest of us had no ears for him. We would fight without him.

When it came to fighting, our people never brought our families along. We wanted to make sure they were protected. So, for that reason, we kept our women and children in a camp about a full day's ride away in the Wolf Mountains near what is today the Montana and Wyoming border. By camping there, our families were away from the fighting but near enough for our warriors to visit and make sure they were fed.

In contrast, our Cheyenne allies often brought their families to a fight. Their women would sometimes even participate in the fight to the point that if their husbands were killed, they would put on his war paint and carry his name into battle.

We decided to concentrate on Fort Phil Kearny. It was located near Clear Creek which is today called Little Piney Creek by the Americans. Clear Creek flows in present day north-central Wyoming.

Our main objective was to get the soldiers away from the fort and out in the open. To achieve this goal, we burned the grass around the fort so the soldiers would have to go away from the fort when it came time to cut hay for their horses. This exposed them to longer waits if they needed to be reinforced from the fort during a fight. We engaged the soldiers in several skirmishes, including whenever they left the fort to cut logs for building or firewood for the winter months.

Around December 6, 1866, some soldiers and wagons left the fort to cut wood. Once they were out among the trees, our warriors attacked. The soldiers responded by sending additional soldiers from the fort in a counterattack and pursuing our warriors to a place they now call Lodge Trail Ridge.

Lodge Trail Ridge was a tall ridgeline northwest of a rounded hill that the soldiers called Sullivant Hill, which is almost directly west of Fort Phil Kearny. Once we got to the western side of Lodge Trail Ridge, we could not be seen by the soldiers at the fort, who were by then nearly two miles away. We knew this area would be a good place for an ambush. Our objective became to bring the soldiers to this area where we could fight them without anyone in the fort knowing how the fight was progressing. We would also be too far away from the fort for them to fire their cannons at us.

During the skirmish, our warriors were successful in luring some of the soldiers beyond Lodge Trail Ridge, where we were able to wipe a few of them out. After that taste of success, we decided to try to lure a larger soldier unit into the area and take care of them once and for all. So Crazy Horse and some of our elder warriors, like Hump, began to devise a plan.

Meanwhile, Red Cloud took a trip south to do some trading near Fort Laramie and secure extra guns. He also was trading for bacon and coffee. He did not make it back in time to participate in helping us wipe out the soldiers. We did not miss him.

The ground was hard and frozen when we put our plan to work on December 21. Once again we attacked the soldiers' wood-gathering party. As they had done so many times before, the soldiers sent men from the fort to chase us away. Some of the men were on horseback while others were on foot. Crazy Horse and nine other Lakota and Cheyenne warriors had been sent to decoy these men into an ambush.

After some taunting, Crazy Horse and the rest of the decoys were successful in capturing their attention. They flashed their behinds and fired shots at them and then just sat on their horses and watched the soldiers get closer. Soon the soldiers advanced close enough that our decoys were within easy rifle range. The soldiers would stop to fire, and our decoys would ride off. If the soldiers hesitated to continue their pursuit, Crazy Horse and the rest of the decoys would act like their horses had gone lame or had been wounded and hop off and pretend to check their hooves for injury.

Crazy Horse and our warriors rode high on the ridges the entire time so that they could be easily seen. They teased them so that the soldiers pushed beyond where they were safe. The soldiers followed them for nearly two miles until they had journeyed beyond Lodge Trail Ridge.

Our decoys lead them to a place that is today known as the Peno Creek Valley, which is just beyond Lodge Trail Ridge. Upon entering the Peno Creek Valley, our decoys split up. One group rode along Peno Head Ridge on the western side of the valley while Crazy Horse and the rest of the decoys rode to the top of what is now known as Fetterman Hill and sat on their horses in full view of the soldiers and stared at them. The soldiers were so excited about taking out all ten of our decoys that they split up. The soldiers on horseback

Peno Creek Valley from Magpie Creek. In the far distance, the Fetterman Monument is on the third hill from the left and is slightly left of center. Crazy Horse decoyed Fetterman up Fetterman Hill, which is second hill from the left, while the cavalry pursued the other decoys along the ridge on the right side of the photo. Photo by Bill Matson.

rode after the six decoys who chose to ride along Peno Head Ridge, and those soldiers on foot charged up Fetterman Hill to get at Crazy Horse and our other three decoys.

Meanwhile, a handful of Cheyenne women had set up a small camp on the northwestern end of the Peno Creek Valley in front of Magpie Creek, which today is called Peno Creek by the Americans. There was brush all around the creek. The women were pretending to help injured warriors. This was also a decoy tactic. Our six decoys who had been riding along Peno Head Ridge turned down into the valley towards the women. The soldiers who were on horseback left the safety of the upper ridge and entered the valley. Attacking the women and injured warriors was just too hard to resist.

Now we had the soldiers right where we wanted them.

We had about five hundred warriors hiding behind the ridges that lined the valley. They had been monitoring the soldiers' location along the way by listening to the shots exchanged between the soldiers and our decoys. As soon as those soldiers on foot got close enough, Crazy Horse and the three decoys with him rode over the hill and out of sight. As the soldiers' pursuit reached near the top of the hill, our warriors swarmed out from behind the eastern ridges. The soldiers didn't have a chance.

When the horse soldiers in the valley got near the Cheyenne women, about two hundred Cheyenne warriors led by Little Wolf came out from behind the western ridges and circled around behind the soldiers to close off their return route to the fort. A second large group of warriors came out from behind the women and the bushes of Magpie Creek. Suddenly we had the horse soldiers in big trouble too.

The horse soldiers, seeing they were badly outnumbered, galloped to rejoin the foot soldiers on Fetterman Hill. Once they arrived there, we had them all encircled at the top of the hill where they were easy targets. The soldiers backpedaled up the hill, and our Lakota and Cheyenne captured more and more guns from the soldiers they had killed. The fighting lasted about forty minutes.

Our warriors wiped them out to the last man.

Some of our warriors also added to their herds by gathering the now riderless soldier horses. They were distinct because they had a branding that said "US" on their hip.

Afterwards, the Cheyenne women once again repaid the soldiers for their atrocities at Sand Creek, mutilating the soldiers in the same manner that their loved ones had been mutilated two years earlier.

We took many casualties in the fight and had to take time to take care of our dead. We then decided to head back to the warm fires in our family camp for the rest of the winter to heal and get strong again.

Later we heard that a retrieval party of soldiers went out to the battlefield and discovered that their head men in the battle had been killed by soldier bullets. Of course, most all of the bullets shot that day were fired with soldier rifles because Crazy Horse and our warriors had soldier rifles too—either prior to the battle or captured during it.

The following spring, we allowed our ponies to regain their strength and fatten for future battles. After celebrating our summer solstice of 1867, we decided to resume the fighting. However, we were undecided whether to take out Fort C. F. Smith or Fort Phil Kearny first. So we split our warriors up. About half went north to attack Fort C. F. Smith, located in south-central Montana, while Crazy Horse and the rest of our warriors concentrated once again on Fort Phil Kearny.

At Fort Phil Kearny, we observed that the soldiers' behavior had not changed much over the winter and that they had even added more soldiers to their fort. The soldiers still went to cut wood. They were making the fort even bigger. These woodcutting soldiers would stay out at the same place every night, about five miles northwest of Fort Phil Kearny, where they would sleep with their horses in the center of a circle of wagons without wheels.

Around August 2, 1867, we counted about thirty soldiers at this wagon box circle. We had around six hundred warriors. The woodcutting soldiers were spread out all over the area that day. Crazy Horse and our head men decided that it would be a good time to attack, so we did.

One group of our warriors attacked the woodcutters in the forest and burned their wooden wagons while Crazy Horse and a few other warriors attacked their horse holders down by the creek. He had hopes of luring the larger group of soldiers away from the safety of their wagon box encirclement and into the waiting arms of an ambush.

In the attack on the horse holders, Crazy Horse killed one of the soldiers and took his rifle. It was different from anything he had ever seen. It could fire bullets one right after the other, or almost four times as fast as any rifle he had ever seen. Later we learned that it was called a breech-loading Springfield Allin Conversion rifle. Now all of the soldiers carried one. He showed it to some of our other warriors, and they became excited and wanted to capture one of their own.

When our attack on the horse holders became known to the soldiers in the wagon circle, they began to assemble for a counterattack. Unfortunately, some of our younger warriors, in their haste to show their bravery, spoiled our ambush by revealing themselves before the soldiers had left the confines of the wagon boxes. This caused their sentries to race back to the wagon boxes for cover. Now our warriors would have to attack the soldiers in a fortified area.

While all this was taking place, Crazy Horse was in the wooded area to the south of the wagon box camp watching for any additional woodcutting soldiers that might appear from the timbers. Sitting on a hill to the southeast of the wagon boxes were a handful of warriors led by the Cheyenne head man Little Wolf. They stood watch in the direction of the fort, looking for any soldier reinforcements. Corn, Hump, and some other elders watched from a hill northeast of the wagon boxes for any supply trains traveling down from the north.

We thought that this fight would be a good place for our younger warriors to gain some fighting experience. Since we outnumbered the soldiers by such a large number, we thought it would be an easy fight even though we had lost the element of surprise. Many of our younger warriors were in their mid-teens to early twenties and wanted to prove themselves. We allowed them to make the attack with a few of our older warriors to lead them. They represented about a third of our warriors.

It was a disaster.

Our warriors fell like leaves on a fall day. The fight kept our elk dreamers, who watched from the hills with their long, flowing war bonnets, busy. Our elk dreamers were like medics; when they saw somebody fall, they would ride down and administer the elk medicine that would help heal the fallen warrior so they could fight again. Our elk dreamers did not learn that they were to be elk dreamers from a vision; they learned their path at birth. Those of other cultures think these men on the hills with the long, flowing war bonnets were head men or chiefs, but our head men usually just wore two or three feathers.

Prior to this fight, the soldiers had used muskets that required a long pause in between shots, which our warriors used as an opportunity to get closer and closer to the soldiers. Now the pause no longer existed with the soldiers' new quick-firing rifles, and our young warriors were not able to adjust. We lost about twenty percent of our young men, so we withdrew.

Our respect for these new rifles grew, and we became unsure if we wanted to try again. However a Cheyenne elder took it upon himself to show our young men how to be brave. He grabbed a rifle and a pistol and charged the wagons by himself. They cut him down, but his bravery inspired our younger men. So they attacked the wagon boxes a second time, only this time on foot.

They got within a few feet of the wagons, but once again they took such heavy casualties that they had to pull back. We fought the soldiers for about half of the day until we realized that their new rifles made an attack on them too difficult. Nearly one-third of our warriors were either killed or wounded that day. When more soldiers came from the fort firing their cannons, we decided it was time to leave.

We retrieved our dead and headed north so we could heal once again.

CHAPTER ELEVEN

A Family Man

Red Cloud's niece, Black Buffalo Woman, by all accounts was very pretty. She was in her early twenties. She had first met Crazy Horse at a summer solstice when she was around twelve winters old, and had developed a crush on him. When her uncle, Red Cloud, came to our family's camp to plan our strategy for pushing the whites out of our hunting grounds in early 1866, her interest in Crazy Horse was renewed. She went out of her way to get his attention and did nice things for him. He enjoyed her company but never actively pursued her because she was already married to a man named No Water.

However, just because her feelings for him were not reciprocated did not mean she stopped lionizing him. When he was appointed shirtwearer, she talked glowingly of his appointment. When he returned from battle, she bragged about his exploits. It made her husband jealous. No Water saw Crazy Horse as a threat and began to criticize him to his face. Crazy Horse ignored No Water's insults. However, it made our family uncomfortable to see this animosity develop, and we hoped it would pass.

No Water had a habit of over indulging in alcohol and quite often would leave Black Buffalo Woman and their two children alone so he could go to the white man's trading post at the Agency to get a bottle. When he returned home from one of these trips, he was usually drunk in a mean way and would take it out on Black Buffalo Woman.

Crazy Horse's vision to protect our people caused him to become involved in her life. Learning that No Water beat Black Buffalo Woman after getting drunk, Crazy Horse told No Water that if he continued to pursue his drunken habits, he would encourage her to leave him. This made No Water laugh and reply that she would never leave.

No Water had some relatives who camped with Crazy Horse's camp, and when Red Cloud left our camp, No Water and Black Buffalo Woman decided to stay. In 1867, during our fall buffalo hunt when we would kill and store all our meat for the winter months, No Water decided to leave for a trading post to get a bottle of whiskey. This made Black Buffalo Woman nervous for his safety, so she went to Crazy Horse and told him.

After a great deal of reflection, Crazy Horse decided that Black Buffalo Woman could use a new start to her life and invited her to accompany him on the buffalo hunt. He said he knew that her relatives, Black Bear and his wife, would be on the hunt and that they could help her. Her heart swelled with joy, and she accepted his invitation. She left her two children with No Water's mother and accompanied him on our fall hunt in the Stronghold area.

Once they arrived, he took her to Black Bear's tipi and told Black Bear and his wife why he had brought her. Black Bear's wife was a blood relative of Red Cloud, and they agreed to look after Black Buffalo Woman and help her reestablish herself as an independent woman.

When a drunken No Water returned to our village and his mother told him that his wife had left with Crazy Horse, he became livid. He found himself a pistol, mounted his horse, and raced out to our buffalo hunting camp.

It was early in the evening, and our hunting party's tipis glowed with the golden warmth of inner campfires. They could be seen for some distance. The hunt that day had been good, and they had acquired plenty of meat but still not quite enough to last the winter. Our warriors were relaxing in their tipis and telling stories about what had happened that day. Laughter occasionally filled the air. Crazy Horse, his cousins Touch The Cloud and Standing Elk, and Black Buffalo Woman were in Black Bear's tipi. While Black Bear's wife chatted with Black Buffalo Woman in the rear of the tipi, our men were gathered around the campfire pondering the next day's activities when No Water showed up.

"Crazy Horse!" No Water shouted through the tipi door.

The stories and laughter stopped. Black Buffalo Woman knew that voice, and she gave Crazy Horse a worried look.

"Who is it?" asked Black Bear, since it was his tipi.

No Water poked his head into the tipi and asked, "Where is Crazy Horse?"

"I'm here," answered Crazy Horse in a strong voice.

No Water took out his pistol and stuck it inside the tipi door and aimed it at Crazy Horse's heart. Touch The Cloud, sitting inside the tipi to No Water's left, immediately recognized the danger. He brought his hand up and knocked the pistol skyward but not until after No Water had gotten a shot off. The shot hit Crazy Horse in the face by his left cheek and he immediately went down. Black Buffalo Woman pulled the tipi wall up and rolled out in order to hide from No Water.

No Water took off. Three of our relatives at the camp, including Touch The Cloud and Standing Elk, rode in pursuit of No Water. Black Bear and his wife stayed to care for Crazy Horse.

No Water got off to a large enough lead that he was able to ride to Twin Buttes, a place with a flat top that overlooked the surrounding terrain, near what is today Nisland, South Dakota. There he rested his horse until he saw our three relatives coming after him. Desperate to stay away from them, No Water took off again and rode his horse so hard that it died from exhaustion near the White Earth River. With his horse dead, No Water continued to run on foot. Our three family members followed No Water's moccasin tracks for about two miles until they disappeared into the White Earth River near what today is the community of Red Shirt Table. There they found a family camped with a boy watching a herd of horses. They asked the boy about No Water. The boy told them that he had indeed seen him running with a horse bridle in his hand. He said No Water approached him and asked which of his horses was the strongest and fastest and that he had pointed one out.

No Water told him he needed to use it and would return it later. He then threw his bridle on it and rode in the direction of the Red Cloud Agency. Knowing No Water had a fresh horse, our three relatives gave up the chase. A few days later, we heard that he had sent the horse back to the boy's family.

Meanwhile, back at the hunting camp, Crazy Horse was badly hurt and word was sent to Waglula, who came immediately to care for his son. He placed his son on a buffalo robe and found some leaves and flowers from a plant that today is commonly called heartleaf four o'clock and boiled them in water. He placed the dark boiled residue of the plant on his son's wound to help it heal. However, Crazy Horse's face was swollen and he was having a hard time opening his mouth to eat. It was not a good situation.

When No Water shot Crazy Horse, it also wounded the unity of our people. Knowing it to be an urgent situation, Spotted Tail brought his niece Black Shawl the day following the shooting to tend to Crazy Horse and nurse him back to health as quickly as possible. Waglula accepted her help because he had heard that Black Shawl had proven herself to be good at healing bullet wounds.

After two days had passed, Spotted Tail again showed up, only this time with Red Cloud. They were met by Waglula. Red Cloud demanded that Crazy Horse give his shirt to No Water in exchange for offending him. Red Cloud also had personal reasons for doing this.

Red Cloud felt that he had lost his influence over the young men because Crazy Horse had stopped listening to him during the war over the Bozeman Trail. He still harbored desires to be the most revered leader among our people. After all, the white man treated him like a big chief, so why not his own people?

He determined that it was Crazy Horse who was in his way. Red Cloud figured if he could damage Crazy Horse's reputation, then somehow the young men would turn around and listen to him or, at least, one of his close relatives like No Water.

Waglula understood where Red Cloud was coming from. He knew that the shirt was too sacred to be given away. He told Red Cloud that he would only give the shirt to the elder that had originally announced Crazy Horse was to be a shirtwearer during the time when he was appointed. This way he would know that the shirt would end up with the Sacred Calf Pipe Keeper, Old Man Elk Head. Unhappy with his failure to secure the shirt, Red Cloud stopped on his return trip to see Black Bear and took back his niece, Black Buffalo Woman, so he could return her to No Water. He and Spotted Tail then went to see the elders.

It was a sticky situation.

The elders had to devise a solution before tempers got out of control. They decided to take Crazy Horse's shirt away and sent Spotted Tail and Red Cloud once again to visit

Black Shawl, circa 1888. Courtesy Edward Clown family.

Crazy Horse, but this time with the elder who had announced Crazy Horse's appointment. Waglula and Crazy Horse gave the elder his shirt as had been promised. The elder took the shirt and brought it back to the other elders, and then by a decree, they decided it was never to be worn by anyone else ever again.

Back at Crazy Horse's tipi, Black Shawl fed him soup through a hollowed willow stick resembling a thick straw because he couldn't open his mouth wide enough to drink the soup from a bowl. She rubbed bear grease on his wound to help it heal.

Black Shawl was in her mid-twenties, which was old for a Lakota woman to still be single at that time. She had a plain face, an average build, and a beautiful heart. She stood around five-feet-three inches tall and constantly wore a black shawl.

Crazy Horse's wound healed into a star-shaped scar on his upper left cheek. The scar made him self-conscious of his appearance. The time she spent caring for him touched him deeply. Like Crazy Horse, she was very unselfish. They fell in love.

"I have an ugly scar, but you still see me with your heart. You love me for who I am," he told her.

When he asked, she agreed to be his wife and became pregnant a short time later. While she was pregnant, Crazy Horse would occasionally go on hunts and war parties to shake off some of the rust that had set in during his convalescence. He would make sure his lightning bolt paint covered the scar on his cheek.

During this time, five of our family members joined Crazy Horse as part of a larger war party. They were Hump, Touch The Cloud, Talks About Him, Little Crow, and Hump Two. One afternoon, they had left the larger war party for a little while to rest on a hill overlooking a portion of the Shell River when they saw a small group of white men in soldier uniforms riding near them. Seeing them, Crazy Horse climbed on his horse, Wakiyan, and took out his medicine rock from the White Owl Nation. The rock was just soft enough that he could bite off a tiny portion, grind it with his teeth, and then blow its medicine on himself.

"I'm going to test myself to make sure that I am healed," he told his relatives.

Crazy Horse rode his horse out into full view close to the soldiers so he could taunt them with his war cries. The soldiers fired their guns at him. He was not hit, but Wakiyan was shot twice, once in the shoulder and once in the hip. Wakiyan had been a faithful horse to him and had been his companion whenever there was danger. He was as much a part of Crazy Horse as Crazy Horse was a part of him, and now he was hurt. Crazy Horse's family members knew instinctively what to do: they mounted their horses and began to lead the soldiers back to the main war party. Wakiyan, badly hurt and bleeding, gave Crazy Horse everything he had left and gamely kept up with the rest of the family as they galloped towards the main war party.

When Crazy Horse was just about to our main group, he and his relatives fired a few shots at the soldiers to alert our main war party. Within moments, our warriors emerged and chased down the soldiers. They took all but one out who had come with no weapon. They captured him and tied him to a tree. Not carrying a weapon into a fight was something only a brave man would do. They decided he was too brave to kill, so we left him near the trail so his people would find him.

After it was all over, Wakiyan got worse and died. It made Crazy Horse very sad.

"You should have had some medicine to protect your horse," Hump told him.

Crazy Horse agreed and took Hump's advice to heart. He promised him that when he found a horse that he liked as much as Wakiyan, he would find medicine to protect it.

As Black Shawl's belly grew larger each day with their child, Crazy Horse spent more time around our camp. While in camp, he came to notice that his little brother Makah had befriended a dog that was half wolf. When Makah sat down, the wolf dog would lie at his feet. When Makah slept, his wolf dog would sleep next to him. Wherever Makah went, the wolf dog was sure to follow.

Soon whenever we saw Makah, we knew that the wolf dog was nearby. After a while we gave Makah the nickname "Wolf" because of his tight bond with the wolf dog. His nickname would prove to be an important part of his identity in later years.

As the time neared for Black Shawl to deliver their baby, our family moved to our winter camp in the Black Hills. Crazy Horse wanted his offspring to be born in the same place as his grandfather, Walks With Sacred Buffalo.

It was not long afterwards that our family's women came together to help Black Shawl give birth to their baby. Seven women helped with the delivery, including Iron Between Horns, Kills Enemy, Red Leggins, Good Looking Woman, They Are Afraid Of Her, one of Black Shawl's aunts, and Corn's wife. Good Looking Woman and They Are Afraid Of Her were the ones who helped pull the little one into the world. They made sure the birth went smoothly.

Shortly after the birth, Crazy Horse entered the tipi. Black Shawl was already holding their new daughter in a deerskin blanket. Tears of joy welled in her eyes. Glowing with pride, Crazy Horse studied his daughter and touched her little hand. He then proclaimed that he would name her They Are Afraid Of Her because he wanted her to be an independent spirit like her aunt and not depend on anyone to take care of her. He wanted the world to know she was going to stay a Lakota girl. His aunt They Are Afraid Of Her blushed with pride.

Black Shawl gave Good Looking Woman her favorite black shawl in appreciation for helping her deliver the baby. It was a gift that Good Looking Woman treasured because she understood that it had come from Black Shawl's heart.

They Are Afraid Of Her's umbilical cord was put into a buffalo hide pouch shaped like a turtle. Crazy Horse carried it so he would have a piece of his daughter with him everywhere he went.

The world was perfect for Crazy Horse and Black Shawl that beautiful spring day. It was a perfect day for all of us.

CHAPTER TWELVE

Peace and Family Episodes

T he white people had been working on building a road for their iron horse, or railroad as they called it. By late 1867 it was nearly complete. Their iron horse could now take the gold seekers to their gold without passing through our hunting grounds. With the railroad in place, the government no longer needed the Bozeman Trail.

In the fall of 1867, the government asked us for a peace treaty once again. Our elders asked Waglula if he would attend the treaty meetings, but he declined. He told them there was already a treaty (1851) in place, so there was no need for a new one.

Lone Horn represented the family at the 1868 Fort Laramie treaty talks. Left to right: Lone Horn, Pipe, Grass, and Young Elk. Courtesy Edward Clown Family.

Lone Horn at the 1868 Fort Laramie treaty talks. Left to right: Spotted Tail, Dull
Knife (Roaming Noise), Old Man Afraid Of His Horse, Lone Horn, Whistle Elk,
Pipe On Head, and Slow Bull. Courtesy Edward Clown Family.

So once again Lone Horn represented the family at a new peace conference held at
Fort Laramie during the summer of 1868. He knew there would be presents there and
hoped to negotiate for some of the quick firing rifles that he had heard about from our
warriors at the Wagon Box Fight.

At the peace conference, the government agreed to abandon their forts along the
Bozeman Trail and allow us to hunt the buffalo in our traditional hunting grounds.
According to the treaty, our eastern boundary was the east bank of the Muddy River.
The northern boundary was the Elk River. The western boundary was the Shifting Sands
River, while the southern boundary became the Shell River. The Elk River has been
renamed the Yellowstone River by the Americans.

In addition, to guard ourselves against our lands being sold by bogus "chiefs" like
Red Cloud, it now required three-fourths of our men to agree to any boundary changes.
The government also agreed to set up a place where we could get presents every month,
which they now called rations, at places the white people referred to as agencies or reservations. It was a total victory with the exception of Lone Horn's efforts to secure the
quick-firing rifles. However, we knew there were other ways to do that.

Our Cheyenne allies and some of our people joined together to celebrate by burning
the soldiers' deserted forts on the Bozeman Trail to the ground. Unfortunately, we found
we were still not completely free of the white people. There were disturbing things still
taking place.

The white people continued to invade our hunting grounds to kill our buffalo whenever they could. They depleted our herds just to take their hides, and sometimes just
for their tongues, to send to those living in the east. It was a terrible waste. We did our

best to intercept and stop them. However, enough of them succeeded that the size of our herds became smaller with each passing year. We found that there were still things to remedy.

After the treaty was signed, the government told us where the sites distributing our rations would be located and wanted to know which site each of our camps would be visiting to pick them up.

Around this time, Crazy Horse's younger brother, High Horse, had lain eyes on the daughter of Kills The Enemy, a prominent Oohenonpa band head man, and had fallen in love. Her name was Bluebird Woman.

Back when High Horse came of age and went on his hemblecha, he had a vision that told him he would die at a young age at the hands of Crow warriors. High Horse had a strong passion for Bluebird Woman, so he decided he would make her his wife and she would bear his children before his vision was fulfilled.

High Horse was eighteen winters old and was staying at Lone Horn's camp when Lone Horn asked him if he would ride out to Kills The Enemy's camp and find out which government site Kills The Enemy would like to pick up his rations from. At the time, Kills The Enemy's camp was located at a place we called Black Horse Butte between what is today Ekalaka and Broadus, Montana, near the Shifting Sand River. High Horse jumped at the chance and decided when he came back he would bring Bluebird Woman back as his wife. So he took three horses with him to ask for her hand.

When High Horse went to deliver the message to Kills The Enemy from Lone Horn, he took that opportunity to offer his three horses in exchange for Bluebird Woman's hand. Her father looked at him and saw no future. Kills The Enemy refused him, so High Horse found and added one last horse to his tiny herd and approached her father again. Her father turned him down again.

"If I don't have her, I will throw my life away," he told Kills the Enemy.

"Then throw your life away," Kills the Enemy answered.

High Horse left disappointed but undaunted. He was a strong-willed young man and determined to find a way. He vowed to return and steal her from Kills The Enemy's tipi in the middle of the night.

A few nights later, he donned a buffalo robe and crawled into Kills The Enemy's tipi in an attempt to sneak Bluebird Woman out. However, once he was inside the tipi, Kills The Enemy's wife got up to stir the fire in the tipi and add wood to it. So he laid still under the buffalo robe waiting for her to go back to sleep. She stayed up for a long time and continued to build the fire until it was very warm inside the tent. The heat and his inability to move finally put High Horse to sleep. The following morning, he was discovered still asleep; they chased him out of the tipi and whipped him with willow sticks.

It was a humiliating experience, but it made High Horse more determined than ever. He devised a new plan. He had made a friend named Red Deer during his stay at Kills The Enemy's camp. He asked Red Deer to help him paint his face like a skeleton, complete with blackened eyes. Red Deer obliged him. Then High Horse put on a head dress made of turkey feathers so he could enter Kills The Enemy's camp during the night and scare everyone away with his haunting look if he was discovered.

However, some of Kills The Enemy's relatives were either awake or light sleepers, and when he called to Bluebird Woman to join him, they came out of their tipis and tried to grab him. His haunting look had failed to scare them at all, and they chased him out of the camp.

A distraught High Horse believed he had been recognized and felt he would never be with his love, so he decided to ride out to find a Crow camp and throw his life away. After a full day's ride west, he found a Crow encampment along the Elk River. They were in the midst of celebrating a successful buffalo hunt and had left their horses virtually unattended by the river. He rode in without hesitation, still wearing the makeup and turkey feathers.

"Kill me! Crow Nation, fulfill my vision! Kill me!" he shouted as he rode through the encampment.

While he was shouting his desire to die, he noticed the large group of horses along the river. When the Crows looked to see who was shouting, his appearance scared them and made them scatter. They thought he was an evil spirit. As they scattered, he noticed nearly all the men were on foot, and he realized that if he took their horses, they would not be able to catch him.

Seeing a solution to his misery, he rode to the river and cut the mainline of the horses and led them away. He drove the herd several miles from the Crow camp and then left them to go for help. He brought back Red Deer and some additional warriors to help herd the horses into Kills The Enemy's camp.

After he returned with the horses, High Horse went down to the river and washed his paint off. He also took off the turkey head dress so he could present himself to Kills The Enemy once more. He knew there was no way he could be refused now.

Kills The Enemy and his relatives had speculated that the painted intruder from the previous night may have been High Horse, but they weren't completely certain. When High Horse once again presented himself to Kills The Enemy, Kills The Enemy still had suspicions. However, when he saw all the horses, his suspicions evaporated.

"I have brought over one hundred head of horses to give to you and everyone in the camp so that I can make your daughter my wife," High Horse declared.

Kills the Enemy smiled.

"You have done an honorable thing. For a time we thought that it was you that had painted yourself up like a bad spirit and had come to visit us again, but we were wrong. You were out proving yourself," replied Kills The Enemy.

That evening Kills The Enemy consented for his daughter to become High Horse's wife. About eighteen months later they had a son.

Sadly, the Crows finally did fulfill High Horse's vision shortly after his son was born, around 1870. A Crow hunting party encountered High Horse on the trail and killed him. He was dead at twenty winters. His widow, Bluebird Woman, and their son died not long afterwards of a white man's disease that affected their entire village.

Losing High Horse was hard for our family to accept because he was still so young and had always made our hearts light. In fact, he lived so strongly through his heart that we thought he would be with us forever. Our whole family mourned his passing and looked forward to seeing him and his family when we joined them on the other side. In subsequent years, Crazy Horse would feel his little brother beating a rhythm of revenge inside his heart whenever he went to fight the Crows. High Horse was laid to rest near Black Horse Butte.

*　*　*　*　*

During the years immediately after the birth of his daughter, They Are Afraid Of Her, Crazy Horse spent a great deal of time pampering her. He envisioned great things for her. When he wasn't with They Are Afraid Of Her, he would go on hunts to replenish our food supply or raise havoc with white buffalo hunters poaching from our herds.

In the spring of 1870, Crazy Horse went on a hunt to find buffalo and elk with Hump and several other warriors about a good day's ride, about sixty to seventy miles, southwest of Grey Horn Butte. Hump was about fifty-nine winters at the time.

During the ride, they encountered a heavy rainstorm. Once the rain subsided, they happened upon a Shoshoni camp. Hump was still bitter at the Shoshoni for killing one of his wives, so on impulse he rode up on a heavily timbered ridge overlooking their camp with revenge in his heart. Crazy Horse followed right behind him along with the rest of our warriors. Suddenly and without warning, Hump veered down through the mud-soaked ground and disappeared into a stand of trees. He reappeared among a group of surprised Shoshoni watering their horses and killed three of them before one of the Shoshoni took him out with a war club. It all happened before Crazy Horse and the rest of our warriors had a chance to react to his sudden charge.

Upon reaching Hump, Crazy Horse and our warriors drove the Shoshoni away, inflicting five fresh casualties on them while suffering a few wounded of their own. Some of our wounded were forced to ride double with a healthy warrior in order to make the return trip. Hump was put over a horse and taken back up the ridge.

It wasn't long afterwards that they saw the Shoshoni regroup and begin to advance towards them for another fight. Our warriors were greatly outnumbered, so Crazy Horse knew it was time to leave. Since Hump had already left for the other side, Crazy Horse and our warriors decided to take him to the highest butte within the surrounding area and quickly cover him with sage and rocks and return for his body later, after they had bolstered their numbers with additional warriors. The sage was used to disguise the scent of his decaying body from the animals. After hiding his body, they rode back to our camp.

About a week later, Crazy Horse and a large contingent of our warriors returned to recover Hump's body. Crazy Horse knew that his uncle had wanted to lie next to his father at Grey Horn Butte, so he was there to grant his wish. Unfortunately, the coyotes had found Hump despite the sage and had eaten the legs off his remains. Thus Crazy Horse and our warriors decided to bury him where he lay.

Crazy Horse was deeply saddened over losing Hump and remembered a promise he had made to him that he had not yet fulfilled. It was the promise that Crazy Horse would find a good horse like Wakiyan, along with medicine to protect it.

Ever since he had lost Wakiyan, he had been borrowing his father's dark brown war pony with the black mane. Not yet having followed through on his promise made Crazy

Horse feel as though his relationship with his uncle was incomplete, so he vowed to do something about it. He decided to steal a new horse from his uncle's most hated enemy, the Shoshoni.

Later that year, he and some of our other warriors took another trip into Shoshoni country to fulfill his promise, and they stole a herd of Shoshoni horses. Among the stolen horses was a big, strong young black-and-white paint horse that he claimed as his own and brought back to our camp.

Once he had returned with his new horse, Crazy Horse began to train it just as he had trained Wakiyan. While he was doing this, he went to his father and asked him what kind of medicine to use to protect his new horse during battle. Waglula deferred him to his father-in-law, Corn.

Corn spent a great deal of time with a medicine man named Horn Chips. Crazy Horse had seen Horn Chips in camp with Corn and knew he had a special Bear Medicine that could heal the sick and wounded. He asked Corn if Horn Chips might also have medicine that would help him protect his new horse.

Horn Chips spent most of his time at the Agencies, traveling back and forth between the Spotted Tail and Red Cloud Agencies to perform ceremonies. When called upon, he also came to visit our camps to perform ceremonies. Corn traveled quite frequently to see Horn Chips at the Spotted Tail Agency, so he agreed to make a trip for Crazy Horse to see what Horn Chips could do for him. The result was that Horn Chips agreed to accompany Corn back to our camp and meet with Crazy Horse.

Upon their meeting, Horn Chips prayed for a remedy. His prayers brought a sacred black rock to place behind the horse's ear. Upon giving the rock to Crazy Horse, he also told him to rub the earth's sacred dirt on his horse so that he would combine his horse with the Creator's power from our Mother the Earth. He also told Crazy Horse that once he mounted his horse, he needed to use his owl medicine, the crystal-like rock he had been given, and blow it on his horse when he blew it on himself.

"This will make your horse like a rock, so the arrows and bullets can not kill it. You and your horse will be as one," proclaimed Horn Chips.

Crazy Horse thanked him and did all Horn Chips had told him to protect his horse. He named his new horse *Inyan*, which in Lakota means "rock."

Immediately afterwards, he rode out to a Shoshoni camp to test his new medicine. Crazy Horse let them fire at him and Inyan at a close range and found the new medicine worked. Bullets and arrows could no longer harm his horse. It made him happy. He knew that Hump would now be smiling at him from the other side.

When he got back to our village, Crazy Horse learned that his eldest little sister, Shell Blanket, had become the wife of a man named Stands Straddle of the Oohenonpa band. He was happy for her, but when he learned that Stands Straddle worked for the government helping distribute rations, he wondered what kind of man he was. Stands Straddle had taken her to a soldier house named Fort Bennett, which sat on the banks of the Muddy River about twenty miles northwest of what is today Pierre, South Dakota. Today Fort Bennett sits at the bottom of a reservoir named Lake Oahe, which was created by Oahe Dam.

Shell Blanket and Stands Straddle had a daughter the following year, 1871, named All Yellow. All Yellow was Waglula's second granddaughter. It made his heart burst with joy. She was special to him, almost as much as his first granddaughter, They Are Afraid Of Her. He made it a point to accompany his relatives whenever they went to pick up rations so he could visit and spend time with her. It made him unhappy that she was at Fort Bennett, and he, like his son Crazy Horse, wondered what kind of man would give up the buffalo hunt to hand out flour and coffee for the government. He did not like Fort Bennett, but he could not help himself. It was where his daughter and granddaughter lived, and he loved them both.

CHAPTER THIRTEEN

Painful Losses

During the late fall of 1871 there was plenty of snow. Two of our young Lakota boys had ridden a short distance from our camp because they had heard there was a great big bull buffalo and they thought they would kill it. They brought their bows and crawled near to the buffalo.

Finally, when they thought they were close enough, they fired and hit it in the flank, but did not kill it. Wounded, the buffalo became incensed, and with his tail standing up in a sign of anger, he charged straight for the boys. The boys panicked and hastily mounted their ponies and rode as quickly as they could back to our village, with the buffalo in hot pursuit. The angry buffalo pursued them into our village, bringing an unnecessary danger to our defenseless ones, who quite often wandered within our camp innocently.

One of the defenseless ones was Waglula's youngest son, Comes Home Last, who was celebrating his sixth winter of life. He was a normal little boy who liked to shoot his toy bow at tipi drawings of buffaloes. He was too young to understand the danger he was to encounter.

As the raging buffalo entered our village, it spotted young Comes Home Last and made a beeline for him. Comes Home Last didn't have chance. He was killed before any of our relatives could save him. The buffalo continued to run through our village and then ran back out onto the plains. Our women rushed to Comes Home Last's aid but saw there was no hope. It broke our family's heart and we grieved enormously, Waglula more vehemently than anyone.

Within a short time, Waglula's grief turned into a burning anger at the great big bull buffalo that had taken his boy from him. He hopped on his horse to settle the score.

He found the buffalo in the middle of a field. The buffalo was still angry, but so was Waglula. Waglula urged his pony at a gallop out towards the buffalo and then he pulled an arrow from his quiver and placed it in his bow. He pulled the bow back with an extra surge of emotion and let his arrow go. It entered deep into the buffalo's heart. He dismounted and stared at the buffalo and remembered that the buffalo was his brother.

He prayed.

He cut the meat up with clouds of tears in his eyes in a vain attempt to block out what had happened that day. But his heart continued to bleed grief. He thought about the rest of his family and how much his eldest son, Crazy Horse, cherished They Are Afraid Of Her. He hoped his son never had to endure losing a child. It was the hardest ordeal he ever experienced and now he had experienced it five times, beginning with Sacred Girl, followed by Kills Enemy's twins, High Horse, and now Comes Home Last. Each loss felt like his first all over again.

Once Waglula returned to our camp, he shared the buffalo meat with all who would have it, but he lacked the appetite to partake himself. He also thought about how the two young Lakota boys had not been properly taught on how to hunt for buffalo and how the influence of the white man's spirit water and rations were starting to make some of our people lazy. He thought about how there had been sightings of miners entering our sacred Black Hills looking for the shiny metal that some of our people who had become lazy had told them about in order to get a drink of spirit water. These were all things that occupied his mind as he prepared a scaffold for little Comes Home Last to send him off to the other side. Once he had finished preparing it, he laid Comes Home Last's little toy bow next to him on the scaffold and sobbed. (A scaffold is like a litter whose outer corners rest on four poles about four to five feet off the ground. The poles are imbedded vertically into the ground. The body lies on the litter and is usually covered with a buffalo robe. In some cases, the litter can also rest in tree branches when good poles are not available. Our family left Comes Home Last up on the scaffold for four days before putting him into the ground.)

Crazy Horse's heart also fell to the ground upon learning of his little brother's death. When some time had passed, he and Waglula talked, and his father expressed his concerns about what the new ration system was doing to our people. They both knew there was little they could do to change the minds of those who had accepted it. So they pledged to do the only thing that they could. They would keep our family living in the ways of our grandfathers and vowed not to trade that life in for the white man's gifts.

Not long after our family's loss, Crazy Horse left camp with Little Hawk and some of our warriors for a buffalo hunt. There were also a few young boys who had been invited to go so they could learn to hunt in the right way.

Crazy Horse told Little Hawk of his conversation with his father and how they both believed the influence of the white man was becoming too strong.

"I too have seen the miners in our sacred Hills," replied Little Hawk.

"It would be good to teach them a lesson," Crazy Horse suggested.

And with that, Little Hawk gave him the grin of a young boy who had just been handed a bag of sweet-berried wasna and exclaimed, "That would be fun!"

It made Crazy Horse laugh a little more than he thought was possible at the time. Going on a hunt with Little Hawk was always good when he was feeling bad. Within a few days, one of our warriors who had been scouting ahead of them came back to tell Crazy Horse and Little Hawk that our Creator was smiling on them, because a large buffalo herd was grazing just a short ride ahead. Word passed quickly and everyone prepared for the hunt.

The buffalo were just beginning to grow their shaggy winter coats. Each warrior picked out a fat young buffalo about a year or two in age because their meat was the most tender. The first-time hunters were instructed to stay back and watch the older hunters so they would know what to do.

Little Hawk lit out into the herd with two arrows in his mouth, and suddenly the buffalo, realizing their danger, stampeded. Little Hawk pulled the arrows from his mouth in rapid succession and brought down two buffaloes with arrows shot into their hearts. Little Hawk whooped and trotted back towards Crazy Horse with a swagger. Crazy Horse smiled and recognized the challenge. He urged his horse forward and galloped headlong into the herd. He picked out a young bull buffalo and rode up alongside it. The young bull suddenly turned to try to gore his horse, but Crazy Horse was too much of a horseman to allow that to happen and dodged the attempt.

As the young bull resumed running, Crazy Horse slid down the side of his horse keeping only one foot gripping the horse's back and fired his bow from underneath his horse's neck right into the buffalo's heart. As the buffalo fell, it revealed that the arrow had gone completely through its body and had hit a second buffalo on the other side of him. The second buffalo teetered and fell. Crazy Horse trotted out from the herd and smiled at Little Hawk. Little Hawk just shook his head and smiled. Little Hawk then rode back out into the herd while motioning our first-time hunters to follow his and Crazy Horse's examples.

Our first-time hunters did well, except that a wounded buffalo nearly killed one of them who had fallen from his horse during the hunt. A well-placed arrow from Crazy Horse averted a repeat of what had happened to his little brother back at our village. From this buffalo, Crazy Horse cut out liver and presented it to our first-time hunters to share and they all took a bite. And so the hunt ended well, with laughter and joking and plenty of meat. It filled their hearts with great joy.

On the journey home, Little Hawk left Crazy Horse to go visit with his sisters. Crazy Horse and the rest of our warriors continued on with several travois loaded with buffalo meat. A few hours later, the wakiyans, or thunder beings, came, and it rained so hard that they could not see. So they camped under some cottonwoods.

As he waited for the wakiyans to pass, Crazy Horse thought about They Are Afraid Of Her's little smile and wondered if she had grown any new teeth since he had been away. He was keeping count.

When they approached our village at our winter camp, we could hear Crazy Horse and the rest of our warriors singing and laughing. But we could not sing or laugh with them. Something had gone terribly wrong.

Upon entering our village, Crazy Horse sensed something wasn't right. Our people avoided looking into his eyes as he rode through our village. It made his heart race and he quickened the pace of his horse towards his tipi. His mother, Good Looking Woman, was standing in front of his tipi with puffy eyes. He could hear Black Shawl weeping inside his tent. His heart sank as he got off his pony and went to his mother. She grabbed his arm and solemnly looked him in the eyes.

"Go see your father," she told him as she motioned to his tipi.

Crazy Horse rushed to Waglula's tipi. He sensed the gravity of what he was about to learn. Inside his tipi, Waglula was waiting for him with a heavy heart.

"Be strong, my son. The white man's sickness has visited your daughter. Your woman needs you now," Waglula told him.

His face turned into a broken heart. Tears welled in his eyes and he charged back to his tipi. Waglula had waited and thought for a long time after little They Are Afraid Of Her had passed to the other side on how to tell his son to somehow make it easier for him, but in the end, he could only give him his heart.

Inside the tipi, Black Shawl, her hair cut short, was mourning their child. Good Looking Woman, Iron Between Horns, Kills Enemy, and Red Leggins mourned with her. The tipi smelled of sage smoke, which they had burned for his daughter in an effort to try to protect her and keep her alive. We call this smudging. Crazy Horse studied his limp daughter, now wrapped in a hide, and knew he would never see her smile again.

Good Looking Woman opened the hide and revealed her tiny body to him. She was dressed in her very best dress and was holding her favorite doll. She had been prepared for her trip to the other side. On one side of her body was a lock of Black Shawl's hair that she had cut from her head and tied together with sinew. With the heaviest of hearts, Crazy Horse pulled his knife from its sheath and cut his hair. He tied it and placed it on the opposite side of her body from his wife's. Their hair carried their wisdom and knowledge, for it had been with them for a long time. It was something their daughter could take with her so she could continue to learn from them on the other side. Crazy Horse then pulled out the little turtle-shaped pouch that held her umbilical cord and placed it in his daughter's little hand.

Good Looking Woman rewrapped her. He then knelt by Black Shawl's side and gently picked up little They Are Afraid Of Her and held her close to his aching heart. Then he and Black Shawl held each other with their little girl in between them for a long time. Finally Black Shawl spoke and told him that their baby had died from the white man's coughing sickness.

As he held his little girl, he knew why it had happened. When our people visited the white men to get rations, they also brought back their diseases to our people. Crazy Horse laid his daughter down and left to see his father. Waglula gave him a medicine to place on her scaffold to protect her on her journey to the other side. Her scaffold stayed up for four days before she was put into the ground. They laid her to rest on a butte. Crazy Horse had loved her more than his own life, and now she was gone.

They Are Afraid Of Her's death was hard for Crazy Horse to accept. The four-leggeds watched him night after night praying on the butte with his pipe. They could only watch as the wakiyans showed their power and talked to him through their lightning and thunder. Something was going to happen. His ears danced to the Creator's will, and suddenly he knew what he must do. He grabbed his bow and a rifle, mounted Inyan, and rode into the Black Hills carrying a storm in his heart.

CHAPTER FOURTEEN

Prelude to a Showdown

The cottonwood trees in our Black Hills were turning into their bright yellow and red fall colors as Little Hawk rode to see his sisters. He smiled as he thought about Crazy Horse swaggering towards him after taking out two buffaloes with one arrow. It was that kind of competitive passion that caused all our warriors to respect Crazy Horse so much, including his step-cousin, Little Hawk.

As Little Hawk continued his ride through the Hills, his mind wandered, and he caught himself trying to think of a new maneuver to top Crazy Horse's feat. Suddenly, a hawk caught his eye and led his sight line to the smoke of a miner's campfire. He gave the miner a wide berth and thought to himself that he would return to chase him away when he had Crazy Horse to watch his back.

His sisters were waiting to meet him at Slim Buttes. Although they were older than he was, for some reason they had not found a man yet. They still depended on their step-father, Corn, to take care of them. But Corn was getting old and could not do as much as he used to, and that left their little brother to take on the role of a big brother.

Upon reaching Slim Buttes, there were already several other families there. These families were preparing for the fall buffalo hunt. During fall time, there were normally plenty of buffalo in the Slim Buttes area.

Slim Buttes has many massive limestone uplifts that shielded our camps from the early cold northern winds. When we stood on those buttes, they gave us a commanding view for miles of the surrounding area. These vantage points allowed us to see other buttes in the distance, like Rabbit Butte to the east, where we had scouts stationed who could signal us with small mirrors that we had acquired from the traders and that would reflect the sun's rays great distances to warn of approaching enemies.

After Little Hawk and his sisters exchanged a warm greeting, his sisters began to plan his time. However, Little Hawk wanted to prepare for the fall hunt, so he snuck into the woods and away from their agendas. Once hidden away, he began to tie metal barbs onto arrow shafts with sinew so he could add additional arrows to his quiver for the hunt.

When a messenger arrived at camp and announced that the government would be handing out blankets at the Spotted Tail Agency, his sisters became excited. Blankets were not always included with the rations and everyone in camp knew that there would be a limited supply.

The Spotted Tail Agency was not the closest ration point to Slim Buttes. It was located on the upper White Earth River about twenty miles north of what is today Chadron, Nebraska. But they had the blankets; this was important news to our women. His sisters searched and found Little Hawk's hiding place and asked him to accompany them to the Agency so they could each collect a blanket.

Riding to the Agency was not a popular idea with Little Hawk. It was about a three-day round-trip ride, and he worried a buffalo herd would be found while he was gone and he would miss out. Buffalo herds were not as plentiful as they once had been, and so they were not to be taken for granted. However, he also knew the miners were showing up in the Black Hills with more frequency, and his love for his sisters and their safety really left him no choice. They took off for the Agency the following day, with Little Hawk leading the way.

On their trip, Little Hawk watched for dangers and rode with his rifle cradled in his arms. Suddenly they came upon a group of prospectors mining gold on the Good River, about fifty miles southeast of what is today Rapid City, South Dakota. The miners spotted them.

Immediately sensing danger, Little Hawk instructed his sisters to ride into a nearby stand of trees and then continue to ride as far away and as quickly as possible. In an attempt to buy time for them, he rode towards the miners with his hand raised in peace. The miners opened fire and shot him off his horse. His call for peace had only made him a better target. His sisters glanced back and saw him fall. They then redoubled their flight to the Agency in hopes of bringing back help for their brother. The miners, not wanting anyone to know what they had done, took his body and hid it in a gully.

Meanwhile, during their flight, his sisters encountered a soldier patrol traveling north to another ration point. They recognized that six of the eight soldiers were Lakota scouts working for the government, and being desperate for help, they flagged them down. The soldiers, including two white officers, agreed to follow the women to their brother's location. Once they arrived at the place where the miners had killed Little Hawk, they discovered no signs of either Little Hawk or the miners. They then saw Little Hawk's horse standing over a newly cut pile of brush. They found his body buried there.

News of his death traveled fast. Crazy Horse, still wearing the pain of his daughter's death, was riding near the edge of our sacred Black Hills when some of our people carrying new Agency blankets back to Slim Buttes stopped to deliver the bad news to him about Little Hawk.

His vision as a youth had told him he would be a protector of our people. But after losing his daughter, and now Little Hawk, he knew he had not fully lived up to it and vowed that would change. The time had come for action. He would start with the miners.

Over the next three years, he exacted a retribution on the waves of invading white men that amazed us all. He killed nearly three hundred miners, and then went to the trouble of laying their bodies out on the entrance trails into the Black Hills to warn other miners to stay out. He became the talk of our Nation. But once again the white people had no ears and they kept coming. He found that most of the miners were so intent on panning for gold that he could easily sneak up behind them without them being aware of his presence and then silently kill them. Sometimes if it was just one or two miners, he would shoot them with their own rifles, which they often left up on the riverbank in their haste to pan for the shiny metal. However, he never took their scalps.

The white man had introduced scalping early on to prove that they had killed one of us so they could collect a bounty from their head men. So our people began to scalp their people and we learned to do it better. However, by taking a scalp, it also meant in our Lakota way that we would be taking a man's spirit so that he would not be whole on the other side. Crazy Horse wanted no part of that. He just wanted us to keep what had always been ours.

After killing these miners, Crazy Horse took the little pouches which they stored the shiny metal in off of their bodies. He believed that the shiny metal, or gold, belonged to our Mother the Earth. But rather than dumping their findings back where other miners would find it again, Crazy Horse took their gold bags to a small, secluded cave located in the northern Black Hills and emptied them onto the floor of the cave. He then mixed the gold dust and nuggets into the earth by covering them with dirt.

During this time, Crazy Horse would often come back and visit our family camp. We were always excited to see him. He would bring presents for us from the things he had taken from the miners, things we could use, like metal cooking pots, knives, ropes, guns, and horses. Sometimes during these visits Waglula would appeal to him to not fight the miners by himself. To make his father happy, Crazy Horse would respond by inviting our younger male relatives and his friends to join him, but after a while he would go off and fight the miners on his own once again. It was his way.

Around the same time, Corn took his grandson Bear Pipe on his first hemblecha. Corn was a very spiritual man and wished to impart that spirituality to his grandchildren. He prepared Bear Pipe with a purification ceremony and then placed him on a hill to be at one with our Creator.

While praying with his pipe during his hemblecha, a bear appeared to Bear Pipe and stood very close to him. Bear Pipe could feel its breath on his face for a long time. After he finished his hemblecha, he told his grandfather about this. Corn listened to him intently and then helped him interpret what he had seen.

The bear is known to our people as a healer. When a bear is sick, it shows in his droppings. By following the sick bear's trail, it can lead us to special places where the bear digs up roots and plants to make itself well. When we see this, we know that we two-leggeds can use these same roots and plants to heal ourselves. Thus, the vision told Bear Pipe that he would be a healer and a medicine man. It was good to know that we would have a medicine man in our family, and nobody was happier than Corn.

However, not everything was going well with all of our family. One sad day in 1873 Waglula's eldest daughter, Shell Blanket, returned to our family camp desperately sick and in tears. Her daughter, All Yellow, had died after just two winters, and right after her death, her man, Stands Straddle, left her. Stands Straddle had moved to the Red Cloud Agency to work for the white men down there. Once he arrived there, he took a new woman named White Nation Woman.

All Yellow had taken a special place in Waglula's heart. Now the white man's disease had taken her and left his eldest daughter and our family with a broken heart once again. There seemed to be no end to the misery the white man's diseases caused us.

When Crazy Horse returned to our camp, he saw how sick and depressed his sister was. He saw what Agency life had done to her. He also heard how Stands Straddle had thrown her away during her darkest hour. The episode created nothing but contempt for his former brother-in-law. Stands Straddle had let his heart become selfish and uncaring while working for the white man. He had forgotten how to be Lakota. Crazy Horse saw how the white culture had taught Stands Straddle that the ways of the paper money were more important than the ways of the heart.

Shell Blanket died of the white man's sickness the very next year. Our family was deeply saddened, especially because she had died so young and so unhappy. After that, Waglula no longer asked Crazy Horse to stop fighting the miners by himself. He only prayed that his son's efforts would rid our people of the white man for good. He was tired of burying his children and grandchildren who had been taken from him by the white man's diseases.

Soon word spread throughout the white man's world that many of their miners had lost their lives to a Lakota warrior. Their soldiers became anxious to protect their miners and their government schemed for a way to take away our Black Hills gold.

Tensions were rising and nearing the boiling point.

Our family's head man on Crazy Horse's mother's side, Lone Horn, had designs on a diplomatic solution. The American government had appointed Red Cloud and Spotted Tail as the head chiefs to our people. But our people did not see them that way. Red Cloud presided at the Red Cloud Agency, which was originally on the Shell River about one mile west of what is now Henry, Nebraska, while Spotted Tail held sway at the Whetstone Agency, which later became known as the Spotted Tail Agency, located about twenty miles northeast of Chadron on the upper White Earth River. Both were long distances from the areas our people liked to roam.

Lone Horn proposed a third Agency for our people that would take in all of our Black Hills. His proposal would contain our family's burial grounds within the Agency's boundaries, including Rattling Blanket Woman's grave along the White Earth River, Black Buffalo's grave near Grey Horn Butte, and Hump's grave in southwestern Wyoming, to name a few. Lone Horn also proposed that he be the new Agency's head man.

Lone Horn desired to get his boundary proposal into the hands of the government. It was something he had discussed with government officials at the 1868 Fort Laramie treaty signing, but it had not been acted on. Toward that end, he sent an elder who was not from our family's band, named Black Tongue, to deliver his proposal to the American government, because he did not feel up to the train ride to Washington, DC, at the time. Besides, Black Tongue understood the white man's language and Lone Horn trusted him. Black Tongue's camp was located near the Spotted Tail Agency.

After Black Tongue delivered Lone Horn's proposal, he returned and reported to Lone Horn. Once he finished telling Lone Horn of his experiences in Washington, he returned to his own camp while Lone Horn awaited the government's decision.

Following our summer solstice gathering in 1874, Crazy Horse spent a few days checking on our family's burial sites as our elders from the south had asked him to do during his hemblecha over fifteen years earlier. While making the rounds, he spotted over one thousand soldiers just west of what is today Sturgis, South Dakota, invading our Black Hills. He watched them survey the land and take pictures with a camera. He also noticed that they carried mining equipment. He was not sure what to make of such a large invasion, so he went to see Lone Horn, who was camped at our family's winter camp, to see if something new had been agreed upon.

Lone Horn was puzzled, he thought that they might be surveying the land so they could draw the boundaries he had proposed for his new Agency, but just in case, he sent a messenger to Black Tongue asking if anything additional had taken place during his trip to Washington, DC, in 1872.

Crazy Horse continued to spread the word and rode to see his father, who was camped at our family campsite on Bear Creek. Upon hearing the news, Waglula became angry and set out to see Lone Horn at once. Crazy Horse stayed behind and gathered six of our family's young men and led them back out to watch the soldiers and make sure our people's burial areas were not disturbed. A few of our family members rode to the Agencies to ask white agents what they knew about the invasion and found the agents had no answers.

Some of our elders hurried into the Hills to get ahead of the soldiers' advance so they could take down our scaffolds and bury the bodies before the soldiers could rob them in their quest for souvenirs, or chop up the scaffold poles to make wood for their campfires.

When Waglula entered Lone Horn's camp, he was not the only head man to do so. Word had spread quickly, and nearly all of our band's head men were there to find out what this soldier invasion was all about. When they learned at a council meeting that Lone Horn had sent someone who wasn't even a member of our band to Washington in his place, many of our head men expressed disappointment. Waglula told Lone Horn that he should have gone himself.

Humbled, Lone Horn began to worry privately that the Black Hills may have been signed away. When word came back that Black Tongue had not been invited to an important meeting back in 1872 between the white man's Great White Father and Red Cloud, our concerns heightened. Our council meeting ended in disarray, as many of our elders were incensed at this turn of events.

Lone Horn fasted and prayed. He was upset with himself for not having gone to Washington when he knew it was his responsibility to do so for our people. He hoped to find a solution with his prayers.

The army marched through our sacred Black Hills for about a month. They killed our game, burned our wood, left their garbage, and played their horns, which disturbed the peace for miles. However, they never rode up on the ridges where our dead were lying and we were thankful for that. We think that may have been the Creator answering Lone

Horn's prayers. After the soldiers left, we expelled a sigh of relief until we found out that they had told their nation that gold was in our sacred Black Hills. After that, the miners flooded in like never before.

Lone Horn continued to pray and fast, blaming himself for all that had happened, and within two months he died of a broken heart. His sacred bundle was passed to his son Touch The Cloud, who vowed to get to the bottom of what had happened. He asked us to not take any rash action until he had gone to Washington himself to see what had been said and done. He hoped to clear his father's name, and out of respect, we decided to be patient.

The following spring, Touch The Cloud went to Washington, along with Black Tongue, to learn if there were any new agreements that our people did not know about. They learned that the Black Hills had not been signed away, which cleared Lone Horn's name. However, Touch The Cloud became quite concerned when he found that the government was indeed interested in obtaining the gold located in our Black Hills, and he was even more concerned when he learned that Red Cloud and Spotted Tail were willing to entertain government proposals of ways to mine our sacred Black Hills.

Upon Touch The Cloud's return, he called together our head men to tell them what had transpired.

"One does not sell the land that the people walk on," stated Crazy Horse. It was all that he said.

It was all that needed to be said.

We now understood that the white man was eventually going to try to take away our Black Hills. We knew that if they were successful, they would be taking away our way of life and our deep-rooted connection to our ancestors. We understood that in the coming days we would have to fight for our way of life. We would have to fight to keep them from building their houses on top of our grandparents' bones. We would have to fight for our very existence as a people. As a people, we needed to establish a way to defend our Nation, our spirituality, and our way of living.

To the north, the Hunkpapa band was also getting pushed out of their traditional hunting grounds by the soldiers. The Hunkpapa were led by a revered spiritual leader named Sitting Bull. His devout spirituality was well known among all our people.

Sitting Bull and his Hunkpapa band came to join us during our summer solstice gathering of 1875. The Hunkpapa was another of our Lakota bands and usually roamed farther north. There were about four thousand of our people who attended the summer solstice that year. The main topic of discussion was how we should defend our way of life.

Our head men told us we should prepare our families for war. They told us that over the next year we should save half our rations each month so we could give it to our warriors to carry with them to help keep them sustained in our upcoming fights. They told us to search and gather our healing medicines so that we would have them if someone got hurt. They told us to begin to make our arrows and gather our gun powder. They told us that after the upcoming winter we needed to be ready.

The stakes were high and it was no time for politics. Our head men had to choose those who would lead us wisely. They asked Sitting Bull to show us how to keep our nation strong spiritually. They asked Crazy Horse to show our young men how to be strong in battle. Both of them accepted their roles and our confidence became sky high. Our family was proud to see that Crazy Horse was chosen to lead our young men. There was no question that he was our people's most experienced fighter.

However, that was not the only thing that happened during the summer solstice. Bear Pipe had found himself a woman and they got married. Her name was Comes Home Hard Times. Their newlywed bliss and our heartfelt celebration for them reminded us of how lucky we were to be a Lakota family. Our joy was beyond words.

The rest of that summer, our people began to prepare for the following year, and we prayed like never before. Our prayers were answered when all of a sudden the game began to return. Large herds of buffalo came down from Canada and our hearts jumped for joy. The Creator was with us.

That fall the government asked for a meeting with us to devise a plan to either lease or buy our Black Hills. Unfortunately, some of our people, like Red Cloud and Spotted Tail, thought that because the white people numbered more than we could possibly count, we were already beaten.

When we saw that Red Cloud and Spotted Tail showed interest in the white man's requests to take our Black Hills at an outdoor meeting, we sent some of our warriors to remind them that the rest of our people were willing to make a stand to save our way of life. It scared Red Cloud, Spotted Tail, and all the government representatives. Our warriors' display made them shut the meeting down.

This made the government angry. During the winter, the government sent us word that all our people had to be living at the Agencies by January 31, 1876. To us it was merely their acknowledgement that a big fight was coming, and their way to make it seem like we started it.

That winter was extremely harsh, and chances are that even had we wanted to come into the Agency, the weather conditions would have prohibited it. But it really didn't matter. We had no intention of changing our way of life and moving to the Agencies.

CHAPTER FIFTEEN

Summer Solstice

During a severe cold spell in mid-March 1876, the Cheyenne head man, Little Wolf, and his people were camped along the Shifting Sands River about 35 miles southwest of what is today Broadus, Montana. Ice and snow were everywhere. In the early morning hours of March 17, about three hundred soldiers quietly rode down the bluffs into the Shifting Sands River Valley and attacked Little Wolf's camp.

Awakened by the attack, the warriors rushed from their tipis to meet the soldiers long enough to allow their women and children to escape into the surrounding timbers. In their haste, they left behind all their possessions. As a result, the soldiers captured their entire village along with their winter supply of food and clothing. They also captured nearly all their horses, which numbered close to twelve hundred head.

Later that same morning, the soldiers burned all the belongings that the Cheyenne had left behind. Some of the Cheyenne watched them do this from the surrounding woods. It depressed them. They had been left with nothing but their beating hearts.

Having to endure late winter's still-freezing temperatures, the Cheyenne were in desperate need of everything. Late that night, the Cheyenne warriors were able to recapture most of their horses to make themselves mobile once again.

During that same evening, nearly all the Cheyenne villagers journeyed north and staggered into our family's camp, which was located at a place we called Twin Buttes. Today Twin Buttes is known by the Americans as the Missouri Buttes and is located three miles northwest of Grey Horn Butte.

When they arrived, many of them had frostbitten hands and feet. Our hearts went out to them. We gave them warm clothing and hot soup. We shared our tipis with them, and because we did not have enough room for all of them, we helped some of their families get situated in nearby caves with warm fires and bedding. They were extremely grateful and most of them stayed with us the rest of the winter.

Once their people were situated, Little Wolf led a group of his warriors out to warn the rest of the Cheyenne camps that the soldiers would now attack them without reason and that they were better off joining our village so we could defend ourselves with better numbers.

Meanwhile, the soldiers returned to their fort on the north side of the north fork of the Shell River, which they called Fort Fetterman, to get resupplied. Fort Fetterman was located about eleven miles northwest of what is today Douglas, Wyoming.

Toward the end of March, we made our offerings for our spring solstice by placing rocks on top of a butte in a circle that measured about the same circumference as the base of a tipi. We then built a fire to heat a second set of rocks. Once the second set of rocks were red hot, we put them in a pit within our circle of rocks. At that point, one of our elders would bring an offering and bend over the red hot rocks while another elder poured water on them to create steam, which in turn enveloped the elder and his offering. This is another form of smudging.

During the smudging, we said a prayer thanking the Creator for the blessings of our past year and asked a blessing for the upcoming year. We also prayed for the Creator to protect our people as we continued to prepare for the inevitable fight against the soldiers.

Once we had completed our spring solstice ceremony, our family and people, along with the Cheyenne, returned to Slim Buttes to concentrate on gathering food, making new bows, and raiding anybody or any place that might have guns. Guns were what was needed for the good fight ahead. They had greater range than our arrows did. We also made sure our ponies had plenty to eat so they would be strong and healthy for the upcoming struggles. We did this the entire month of April and the first part of May.

Around the middle of May, our scouts reported that they had seen buffalo herds to the west. It was a welcome report. So our camp moved to Black Horse Butte along the Shifting Sands River in hopes of securing buffalo meat.

Around this time, soldiers led by a head soldier named George Armstrong Custer left Fort Abraham Lincoln to find us and drive us onto the reservations as if we were cattle.

Slim Buttes area, a place to hunt buffalo and camp. Photo by Bill Matson.

Fort Abraham Lincoln is about four miles southwest of what is today Bismarck, North Dakota. When some of our Dakota tribe members, who had camped near Fort Lincoln, joined Sitting Bull's camp near the Bigger Than You See River, they told Sitting Bull about the soldiers that had left the fort. (The Bigger Than You See River got its name because it often spilled over its banks and flooded in the spring. The Americans renamed it the Grand River.)

While we were camped at Black Horse Butte, Sitting Bull's camp decided to join ours. His camp consisted of about two thousand five hundred Hunkpapa and Dakota warriors and their family members. After they arrived, they told us about the soldiers coming to get us from the east. It worried us.

Once Sitting Bull's people had settled in to our camp, it increased our camp size substantially. It meant there were more hungry mouths to feed, which kept our hunting parties very busy.

Now that our camps had come together, Crazy Horse and Sitting Bull sat down to figure out what to do next. Determining the soldier movements was critical toward that end. So they sent a message to our Lakota still at the Agencies to keep an eye out for any soldier movements and send word back to us if they saw anything, because we needed every advantage we could get in our battle to save our way of life. After our Lakota at the Agency received this message, they came to understand that we were in a do or die situation, and most of them gave their hearts to us. Many of them even left the Agencies to join us.

One of Lone Horn's sons, Frog, was an agency policeman at the Red Cloud Agency. We called these Agency policemen "metal breasts," due to the fact that they were given metal stars to put on their chests. Frog was one of those who would visit our family and tell us about soldier movements and anything else that he may have heard.

When Frog left the Agency to tell us of the soldier movements, he would give his metal breast, or policeman jacket, along with his Agency horse to one of his younger relatives. He would then instruct them to wear the metal breast jacket while riding his Agency horse high on the ridges so that the Agency officials would still think he was performing his job.

In preparing for the fight, many of us still remembered the Wagon Box Fight. With that memory in mind, we wanted to make sure we had up-to-date guns and ammunition. To accomplish this, Crazy Horse and Sitting Bull discussed ways of bringing in better rifles and gun powder to help our people and even our chances with the soldiers. Crazy Horse learned that Sitting Bull knew a Dakota head man named Two Bears. Two Bears knew a trader up north whom we called Jeanineau (we are unsure of the spelling, as our family history has always been spoken), who was willing to trade better guns and ammunition for gold. Unfortunately, our people did not have any gold. It was not something our people had ever seen any need to accumulate. That's when Crazy Horse remembered the cave where he had hidden the gold taken from the dead miners.

This news made all our head men very happy. We all knew that if the gold was still in Crazy Horse's cave, our weapon worries would be over. Crazy Horse devised a plan to send two of our relatives to get the gold from the cave. He told them to bring a pack horse to carry it all back.

Once his relatives arrived at the cave, they found the gold was still there under the dirt. They loaded the pack horse so full that it almost gave out. As a result, they transferred a portion of the pack horse's load to one of their personal mounts. Our two relatives then rode double on the remaining mount in order to continue their journey back.

In the meantime, our horses had eaten all the grass around our camp at Black Horse Butte, forcing us to move to a new campsite in order to keep them in fresh grass. We chose Twin Buttes near Grey Horn Butte. This is also where Crazy Horse's two relatives arrived with the gold. When our head men saw the gold, they were euphoric. Now we knew the traders would furnish us with all the weapons we needed.

Near the end of May, Sitting Bull and Two Bears, along with his Dakota warriors, took charge of the gold. It was brought north to trade for rifles and ammunition at the place where Jeanineau worked. When they presented it to the traders, the traders' eyes popped out of their heads. They had never seen so much gold. The trading post was located where the Muddy River crosses what is today the Montana and North Dakota border.

The traders took some of the gold to other traders in the area and bought all the guns and ammunition they could. It made us very happy. Jeanineau volunteered to come back with our people to insure that all our future gun and ammunition needs would be fulfilled. In the process, he and Two Bears became fast friends.

While our village waited for them to return with the guns and ammunition, our horses ate all the grass around Twin Buttes and we had to move our camp once again. We moved it to a new site along Otter Creek, which is located today a few miles south of Ashland, Montana. Our Otter Creek camp sat in a valley filled with dense pine trees. Today those thick pine trees have been thinned out by government agencies and wild fires.

Meanwhile, reports delivered by those leaving the Agencies to join us said that Custer's men had discovered our trail and were following it. As more and more of our people joined us from the Agencies, our numbers swelled and our horse herds grew to the point that we had to move from Otter Creek after just a couple of days. This time we moved to the area around the Rock Belonging to the Black Tail Deer, the place where Corn's son Bullhead had given his life to the Creator to insure that our family and our people would continue to live. The Rock Belonging to the Black Tail Deer is a group of tightly connected rocks that thrust their rounded tops skyward for about twenty feet out of a grassy incline. The rock overlooks a valley surrounded by rocky buttes and wooded hills from the valley's west end.

It was here that we knew we would learn the fate of our people and our way of life. The black-tail deer had foretold this would be the case to Lame Deer's relative in 1844. Knowing this, the Rock Belonging to the Black Tail Deer was where we decided to begin our summer solstice and hold our Sundance. The Rock Belonging to the Black Tail Deer is located about six miles north of what is today Lame Deer, Montana, near Red Flower Creek. Red Flower Creek was renamed by the Americans as Rosebud Creek.

Once we arrived at the Rock Belonging to the Black Tail Deer, our women assembled our tipis primarily south of the rock and gathered dried buffalo chips and wood to feed our campfires. Many of our men went hunting to keep our camp supplied with meat, because our camp had grown to about twelve thousand people, with new arrivals coming

Deer Medicine Rock overlooks the Sundance grounds. Photo by Mark Frethem.

from the Agencies at an ever-increasing rate. The new arrivals brought their saved-up rations to help feed our camp. Frog was one of those new arrivals. He had put away his police jacket for good to come and fight with us.

The day before our Sundance, Little Wolf returned with some additional Cheyenne bands who decided to join us after learning of the soldiers' attack on his village. They brought five Arapaho warriors with them. The Arapaho joined us for their own safety when they learned that the soldiers were out to attack anyone off Agency lands.

There were some warriors among the Cheyenne who did not believe the soldiers were coming for them. They held out for a peaceful solution. Some of these holdouts had been present to see Custer smoke their sacred pipe in a pledge of peace and unity with one of their holy men in 1869. They were sure Custer would honor his pledge. So they proposed to send out five of their young scouts, along with one of those who had been at the sacred pipe smoking ceremony, to talk to Custer. We agreed that it could not hurt anything and so they went.

It wasn't long afterwards that one of our Lakota families who had traveled from one of the Agencies brought the six Cheyenne back to our camp. They were dead. They had found them lying on the plains. We learned that they had been killed by Custer's scouts. It seems the Cheyenne scouts had approached a group of Custer's Arikara scouts on the prairie lands in what is now the most northeastern part of Wyoming. The Cheyenne were waving a flag of truce. The Arikara ignored the white flag and brutally cut them down without giving them an opportunity to talk with Custer. Upon hearing this, those Cheyenne who had been hoping that Custer would keep his pledge of peace became convinced that he had smoked the pipe without opening his heart. It cemented their desire to join our fight.

One of the Cheyenne warriors killed on the mission had a woman waiting for him back at our camp. They had planned to be married. However, when she discovered that he had been killed, she jumped off one of the high buttes surrounding our camp and killed herself.

When our guns and ammunition finally arrived, it made us very happy. We passed them out to our warriors. We also passed out our newly acquired gun powder and lead for those that needed to make their own bullets for other guns.

As the time for our Sundance approached, Crazy Horse prepared himself for it and prayed to the Creator. He asked for guidance in helping to protect all our people, including those who had lost their spiritual ways. The Creator told him that if he continued to live in the spiritual ways of our ancestors, they would help him succeed from the other side.

Prior to the Sundance, he went two rounds in one of our sweat lodges to purify himself. (A round begins each time the sweat lodge door is closed and we breathe the Creator's air.) He then placed an offering of chanshasha at the base of the Sundance tree and joined our other warriors participating in the Sundance. He danced the entire first day, looking at the sun the entire time. During his Sundance, he asked the Creator if he would be giving up his life in the upcoming fight. He did not get an immediate response.

While our Sundancers danced, a group of our elders beat a stretched-out buffalo hide attached to wooden stakes pounded into the earth and sang our Sundance songs for them. The beat of this makeshift drum sounded like the bellow of the buffalo and vibrated the earth that they danced on.

Eagle bone whistles were heard from members of the Itazipco band (today nearly all Sundancers blow eagle bone whistles). The Itazipco band is another band in our Lakota Nation and are sometimes called the Sans Arc band. The Itazipco is the band that included our Sacred Calf Pipe Keeper, Old Man Elk Head.

Our elk dreamers also participated in their own way. Piercing two holes in the skin of their upper chest, they attached themselves to the Sundance tree with a rawhide, or sinew, rope tied to a small buffalo bone pushed into the open cavity created by the piercing. They wanted a greater spiritual understanding because they knew when the fighting started, it would be their job to save our wounded. They danced for two days, or two red (sunny) days and two blue (night) days. At the end of their spiritual union with the Creator, they leaned back and pulled themselves away from the tree, which ripped the buffalo bones out of their chest. Today nearly all our Sundancers pierce and dance four full calendar days.

Our people watched and encouraged our Sundancers from beneath the chokecherry arbors that we had built around our Sundance arena. Sitting Bull had a key role during our Sundance. He sat on a hide close to the Sundance tree. He was giving the Creator a crimson blanket of one hundred pieces of flesh carved from his arms by his hunka, or adopted brother, Jumping Bull, in a sacrifice and prayer for our people. He sacrificed his flesh to the Creator during the Sundance because that is all he had to give that was his. The Creator already owns everything else in this world.

Sitting Bull danced all four calendar days of our Sundance. Most of the rest of our Sundancers danced only one day. About one hundred and fifty dancers danced shoulder to shoulder each day. Crazy Horse was one of the dancers that danced only one day. The evening following his Sundance, Crazy Horse rested. It was during his rest that he had a vision. It was not good.

The following day, he carved this vision on a rock; it had the shape of an owl. This rock is located a few yards west of the Rock Belonging to the Black Tail Deer. Today we

Looking at Owl Rock from Deer Medicine Rock. Photo by Mark Frethem.

Crazy Horse carved this vision into Owl Rock located near Deer Medicine Rock. Photo by Kim Donau.

refer to this rock as simply the Owl Rock. The vision was of his death. It depicted a line of horse hooves arching towards the sky, which signified life. This trail was interrupted by a carving of a small Lakota man and then again by a white doctor. The horse hooves of life ended with a carving of himself showing two stab wounds to the kidney and liver regions of his body. Leading away from his body, the horse hooves of life continued but were now lying sideways, signifying his death. The death trail led to a carving of a soldier holding a bayonet.

His vision told him that when his time came to die, it would be with the blessings of his own people at a place that housed soldiers. It also told him a white doctor would try to save him. Finally, it showed him that a white soldier would cause two fatal wounds with a bayonet, which would ultimately kill him. His vision also told him that he would not die in the upcoming fights. This part he celebrated. He was told he would live as long as he roamed free and stayed clear of places where our people and the soldiers stayed together.

One of our relatives on our paternal grandfather's side named Bear With Horns also Sundanced. He was a member of our Minnikojou band. He danced the second day and also carved his vision. His carving is located on the Rock Belonging to the Black Tail Deer. It is a carving of a bear with horns with another bear carved inside the horned bear. His vision signified that he was going to help heal our people by fighting for our survival, like a grizzly bear protecting her cubs.

Doug War Eagle points out Bear with Horns' prophecy located on Deer Medicine Rock. Photo by Mark Frethem.

Bear With Horns' father, Red Thunder, also carved a picture on the Rock Belonging to the Black Tail Deer. It was a circle with a "plus" sign inside it, signifying the four directions. A lightning bolt spiked downward out of the circle. The drawing signified that Red Thunder's family was present. Red Thunder and his wife, Melts None, were also the parents of Fights The Thunder, who fathered Crazy Horse's youngest sister Iron Cedar's future husband, Old Eagle.

On the third and fourth days of the Sundance, the young men who had come from the Agencies to prove themselves as worthy warriors participated. By Sundancing, they became worthy of carrying their fathers' or grandfathers' sacred names. Once they were able to carry their families' sacred names, they were expected to distinguish themselves in battle. This would make them full warriors.

Their families celebrated their commitment by making them new warrior shirts and giving them family heirlooms, which they wore every day along with their individual war paint. They were to be ready for battle day and night. Everybody understood that they had pledged their last breath to our people. We referred to them as our Suicide Boys, meaning they would fight until either they killed the enemy or the enemy killed them.

On the fourth day of the Sundance, Sitting Bull's whole being was with our Creator. His devotion amazed us. After several hours in that state, he collapsed.

A hush came over our people.

In a weakened state, he told us of his vision. We listened with bated breath. He revealed that the soldiers would fall into our camp upside down, meaning that they would fall off

Left to right: Bill Matson, Doug War Eagle, and Delmar Clown gaze out at the 1876 Sundance grounds as Doug describes how it was. Photo by Mark Frethem.

their horses and die. He said that the Creator had told him, "I give you these because they have no ears." This meant that because the soldiers had not listened to us, the Creator would give us their lives.

However, Sitting Bull also told us not to take any spoils from the soldiers' bodies. This meant not to take any of their belongings. If we did, a curse would befall our people for seven generations. His vision made us very excited because we knew that it meant we would be the victors in our fight to save our Nation. Our hearts swelled with joy. For the next few days, his vision was all anyone in our camp could talk about. It energized our people. The fate of our people and our way of life was now told, and it was good.

We went about our daily activities with a new purpose. We still had twelve thousand mouths to feed. Our hunters brought in travois after travois filled with fresh meat, and after a few hours' rest, they went out and did it again.

Our women cooked and cooked. They dug wild turnips until they could find no more. They scraped buffalo hides and sewed new tipis. We ate deep into the rations that had been brought from the Agencies. It was a very busy time for all.

While coming back from scraping buffalo hides with a relative, Good Looking Woman happened to see her son's carving on the belly of the Owl Rock. She came to understand it. It frightened her. She hastened to find a place to pray and asked the Creator to take her life in place of her son's. It was a prayer she would repeat over and over the remaining days of her life. She had faith that the Creator would listen to her.

After having camped at the Rock Belonging to the Black Tail Deer for six days, our horses had once again eaten the grass down to dirt. Around the fifteenth of June, we moved our camp westward toward where the buffalo herds were migrating. Keeping so many horses in fresh grass was not easy. We moved up Red Flower Creek about ten miles, to a place that today is called Busby, Montana, a community located in the western portion of the Northern Cheyenne Reservation.

As our women began to set up our tipis at our new camp, another group of Cheyenne rode in with news of a large force of soldiers heading our way from the south.

CHAPTER SIXTEEN

The Red Flower Fight

We thought the soldier force coming from the south was Custer and that he had somehow taken a shortcut through our Black Hills. However, we soon discovered that it wasn't him at all, but soldiers led by a man we knew as Three Stars, or George Crook.

In the late afternoon of June 16, Crazy Horse mounted Inyan and led about twelve hundred warriors to meet these soldiers. His younger brothers Combing and Bear Pipe were among these warriors.

On the way to meet the soldiers, a large group of Cheyenne warriors joined us. The Cheyenne told us that earlier in the day they had found a buffalo herd halfway between the Beaver Tail River and Red Flower Creek and had been preparing to hunt them when they stumbled on some Crow and Shoshoni scouts preparing to do the same thing. They had exchanged visual insults with them. Once they realized the Crow and Shoshoni were part of the larger soldier force belonging to Three Stars, the Cheyenne decided to join us to even the numbers so the Crow and Shoshoni could be repaid for their insults and for poaching our buffalo. The Cheyenne rode a few miles apart and parallel to us as we rode along Buffalo Berry Creek, which today is known to the Americans as Reno Creek.

Along the way, our warriors would dismount and run alongside their mounts while going up inclines. They would remount while going downhill in order to save our horses' energy for the upcoming fight. Our warriors did this quite often because it kept our horses fresh for a longer distance.

Riding in groups spread out over a wide expanse, our warriors' paths finally led us to Red Flower Creek. Red Flower Creek is a slow moving, gurgling stream that averages ten to twenty feet in width. Its banks contain long stretches that are populated with dense growths of trees and wild rose bushes. When the bushes and trees are absent, the banks are populated by tall grass and pockets of brilliantly colored wildflowers.

A light rain fell as we neared Three Stars' army. We stopped at a narrow spot near a Lakota sacred burial ground that Crazy Horse had known of since his youth, in what is today the Rosebud Valley. We watered our horses by the light of the morning star. While we were there, many of our warriors put their paint on, and some prayed on the hills lining this narrow place in the valley.

Crazy Horse prayed on the western valley ridge bordering the Lakota sacred burial ground, which was populated with buffalo bone altars. (The Montana State Park Service has mistakenly labeled this same ridge a buffalo jump.) Crazy Horse prayed that we would push away the soldiers without any loss of life and that our people's way of living would endure forever. When he was done praying, he recognized that this narrow, wooded part of the valley would be a good place to decoy the soldiers into an ambush. He also knew that with the burial grounds to our backs, it would inspire our warriors to fight harder to protect the spirits of our grandparents who would be watching us.

He had the word passed among our warriors.

Once everyone learned of his plan, we went into the fight with the intention of luring the soldiers into our ambush. We appointed certain groups of warriors to hide along the densely wooded valley walls when the time was right.

Once our horses had rested and satisfied their thirst, we tied their tails in a knot to prepare them for battle. The knot quieted the swishing noise of their tails, so our positions would not be given away when we needed silence. Knotting them also kept the horses from tangling their tails in the mud and branches or anything that might impede movement. We then rode into the trees along the valley ridges to keep our presence hidden from the soldiers.

While we were riding through the trees, our lead riders were spotted by the Crow and Shoshoni scouts. They exchanged a few rifle shots, and then our lead riders high-tailed it back towards our main force. Hearing the shots, the main body of our warriors converged towards the gunfire and discovered the Crow and Shoshoni. We quickly formed a makeshift ambush for them to ride into. However, before they got deep enough for us to spring our trap, some of our young men jumped the gun and fired early, which spoiled everything. Now aware of their danger, the Crow and Shoshoni turned their horses around and rode as fast as they could back to the soldiers' camp, which was about eleven miles south. We pursued them at a gallop the entire way.

The soldiers had been resting along Red Flower Creek. They had unsaddled their horses and were completely unprepared for us. The Crow and Shoshoni scouts raced through their camp and alerted them while trying to get away from us. We rode toward the soldier camp from three directions, the north, west, and east. We followed the scouts to within five hundred yards of the soldiers, when a group of their soldiers hustled to high ground and started firing at us from behind rocks and bushes. We veered away, slid down the sides of our mounts while holding onto their necks with one arm and hanging onto the horses' backs with one foot. This gave the soldiers no targets to shoot at. We fired at them while still on the move from underneath our horse's necks.

Our sudden appearance confused them. Some of their horses and pack horses ran off during the melee. Our warriors saw this and captured them. Some of these pack horses had wooden boxes tied on their backs. Upon opening them, we discovered they were full of ammunition. It made us very happy.

As the soldiers regrouped and began to regain their confidence, we tried to decoy them back to our appointed ambush site in the Red Flower Valley. As they chased our decoys towards the site, one of their soldiers fell off his horse. Seeing this, some of our decoys turned around to count coup on him. With our decoys riding towards them, the soldiers rescued their fallen soldier and scurried back in the direction of their camp, which effectively scuttled our ambush efforts for the time being. With their backs to us, the rest of our warriors rushed after them.

Our smaller horses were much faster than their larger ones, and we were nearly able to not only catch the soldiers but encircle them. In an effort to escape that encirclement, the soldiers turned and charged us in order to push us away. This was done several times, until soon their forces were spread out for nearly three miles, which caused them to splinter into smaller and smaller groups. Once their groups became small enough, we started to work on them.

Unfortunately, as soon as these smaller groups realized their danger, they would immediately fall back towards their camp to gather their numbers once again. As we chased the soldiers, we could see Three Stars on top of a hill on a black pony. We were closing on him fast when another group of soldiers came over the hill from behind him and began to charge us. Not wanting to take too many casualties, we backed off, only to find these soldiers galloping after us on horseback. As they closed in on us, some of the warriors in our group dismounted and put up a blistering barrage that broke the soldiers' charge and sent them back towards Three Stars.

It was back and forth the entire day.

We continued to try and decoy the soldiers into our ambush. Just when we started to become discouraged that our ambush would not work out, a large body of soldiers tried to sneak past us by riding through the very valley where our ambush site was located. When we saw this, we became excited and sent word to our appointed warriors to take their places at the ambush site.

As the appointed warriors left to spring the ambush, Crazy Horse and some of the rest of our warriors continued to keep the remaining soldiers at bay. In fact, we had one large group of soldiers pinned down in an open draw. For a time it looked as though we might be able to wipe this group of soldiers out. However, seeing their situation turn desperate, Three Stars sent a message out to those soldiers riding towards our ambush.

Having ridden to the very jaws of our ambush, the soldiers in the valley stopped. They sensed that the narrowness of the valley would likely be a good place for an ambush, so they dismounted to tighten their saddle girths in case their fears were realized. At that point, Three Stars' messenger arrived. After a brief exchange, the soldiers suddenly turned around and headed back to rejoin the rest of Three Stars's command. Our warriors waiting to spring the ambush were very disappointed and discouraged.

Not long after that, Crazy Horse called off our attack. He saw that the soldiers were thoroughly confused and disorganized, and at least for the time, no longer posed a threat to our village. Besides, it was late in the day. He asked some our warriors to gather our dead and wounded and bring them back to our camp.

"It is late and we are hungry," Crazy Horse told us. He assigned a small group of our warriors to keep the soldiers busy and act as our rear guard. The rest of our warriors went back to our camp that night. Our losses were about twelve warriors killed and about twenty wounded.

Our Cheyenne allies called this fight "The Fight Where the Girl Saved Her Brother" because during one of the soldier advances, one of their warriors, named Comes In Sight, had his horse shot out from underneath him. It appeared certain that the soldiers would swallow him up in their counter attack. However, his sister, Buffalo Calf Road Woman, galloped out and helped him onto the back of her horse and brought him to the safety of our warriors.

It turned out to be a good fight for us because we had stopped Three Stars and captured many of his pack horses loaded with bullets.

One of our rear guard warriors, named Long Road, was shot while covering our exit and died after reaching what would become our camp four days later at the Greasy Grass River. The Greasy Grass has since been renamed Little Bighorn by the Americans. Long Road made it as far as what is today called Reno-Benteen Hill. His family set his body up in a tipi outside our village to honor him. Unfortunately, Custer's soldiers looted his burial site on their way to fight us.

The Red Flower fight did not produce the victory that we had been promised in Sitting Bull's vision. That was yet to come. However, we had done what we had set out to do, and that was to keep the soldiers away from our families. So we rode back to our camp to enjoy the last few days of our summer solstice.

The soldiers did not follow, and as a matter of fact, they went into the Bighorn Mountains and camped there for a long time. They seemed to have lost their appetite for fighting, as they spent most of their time fishing and hunting.

Upon returning, we noticed that our camp, which was now situated on Buffalo Berry Creek, had grown larger. Our people were joining us from the Agencies in increasing numbers. None of us had ever seen our camp so large. These new arrivals told us that the Agency officials were starting to notice that most of our people were no longer at the Agencies and they were becoming alarmed.

One of these new arrivals was an elder Dakota warrior named Inkpaduta. Inkpaduta had come because there had been an outbreak of a water disease back at one of the Agency villages, most likely cholera. He had brought with him a medicine man named Red Fox, whom he vowed to protect with his life. They hoped to get a special medicine that would cure the disease from another medicine man who was traveling with us and who they knew possessed the medicine.

All of these new arrivals had left trails to our village that were easy for the soldiers to follow.

CHAPTER SEVENTEEN

The Greasy Grass

The rolling plains of eastern Montana stretch as far as the eye can see. In the early spring, the grass is lush and the wildflowers are plentiful. Bees can be seen pollinating the flowers to ensure the beauty will be there again the following year. The river known as the Greasy Grass sweeps by islands of cottonwood trees lining its banks. The stands of cottonwoods are interrupted by patches of grass that sprout from the surrounding sandy soil. When it rains, the sandy soil supporting these grass tufts becomes slick, making it easy to slip and fall. That is why we call it the Greasy Grass.

Greasy Grass River. Photo by Mark Frethem.

When we arrived at the Greasy Grass on June 20, it was hot. The women built our village quickly. Our teenage daughters gathered wood for the campfires so they could cook. They picked berries to make wasna. Laughter and good feelings echoed throughout the camp. Our young boys raced their horses and ran foot races, creating a stir of excitement throughout the camp. Our smiling children splashed each other and cooled themselves in the river.

Our men poured our newly acquired gun powder into empty bullet casings, placed them into bullet molds, and squeezed them shut to make bullets for their guns. They practiced firing our new Winchester repeating rifles with the fifteen-round magazines that the gold had purchased from the traders. It brought smiles to our men's faces. There was something for everyone.

It was a great time to be Lakota.

Many of our men went looking for game. The buffalo herds were near and the hunger of our village was without end. In addition, with all the new arrivals that kept pouring in, we needed plenty of new buffalo hides to make tipi skins. It normally takes about five to six skins to make a tipi.

There are many books written by other cultures that say we camped according to our band affiliation as though we were regiments in an army. The fact of the matter is that we most often camped next to our friends and relatives. Sometimes these friends and relatives were in our Minnikojou band, and sometimes they were in another band. Summer solstice was a chance to visit those we hadn't seen for a while. It was one of the reasons we attended. There were no hard and fast rules where to set up our tipi.

On the eastern end of our camp were sixty-eight Minnikojou head elders. They stayed at the edge of our camp to keep their medicines separate from any impurities, such as a woman's moon, or also known as her period. During a woman's moon, she expels her impurities so that she is clean for another month, while a man must sweat out his impurities in a purification ceremony. Our women were good at keeping themselves separate when they were on their moon, but there was always that time just prior to their moon that made our head elders cautious enough to keep their medicines separate. Waglula and Corn were among those who camped with our elders. We called this camp The Old Man's Camp.

On the western side of the river, our younger boys watched our horses and made sure they did not wander away. Our horse herd numbered over ten thousand head. Makah and his friend Old Eagle were two of the horse herders.

Our main camp was positioned around our Sacred Calf Pipe and our Sacred Calf Pipe Keeper, Old Man Elk Head. Crazy Horse and Black Shawl were camped close to Sitting Bull's tipi near the center of our village. Our village numbered close to fifteen thousand people now and stretched nearly continuously for six miles along the Greasy Grass River.

Down by the river, near the center of our encampment, our elders built twelve sweat lodges with their entrances facing one of the four directions, west, north, east, or south, depending on who built it. They were there to help heal and renew the spirits of our warriors who had been injured at the Red Flower Creek fight. We also prayed in them for those warriors that had journeyed to the other side.

Our young men who had joined our camp from the Agencies and had Sundanced the previous week at the Rock Belonging to the Black Tail Deer were brought into our sweat lodges by our elders to purify themselves. They were given buffalo horns of hot medicines to drink. During this time, our young men told of the visions they had received during the Sundance. After telling of their visions, their Sundance was considered complete and they received their fathers' or grandfathers' names to carry as their own. It was a proud moment for them all.

The young men who came to us too late to participate in the Sundance were also taken into a purification ceremony by the head of their family, or one of our head elders. There they were prepared to become spiritually strong enough to become a warrior through the purifying of their hearts so they would have a better path to the Creator. These young men would receive their fathers' or grandfathers' sacred names, too but only after proving themselves in battle. Until then, they still had to carry their childhood names.

Back at our family's camp, things had taken a dark turn. Good Looking Woman had become quite ill. She had developed a fever and cough. The medicine that she needed to get well was found back at the Northern Agency (later known as the Cheyenne River Agency) along the Owl River, which has been renamed the Moreau River by the Americans, after a white trader. At the same time, we knew the soldiers were coming from the east and we were going to be in for a big fight. We estimated that the soldiers would engage us on June 26. So we prepared to send our elderly, women, and children back to the Agency with some of our warriors. With her illness getting progressively worse, Good Looking Woman was one of those being sent.

Good Looking Woman knew why she was ill. The Creator had listened to her prayer. Now she wanted to see her son one more time. When Crazy Horse heard she was sick and wanted to see him, he came immediately. When he got to her tipi, her pale face brightened. She knew that this would be the last time she would ever see him. "You are the heart of my heart," she told him.

Crazy Horse had seen his mother feeling under the weather before, but this time he sensed it was different. She was very weak. There was a resignation in her eyes that he had never seen before. It made him feel helpless, like he might actually lose her this time. He tried his best to give her his strength, but instead she gave him hers. Her life had always been one of giving.

She prepared him to think of her as someone who would stay part of his life and not someone who had left it. She gave him a smile so he would always remember her—a smile that could carry her in his heart forever. And with that, she told those around her that she was ready to leave for the Agency.

On the evening of June 23, Talks About Him and his father-in-law, Dull Knife, prepared what was approximately half of our camp for their return to the Agency. With the help of the younger men, They Are Afraid Of Her settled Good Looking Woman onto a travois for the long trip back.

Some of the younger men were sent ahead to mark the trail in the moonlight. The crickets became quiet. The night sky held a nearly full moon.

Crazy Horse held her hand as long as he could, and then it was time for them to go. Black Shawl watched from the shadows. Combing and Bear Pipe said their good-byes and stayed behind with our warriors. Waglula and his wives, along with Corn, Makah, and Iron Cedar, also bid her farewell and they, too, stayed behind. Once the good-byes were said, the procession started.

Crazy Horse watched her go for a long time, even after her travois had traveled so far away that he could no longer see her. He felt he had not done enough to show his appreciation to her for helping him to have a good life after he had lost his birth mother.

Seeing his uneasiness, Black Shawl stepped from the shadows and placed her hand on him in a comforting manner. She reminded him that he had grown into what Good Looking Woman had wanted him to be, and that was the biggest thank-you he could ever give her. Crazy Horse appreciated his wife's intentions, but he still felt he owed the woman who had raised him much more. As the crickets renewed their song, Crazy Horse and Black Shawl retired to their lodge.

Our elderly, women, and children's journey back to the Agency was fraught with dangers. After a few miles, the young men who were sent ahead came back and informed Talks About Him that a group of Crow had been discovered watching our village from a butte overlooking the valley. The butte was about fourteen miles outside our village. Today that butte is called the Crow's Nest.

Anxious to get by the Crow without being noticed, Talks About Him said a prayer to the Creator asking for help. Then he began leading the party around the butte in the dim moonlight. They walked in each other's footsteps to diminish the rustle of the grass. Two of our men picked up Good Looking Woman's travois and carried her to minimize the sound. Once they had gotten around the Crow without being noticed, they journeyed to the south into the Wolf Mountains by way of a place known as Sioux Pass, and then continued on in a straight line east toward the Agency.

The following morning at the Greasy Grass, the people in our village awoke to see Sitting Bull appear from the northeast side of a hill, which today is known as Last Stand Hill. He was holding his sacred pipe in one hand and what we saw as a spirit rock in the other. We saw him place the rock near the crown of the hill. We did not know why he did this, but we knew there had to be a reason.

Inkpaduta and Red Fox left that morning for the Agency. They had finally obtained the medicine from the medicine man they were seeking so they could combat the sickness at their Agency village. Later on we heard that on their way back, they had come across some abandoned army boxes of hardtack and opened one of them. Some soldiers spotted them doing this and fired shots at them, but they escaped without injury. After that, Inkpaduta and Red Fox continued on to the Agency in order to deliver the urgently needed medicine.

As a precaution regarding the scouting reports we had received of soldiers coming from the east, we sent a group of about sixty Suicide Boys to decoy them away from our village. Our Suicide Boys took off on this mission with an enthusiasm that is reserved only for the young. Their eagerness made us proud. Unfortunately, we did not recognize that their zeal would take them beyond where they could be useful in stopping the soldiers.

The buffalo herds were now in the Bighorn Mountains and most of our warriors, including Sitting Bull, were preparing to hunt that morning. Crazy Horse, Combing, and Bear Pipe joined them. Crazy Horse left Inyan with his father that day to rest him. With most of the men on the hunt, Black Shawl went over to Waglula's tipi for a visit with his wives. After her visit, she wandered outside our camp to dig wild turnips.

We knew that a fight was coming, but anticipated that it would be the following day, so meat was still the priority. We felt that there would still be time to prepare in the late afternoon and evening. We also knew that once the fighting started, there would be no time to find game or other food.

As morning turned to afternoon, our hunters began returning with buffalo meat. Crazy Horse, Combing, and Bear Pipe brought in several pack horses full of meat. Our women descended on the meat like a group of happy ants, cutting it up to let it dry.

The young men coming from the Agencies continued to pour in. It made our hearts swell with pride to see that so many of our young men cared about our Nation. The entire morning and early afternoon our family head men and elders helped our newly arriving young men get spiritually strong in the sweat lodges. By mid-afternoon Waglula had returned to the Old Man's Camp while Touch The Cloud continued to conduct purification ceremonies for our new arrivals.

There were a few of our men who had skipped the buffalo hunt in order to stay close and hunt nearer to our camp. Deeds was one of these men. He had taken his young son with him and was about two-and-one-half miles southeast of our camp when he heard the soldiers' canteen cans and other hardware rattling in the near distance. He rushed to a vantage point where he could see a long distance and saw their metal flashing and moving in the sun. They were early, and he knew he had to warn our camp right away.

Deeds and his son had just killed a deer and had been in the process of dressing it. But now there was no time to finish. He hid the deer in the bushes and instructed his son to hide in the brush while he went to warn our village. His warnings were first heard in the Old Man's Camp. It would be up to our elders and our young horse herders to meet the soldiers' charge and hold them at bay in order to save our village.

Sweat lodges emptied. Tipis emptied. Women and children who were at the Old Man's Camp ran toward our main camp for safety. The youngsters watching our horse herds brought horses for our elders to ride into battle.

Makah and Old Eagle brought Waglula, Corn, and the rest of our family's mounts. Iron Between Horns, Kills Enemy, Red Leggins, and Iron Cedar mounted to ride to our main camp. The boys brought an extra horse for Black Shawl, but she was nowhere to be found.

As the soldiers charged toward our camp, the ground shook and the dust flew. The Arikara scouts riding with them fired toward our camp without caring where their bullets landed. Our family's women, with the exception of Black Shawl, took off for the main village.

Waglula and several of our elders knew they needed to divert the soldiers' charge from our village, so they had our young horse herders cut limbs from cottonwood trees and tie them to the backs of their horses. Our horse herders then galloped away from our camp towards the river, creating huge dust clouds. These horse herders' ages ranged from eight to sixteen winters. Many of our elders positioned themselves in the dry creek beds that lined both sides of the dust clouds and waited for the soldiers. Waglula, Corn, and Red Thunder were among these elders. When the soldiers saw the dust cloud, they thought it was our people trying to escape and turned their horses to pursue. Once they got to the dust cloud, our elders opened up with their rifles and bows, which confused the soldiers and stopped them cold. The soldiers dismounted to return fire.

Once our elders sprang the trap, Makah and Old Eagle cut the branches loose from their horses and rode back to the horse herd to bring additional mounts for our elders.

The soldiers tried to push us back but soon discovered we had surrounded them on three sides and had put them in a cross fire. They withdrew to a wooded area along the Greasy Grass River. Later we learned that these attackers were led by a head soldier named Reno.

Meanwhile, the word of the soldiers' attack spread throughout our village. Upon hearing the news, Crazy Horse and many of our other warriors prepared themselves with their protective medicines. Once they were prepared, they rode to the fight.

Crazy Horse hopped on his father's bay hunting horse and raced to the fight with about two hundred warriors following him. Combing rode with him so he could be there in time to fight at his father's side. Bear Pipe high-tailed it to the horse herd to bring back several head so more of our warriors could ride and have a part in the fight.

As Crazy Horse raced toward the fighting, he saw our family's women. He stopped for them, and they told him they had left Inyan back at Waglula's tipi and that Black Shawl had not come back in time to join them on their flight to our main camp. With that news in hand, Crazy Horse sped toward the fight while watching for his wife. Along the way he spotted her running toward our main camp. He picked her up and galloped back to our family's women to drop her off so she could join them on their ride to safety. Crazy Horse then continued his charge into the battle.

As the fighting intensified, our elders and young herders, now joined by several of our young men and Cheyenne, began to sneak into the trees where the soldiers were hiding to get better shots at them.

When Crazy Horse arrived, our elders and young herders already had the soldiers nearly surrounded. He joined his father and Combing. Combing had arrived at his father's side just prior to Crazy Horse's arrival. Seeing that his father did not have a gun, Crazy Horse offered him his lever action Winchester and explained that he had another gun in the form of a pistol. Waglula thanked him and accepted it.

One of our strategies was to try to kill the soldiers' head man. From past fights we noticed that if we killed their head men, then the soldiers became confused and did not fight as well. So we always tried to pick the head man out. We detected a soldier in a white hat that seemed to be that head man and we targeted him. The soldier in the white hat was Reno.

Waglula snuck into the wooded area and found a clear vantage point to take a shot at Reno. He aimed his Winchester and had Reno in his sights when he pulled the trigger.

At the last second, an Arikara scout leaned forward and spoiled Waglula's shot. The Arikara scout went down with a bullet through his head, leaving pieces of his brain all over Reno's face. Reno froze for several seconds. Then he mounted his horse and rode up the hill with most of his men.

However, some of Reno's soldiers did not make it to their horses and were left behind in the wooded area. Crazy Horse found one of these men and killed him with a war club. Upon finishing the soldier off, two boys rode up to Crazy Horse and told him that a second group of soldiers was attacking our main village. Crazy Horse looked to his father. "Go. These are beaten," Waglula told him.

With that, Crazy Horse remounted and galloped off towards our main camp. Combing stayed with Waglula and helped chase the soldiers up a hill that is today referred to as Reno-Benteen Hill. They took out soldiers and counted coup all the way up. Reno and most of his men made it to the top and set up a perimeter. We lost nine elders and five horse herding boys in the fight with Reno.

On his way to fight soldiers at our main village, Crazy Horse stopped at Waglula's tipi to get his war pony, Inyan. He prepared him for battle. When he heard gunfire to the north, he quickly mounted Inyan and headed that way with about two hundred warriors. There they spotted some of Reno's men trying to reach another group of soldiers. They pursued them, traveling west, and overtook them. Crazy Horse then rode toward the northwest where he had seen some more soldiers disappear over a ridge.

In the fight at the main village, a second group of soldiers were on the attack. They were led by a head man by the name of George Armstrong Custer. Most of us had heard of him and he was known to be a good fighter. The survival of our people truly hung in the balance.

At about the same time, Talks About Him and Dull Knife were making good time leading our defenseless ones back to the Agency and had put plenty of distance between themselves and our village. Our warriors who were with them rode up on the ridges and watched for dangers while our elderly, women, and children rode in the valley below. Good Looking Woman had tired of lying on her travois and insisted she was well enough to walk. So she did.

At our main village in an area where many of the Cheyenne were camped, another group of soldiers attacked them. The soldiers were trying to be sneaky. They had hoped that all our warriors would be so busy fighting Reno that they could slip into our village and take out our women and children. The whole idea made us angry. A group of Cheyenne who had stayed behind to watch over their tipis had shot the soldiers' head chief off his horse as he was leading his men across the Greasy Grass River. The soldier wore a buckskin jacket. Later we found out that head soldier chief's name was Tom Custer. He was the brother of George Armstrong Custer.

Shooting their leader sent the soldiers into disarray. They scrambled to get their head man back on his horse, but the gunfire was too intense and they fell back. Their main soldier chief, George Custer, watched us from just below the crest of Last Stand Hill. The soldiers who had tried to enter our village reformed into a skirmish line farther up from the riverbank. Several Cheyenne and Lakota warriors, including Touch The Cloud and Hump's son, Hump Two, along with the Hunkpapa warrior Gall, joined together to put pressure on them.

At the same time, our elderly, women, and children who had fled our camp made their way west to a seasonal creek that today is called Squaw Creek, where our elders formed a perimeter to protect them. Black Shawl, Iron Between Horns, Kills Enemy, Red Leggins, and Iron Cedar were among those who had gone there for protection.

With our continued pressure on the soldiers' hastily formed skirmish line, the soldiers' resistance crumbled and they retreated north to join another group of soldiers under a soldier chief named Keough. Our warriors found Keough to be a worthy opponent. Upon attacking, his soldiers stood firm. Our warriors were unable to make any progress. Then the soldiers began to beat us back. At this point, we began to worry that Sitting Bull's vision might not come to pass.

On his way to this fight, Crazy Horse spotted a loose cavalry horse wandering aimlessly and captured it. He found that the horse's saddlebags contained army uniform buttons and decided to keep them as a gift for his mother, Good Looking Woman.

When Crazy Horse arrived at this fight, he immediately surveyed the scene. The eyes of our warriors watched him closely from their hiding places. Touch The Cloud, Combing, Bear Pipe, Quick Bear, and Scarleg joined him moments later. It was in the fight with Keough that Crazy Horse made a never-to-be-forgotten contribution.

With the tide of the fight seemingly turning in favor of the soldiers, Crazy Horse took matters into his own hands. He charged at the center of Keough's skirmish line by himself. Our warriors were in awe. They could not believe their eyes. Every rifle, every pistol, every ounce of fighting energy that the soldiers could muster was directed at Crazy Horse. Yet he rode right through their skirmish line while taking out three of their soldiers along the way. He even ran one soldier over with his horse. Once he got to the safety of the other side, we whooped appreciation. It was one of the bravest feats any of us had ever seen. However, Crazy Horse was far from done.

As if to prove that the first time was no fluke, he rode directly at the center of their skirmish line once again. The soldiers were doubly determined not to let him do it again. They got ready. As he rode towards them, the soldiers emptied every round they could in the direction of our charging leader. As we watched him, we became worried because this time everyone at the battle knew what he was going to do. The soldiers raced to block his path. Once again he rode through their skirmish line. Along the way, he wiped out three more soldiers with his war club and came through unscathed. He then rode toward our warriors and raised his war club in the air to encourage them to charge. We couldn't resist the invitation. It was a sight to behold.

Our warriors charged with so much enthusiasm that the soldiers didn't have a chance. Once again the soldier defense crumbled and they fled toward Custer's remaining platoons on the lower west side of Last Stand Hill. Our warriors took many of them out, as if they were killing buffalo on a hunt.

When Custer saw that so many of his men had already been killed, he became desperate. He sent his soldiers who rode the gray horses toward our remaining defenseless ones in our camp once again. However, most of our defenseless were now at Squaw Creek, where Sitting Bull had joined them after spending time thanking our Creator so that his vision would be completed. From Squaw Creek, Sitting Bull led our defenseless in singing songs of encouragement and victory for our warriors.

When the soldiers on the gray horses attempted to enter our village, about two hundred of our Suicide Boys had gathered under the leadership of one of our warriors named Eagle Hat. More than half of the Suicide Boys took positions along the river. The rest of them, led by a warrior named Crazy Iron Horse, circled around behind Custer from the northwest side of Last Stand Hill and attacked him. As the gray riders got close enough, Eagle Hat and the Suicide Boys opened up, and a great many of the soldiers were either killed or lost their horses in the fusillade.

Those soldiers who lost their horses scrambled for cover in a neighboring deep ravine, which today is appropriately referred to as Deep Ravine. The soldiers who retained their mounts followed them into the ravine to give them added fire power. Our warriors rushed to station themselves on both sides of the ravine and shot down into the ravine, effectively putting the soldiers into a crossfire. The soldiers, realizing their dilemma, tried to crawl up the sides of the ravine to escape. The ravine walls were too steep and most of them slid back down toward the ravine's base.

When Crazy Horse arrived from the Keough fight, the fight with the gray riders commanded his attention and he shouted encouragement to our warriors. We wiped out all but a few of them. Those very few made it back to Custer.

Custer saw what was happening to the south and tried to lead his remaining men to rescue the gray riders. Before he had gone very far, Crazy Horse and some our warriors met his charge. Among those warriors were Bear With Horns, Dark Face, Hump Two, and Touch The Cloud. Hump Two rode up to the soldiers and fired into them at point-blank range. The soldiers returned his fire, and a bullet penetrated Hump Two's leg and killed his horse at the same time. When his horse fell, it pinned Hump Two's leg under its fallen body, leaving him vulnerable to the soldiers.

Seeing Hump Two's dilemma, Bear With Horns and Dark Face urged their horses on and charged the soldiers, firing their rifles as fast as they could load them. They killed two soldiers in the process. They fought like two grizzly bears protecting their cubs. However, during their assault Bear With Horns was shot off of his horse. He took two bullets, one in the stomach and another in the hip. Dark Face was shot in the chest and lower stomach, killing him immediately. Recognizing what was happening, some of our warriors formed a perimeter around Hump Two to protect him while they extracted him from underneath his horse.

We continued pushing the soldiers back up the hill.

While we had Custer backpedaling up Last Stand Hill, Crazy Horse noticed that Bear With Horns was hurt. He rode to see if he could help him. Upon his arrival, Bear With Horns reached up with his rifle and handed it to Crazy Horse. "Take them all out!" Bear With Horns gasped before collapsing lifelessly to the ground.

Crazy Horse took the rifle, said a short prayer for Bear With Horns, and rejoined the attack. As Custer fled to the top of the hill, the Cheyenne cut him off from the north side, and Custer and his remaining men were surrounded.

Seeing that Custer was their leader, Crazy Horse saw a chance to humiliate him by letting him live. In this way the soldiers' head man could go back to the white people and let them know of our strength. So he shouted to all our warriors to kill all the soldiers but Custer. However, Crazy Horse did not count on two heyoka warriors scuttling his plan.

Since a heyoka has the habit of doing everything backwards or the opposite, Crazy Horse's request was treated no differently. Upon hearing him, the first heyoka, Quick Bear, rode his horse straight at Custer and knocked him to the ground with his war club. Custer fell with his head resting on the rock that Sitting Bull had placed on the hill. A second heyoka, Scarleg, who was also the spirit keeper for our Nation, followed Quick Bear and fired his rifle, once into Custer's head and once into his heart. He then dismounted and cut Custer's index finger off and hung it from his staff. By taking his finger, he was now keeping his spirit. Crazy Horse shook his head in resignation.

With their leader gone, the soldiers began to shoot their horses to give them additional protection from our bullets. By shooting their horses, we knew that they had sealed their fate. They now had no transportation to even attempt an escape. As the soldiers paused to reload, Crazy Horse and our elders rose up to lead our last charge over the final

Scar Leg (left) and Hump Two (right), circa 1880. Photo by E. H. Webber. Courtesy National Library of Congress.

few yards. We fired into the soldiers, leaving only about a dozen alive. Many of those remaining soldiers decided to shoot themselves, and the few that didn't, our warriors swarmed and took them out.

Then it got quiet.

From Squaw Creek, our defenseless could see that the soldiers had fallen dead, falling in the direction of our village, just as Sitting Bull had seen in his vision. We whooped and trilled in celebration, but then realized that some of us might soon be mourning a family member. Our celebration became pensive.

With all of Custer's soldiers dead, only Reno's men back at Reno-Benteen Hill remained. Crazy Horse, anxious to let his sick mother know the outcome, took the bag of buttons he had taken from the cavalry horse and handed it to a pair of our young warriors. He asked them to ride out and find Good Looking Woman among those on their way to the Agency, and give her the bag of buttons so she would know that we had won. He also told them to let her know he loved her and that he was still alive.

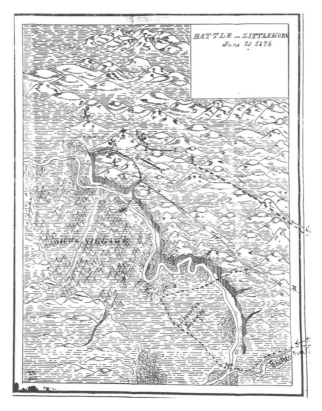

Map of the Little Bighorn battlefield drawn by a New York journalist two weeks after the battle, showing the immense size of the camp. Courtesy Edward Clown family.

CHAPTER EIGHTEEN

The End of the Good Life

After traveling all night and through most of the next day, Talks About Him and Dull Knife's contingent stopped near Grey Horn Butte. They were dead tired. It had been a difficult and tension-filled journey. It was late afternoon and they had found a peaceful place in the trees to nap. Good Looking Woman took her moccasins off so her feet could cool from the long trek. They camped without campfires.

Knowing that those on their way back to the Agency were far enough away from the soldiers that they would be safe, Dull Knife and a few of our warriors rode back toward the Greasy Grass, hoping to get back in time to join in any fighting that still may have been going on.

When it was time to travel again, night had fallen. After a desperate search, Good Looking Woman found she could not find her moccasins anywhere in the darkness. She decided not to tell anyone and traveled to the next destination barefoot.

Meanwhile, back on Last Stand Hill, the nightmare that Sitting Bull warned us to avoid was beginning to happen. Our people went about collecting the spoils off the soldiers' bodies. The Cheyenne women once again mutilated the bodies in the same manner as their relatives had been mutilated twelve years before at Sand Creek. Our warriors stripped the blue coats off the soldiers and wore them as souvenirs. They took everything that was of use from the soldiers and even some things that weren't.

Some of the Lakota and Cheyenne got into a friendly dispute over who the soldier head chief was, so they could lay claim to having been the ones who killed him. The Cheyenne said it was the soldier in buckskin that they killed at the river, which was Tom Custer, and brought his body up and laid it next to George Custer's body to compare. Since one of our warriors, named Rain In The Face, knew them both, he settled the dispute.

The Cheyenne, and our people, were still very angry with Tom Custer for trying to attack our defenseless ones, and some of the women were especially ruthless with his body. They said he had no heart.

When our defenseless ones returned to our main camp from Squaw Creek, some were greeted with news that their loved ones had been killed during the battle. In their grief, our dead warriors' relatives brought large, smooth rocks up from the river to mark the spot where their loved ones had fallen. Some of our fallen were commemorated with a single large river rock, and others with a pile of river rocks that formed a cairn. Many of these rocks still exist on the battlefield today in the very same places that they were placed over a century ago. Today the long grass hides most from view.

Some of our warriors had ridden to Reno-Benteen Hill to join in that fight that had continued into the next day. The white trader Jeanineau, who had traveled with us, had taken up arms against the soldiers when he saw his good friend Two Bears killed while pushing the soldiers up Reno-Benteen Hill. In his anger, he set himself up at a place that is today referred to as Sharpshooter's Ridge and began to fire his long-range rifle at the soldiers with uncanny accuracy. After shooting several soldiers and making them afraid to raise their heads, the soldiers sent out sharpshooters of their own and killed him.

We ended up putting Jeanineau's body on a scaffold in a tree so he could go to the other side. Even though he was not a Lakota, he had earned our respect and proved that he had a good, red Lakota-warrior-type heart, just like we did. We did not know where Jeanineau's family was, or we would have delivered his body to them. We only knew he associated with another trader at the northern trading posts that we knew by the name of Deelee. (Once again, this is what the name sounded like to our ears. The spelling is iffy.)

When Dull Knife and our other warriors returned, they were too late to join in any fights. However, they were happy to learn of the outcome. At about the same time, the sixty Suicide Boys who had taken off on the mission to decoy Custer away from the village prior to the battle returned. They had ridden all the way out to the Rock Belonging to the Black Tail Deer without encountering any soldiers. They were deeply disappointed to learn that they had missed the fight. We joked with them about it, but they did not laugh at all.

Late on June 25 and early on June 26, our people recovered our dead and wounded from the battlefield and put them into special tipis. One of our medicine men, Poor Buffalo, was smudging our dead for burial when one of those who was supposed to be dead, Bear With Horns, sat up. Bear With Horns also happened to be Poor Buffalo's wife's uncle. The insides from his stomach wound unraveled when he did that.

"I want to see my family," Bear With Horns gasped. It was a tall order since his family was camped at Slim Buttes. Poor Buffalo examined his wounds.

"I cannot save you, but I might be able to grant you your wish," he answered.

He pushed Bear With Horns' insides back into his body and then wrapped his body tight with rawhide to keep everything in place. Poor Buffalo prayed to the Creator for help. Bear With Horns was then placed on a travois, and with the help of Bear With Horns' brother Fights The Thunder and nephew Old Eagle, Poor Buffalo escorted him back to Slim Buttes to say good-bye to his family.

Poor Buffalo kept Bear With Horns alive with Bear Medicine. The way he did that was whenever Bear With Horns weakened or started losing consciousness, Poor Buffalo would make a Bear Lodge. A Bear Lodge is a sweat lodge for healing with a door that faces to the south. They would go into the Bear Lodge, and in the middle of the ceremony, Poor Buffalo would leave the Bear Lodge on all fours, acting like a bear. He

Fights The Thunder, circa early 1900s. Photo taken by Frank Cundill. Courtesy Edward Clown family.

would sniff the ground for a while until he found some roots. He would dig one of the roots out of the earth with his hands and then bend down and take it from the earth with his mouth. He then carried it back into the Bear Lodge. Once back inside the lodge, he blew the medicine from the root onto Bear With Horns. His actions brought Bear With Horns' senses back and his eyes became alert again so he could continue the trip until they finally reached Slim Buttes.

The journey took four days. Once Bear With Horns arrived, he spent his last hours with his family and then died a peaceful death. His body still lies near our old Slim Buttes camp.

Meanwhile, the two young warriors who had been sent to deliver Crazy Horse's message of our victory, along with the captured buttons, to Good Looking Woman, had taken two horses each so they could switch mounts whenever one of their horses

Bear With Horns' marker sitting along the roadside inside the Little Bighorn National Monument in Montana. Photo by Bill Matson.

got tired. It allowed them to ride all day and all night at maximum speed. When they finally caught up to Good Looking Woman, she and the rest of her camp were at a sacred hill that we call Bear Butte. It is located about six miles northeast of what is today Sturgis, South Dakota.

Good Looking Woman was suffering from what we now believe was pneumonia. On our way back to the Agency, our people occasionally walked in creeks to cover our tracks. With Good Looking Woman making the journey in her bare feet, this exacerbated her condition.

They Are Afraid Of Her was shocked to learn that Good Looking Woman had lost her moccasins upon arriving at Bear Butte. She admonished her older sister for not letting her know; however, Good Looking Woman told her she had lost her moccasins on purpose in hopes of getting new ones. They Are Afraid Of Her could not help but smile at the attempt to lighten her heart. Good Looking Woman was still her elder sister, even in her final hours.

While They Are Afraid Of Her was attempting to make Good Looking Woman comfortable, our two young warriors sent by Crazy Horse arrived. They brightened both women's worlds when they told them that Crazy Horse still lived and that our people had gained a great victory. What Good Looking Woman had prayed for at the Rock Belonging to the Black Tail Deer was now fulfilled. Her boy still roamed free. Her heart melted into joy.

With broad smiles, the two young warriors presented the bag of buttons to Good Looking Woman. She accepted them and clutched them close to her body as if they were Crazy Horse himself.

"I'm going to make me a victory dress with these," Good Looking Woman told them. She then asked our elder men to sing a victory song. So they sang her one. Once they were done singing, she told them, "Now I can join my father and mother."

She was not afraid to leave our world because she knew she was going to a good place where she would be able to spend time with her parents, brothers, and sister who were already on the other side.

They Are Afraid Of Her clutched Good Looking Woman's hand tightly. Her face transformed into the smile of a satisfied life and she passed to the other side. When her spirit left, our men prepared her for a quick burial. Among her belongings they found a red blanket with very little wear and planned to wrap her in it. It was the one that Lone Horn had received from the Nez Perce elder, which he in turn had given to her. They Are Afraid Of Her stopped them and substituted a thick buffalo robe.

"Let her rest with our buffalo nation. I will keep the blanket for Crazy Horse. She would want him to have it."

The men buried her in the sitting position looking toward our Black Hills. As they finished her burial, the morning star became bright in the eastern sky.

Back at the Greasy Grass, Crazy Horse was praying with his pipe when the morning star brightened. It stayed bright for a few minutes and then it dimmed. He knew what it meant, and tears rolled down his face. His heart fell to the ground. After a while he picked his heart back up and locked his mother inside it.

Life must go on.

Sniping from Weir Point continued during the morning hours. When some of our scouts rode in to report another large contingent of soldiers was coming from the west under soldier chiefs Terry and Gibbon, our head men had a quick meeting. Sitting Bull advocated that we had done enough to the soldiers and that we should leave those still fighting alive so they could tell their people of our might. The rest of our head men, including Crazy Horse, concurred.

Before we left, we prayed for all who had lost their lives in the battle, including the soldiers. We lost about two hundred fifty of our warriors during this battle. We buried many of them on the ridges overlooking Squaw Creek, while others took their dead relatives farther away to bury them in our traditional places.

In the early afternoon, our people left the Greasy Grass. For the next two days, our scouts watched the soldiers to see if they would follow us. But instead, the soldiers stayed at the Greasy Grass to bury all their dead except for the soldier head men. They carried their dead soldier head men to a thunder boat on the Elk River. We did not really understand why they separated their dead in this fashion, but it was their way.

In the immediate days following our departure, Crazy Horse, Sitting Bull, our warriors, and the Cheyenne left an easy path for the soldiers to follow that headed southwesterly into what is known today as the Pryor and Bighorn Mountain areas. Our Sacred Calf Pipe Keeper, Old Man Elk Head, and the rest of our people trekked east towards the northernmost Agencies. Waglula and his wives, along with Black Shawl, Iron Cedar, Combing, and Bear Pipe left with this group. They went to stay at our Bear Creek campsite along the Owl River. Bear Pipe's wife, Comes Home Hard Times, was about to give birth and he wanted his child's first view of the world to be there.

Once our families arrived at the Agency, we noticed the deep scowls on the faces of the white Agency workers. We could see that their attitude toward us had changed, and so we kept to ourselves. We did not say anything about our victory nor did we talk of our losses for fear that the white Agency workers would be able to figure out what families had sent their young men to fight. We did not want to give them a reason to punish any of those families.

When Comes Home Hard Times finally gave birth, she had a son. Bear Pipe was beyond ecstatic and we felt the same way. Babies do that to families. He named his son Comes Home Victorious. The white Agency workers did not understand the meaning of his son's name. But we did.

When the rations were passed out during the first week of July at Fort Bennett, Touch The Cloud and about three thousand of our people came there to collect them. They were mislabeled by the Agency officials as belonging to the Oohenonpa band. But Touch The Cloud and the rest of our people did not care, they only wanted the rations.

Meanwhile, back within our hunting grounds, our warriors still had to look out for Three Stars' men. After Crazy Horse and our warriors led his army scouts in the southwesterly direction, Crazy Horse had some brief skirmishes with them. We finally lost the soldiers by riding through the rivers. After that, Crazy Horse and our warriors began to head toward Slim Buttes. Along the way, they discovered that game had become scarce again. So our people split up to see where the game had gone.

Dull Knife decided to take a contingent of Cheyenne southeast to see if he could find some buffalo, while Crazy Horse, Sitting Bull, and our warriors continued to journey east. Dull Knife's people had some immediate but moderate success.

A few days later, Crazy Horse and our warriors' bellies cried with joy when they finally found a buffalo herd. They killed some of them and then drove the majority of the herd northeast into the Piney Mountain area of the northern Black Hills. Running with the buffalo herd also helped to hide our horses' tracks from the soldiers.

Our warriors sent word to the Agencies for our families to come and rejoin them at Slim Buttes. Our warriors set up two camps in the Slim Buttes area. Most of our family stayed at the southern, or main, camp with Crazy Horse and Sitting Bull. Several of the Cheyenne stayed in a smaller camp at the northern end of Slim Buttes with one of our Lakota head men named Tashunke Wascius. Roughly translated, Tashunke Wascius means Fat Gatherer Horse; however, the Americans translated the name as American Horse. He is not the same American Horse head man that we will encounter later at the Red Cloud Agency.

Once we had spent a few days in our Black Hills, we discovered that there were many more white people living in our Hills than when we had left back in the spring, and only half as much game.

While we had been out defending our hunting grounds, the white people had moved into our sacred Black Hills in large numbers. Some of our people began to wonder if our great victory at the Greasy Grass had really accomplished all that we had thought. Some of our people's hearts fell to the ground and they did not know how to pick them up. They began to take a second look at the white people's reservations and it started to affect our unity.

In addition, our families staying at the Agencies had trouble making it back to spend time with us because the soldiers on the Agencies had taken their horses and guns. The Agencies had always been a good place for us to stash our horses when they got weak from overuse or lack of grass in the winter. But now those horses were also gone.

On top of that, the soldiers had forced some of our Loafers at the Agency to sign away our sacred Black Hills. They told them to sign or they would no longer receive rations. Crazy Horse found this news disgusting. Accepting the white man's gifts had made the Loafers fat and lazy, and now they no longer knew how to live off the land. They had forgotten how to be Lakota. It was what he and his father had worried would happen for quite some time. As a result, the Loafers were willing to give away something that was not theirs so they could continue their lazy ways.

In the 1868 treaty, the government had agreed that the boundaries of our hunting grounds would not change unless three-quarters of our men agreed to it. Now Crazy Horse saw that the government did not even honor their own paper. They had pursued our weak and lazy and had them touch the pen to the paper for all of us. The government's words were like grass in the wind; we could not count on them. Even to this day.

Around late August and early September, we were processing buffalo meat. During that time, it was raining heavily, which created a heavy mud. The mud in our part of the world can be thick and sticky. It will suck the moccasins right off your feet when you lift your leg.

In the early morning of September 9, our lookouts at Tashunke Wascius's camp had gone into their tipis to get dry. During that time, a large group of cavalry soldiers was able to get close enough to surprise the camp with an attack. The soldiers grabbed most of the horses before they knew what hit them. Our warriors ended up fighting a delaying action to allow their families to escape.

Unfortunately, not everyone escaped, and the soldiers captured a few families and found another family hiding in a cave. The fired unmercifully into that cave over and over until they reported killing all of the occupants. They also shot and captured the camp's head man, Tashunke Wascius. He died shortly afterwards. The rest of his camp hurried to Crazy Horse and Sitting Bull's camp for help.

As a result, Crazy Horse and about two hundred warriors charged up to the northern camp to try to rescue everyone and do all that we could. We also wanted to protect our main camp to the south and allow them time to escape any designs the soldiers had to attack it.

By the time he got to Tashunke Wascius's camp in the late afternoon, the soldiers' force had multiplied to about two thousand men. We found we were greatly outnumbered. From the buttes surrounding the abandoned village, we began firing long range at the soldiers to try to drive them away. However, the soldiers were stubborn and charged at our positions. We were able to hold our own, but we were unable to rescue the captured families and decided to try again the next morning.

The next morning it rained. When we came back, we saw the soldiers eating and resting. They had set fire to all the village's tipis and supplies. It made us angry and we fired at them as they packed up and marched away. We followed them, firing at them the entire way until they left the Slim Buttes area. Once they had left, we were relieved that our people back at our main village would now be safe and the soldiers would soon be hungry again.

When we went back to see what was left of Tashunke Wascius's village, there was nothing. The winter supply of meat, the tipis, their horses, and everything else in the village was lost. Our people shared what they had to replenish those from the village. However, the loss took a toll on our people's winter supplies.

Among the village ruins was a toddler boy hiding in a cave under his dead mother's body. There were nine dead women and children in the cave. Having been left for dead, the little one had a bullet wound in his leg. Some of our people decided to take him to one of our villages near what is today the community of Cherry Creek, South Dakota. There he was raised by an Itazipco elder named White Feather. He gave this little boy the name Little Wounded, and he grew to adulthood and even had a son of his own named Jonas Little Wounded.

After the fight at Slim Buttes, Crazy Horse and Sitting Bull decided to go in separate directions. Smaller camps would allow us greater flexibility in our movements, and allow us to contend with fewer horses and people to feed. Our two leaders decided that they would come together again in the spring. Sitting Bull went north toward Canada and

Crazy Horse went west toward the Shifting Sands River. They would never see each other again.

That fall was not kind to us.

We received sad news from those back at the Agency that our Sacred Calf Pipe Keeper, Old Man Elk Head, had passed to the other side. His son, who took his father's sacred name Elk Head as his own, took over his duties.

For the next three months, finding enough game to feed our people was difficult. With the white people's government actively promoting the extermination of our buffalo by encouraging their hunters to take down entire herds just for sport, our people's food supply began to become depleted. It caused our people to be hungry. The soldiers at the Agencies promised the Loafers gifts if they could talk any of our free-roaming people into surrendering or becoming scouts for their army. Scouting against our own people was reprehensible, but once again, the lure of special gifts caused these Loafers to forget that they were Lakota.

Some of the Loafers even came to Crazy Horse's camp disguised as free-roaming warriors, and when our people's bellies were empty, they talked about how the white people could take care of us with their rations of beef and flour. Unfortunately, when our people's bellies were empty, winter's icy winds stung their bodies with twice the impact, making it hard to resist the temptation of surrendering just to have a meal. So some of our people listened and they ended up surrendering.

In early December, a ragged and frostbitten Cheyenne people led by Dull Knife wandered into Crazy Horse's camp looking for food and shelter. Dull Knife's camp, which had been pitched on the Red Fork of the Shifting Sands River about five miles east of what today is Kaycee, Wyoming, had been attacked in the early morning hours by soldiers led by a soldier chief named Mackenzie. Caught by surprise, Dull Knife's camp had lost everything, and once again Crazy Horse's camp shared whatever they had, which wasn't much.

Things were getting stressful. Our memories of this time period are painful. We had to stay on the move and close to areas that had cottonwood trees, because during periods of heavy snow we had to feed our horses cottonwood bark to keep them from starving.

To make matters worse, the soldiers built a new fort in the northern area of our best hunting grounds where the Beaver Tail River flows into the Elk River. The soldiers called this fort the Tongue River Cantonment. A soldier head man named Miles, whom we referred to as Bear Coat because he wore one, ran this fort and spread the word that he planned to hunt Crazy Horse down.

Some of our warriors wanted to ride up to see Bear Coat and talk about some of our people surrendering so they could eat. Crazy Horse did not like this idea, but he was not in favor of seeing our people starve either, and so he let them go. These warriors went waving a white flag of peace. However, Bear Coat's Crow scouts killed these warriors anyway. When word reached Crazy Horse, he was livid. It showed him that Bear Coat had no heart.

Crazy Horse wanted to teach Bear Coat a lesson for what his scouts had done, so he sent decoys out in late December to entice the soldiers at the Tongue River Cantonment to follow our warriors into an ambush. The soldiers followed.

In early January of 1877 it was bitter cold. The rivers were frozen solid. Heavy snow and ice were everywhere. Crazy Horse and our warriors were camped near the Beaver Tail River, about four miles south of what is today Birney, Montana. It was not a good time to be out fighting soldiers, but we really had no choice. We had to get the soldiers away from our hunting grounds.

Around January 7, while on their way to attack Crazy Horse's camp, the soldiers captured nine Cheyenne women and children. That evening one of our Cheyenne warriors told us that Bear Coat was near. Once again our warriors rallied to save our village. Unfortunately, the decoys we had sent out had entered into a skirmish with Bear Coat's scouts, and so the element of surprise had been ruined.

Early the following morning, in 30-degrees-below-zero temperatures, the soldiers were eating breakfast. Our warriors fired on them. The soldiers assembled quickly and fought back. We nearly had them surrounded; however, they charged straight up the bluffs where we were located. They wore very thick buffalo coats over very thick clothing. It was so thick that when we arched our arrows, they would hit the soldiers but many times not penetrate deep enough through their clothing to hurt them.

Up on the bluffs we had built campfires so our warriors could stay warm in between firing at the soldiers. We used up a great many bullets. However, when the soldiers showed us their nine Cheyenne captives, we stopped firing. It made us angry and bitter that the soldiers would even think to use them as a shield against our bullets and arrows. This was not brave on the soldiers' part, and we had no stomach for firing in the direction of our allies' women and children.

When a blinding blizzard made it impossible to see, we left the battlefield and headed back to Slim Buttes. No one was happy. Our people were hungry and cold. Our ponies were weak. And now our warriors were running low on ammunition for the first time since before the fight on the Greasy Grass.

However, Crazy Horse stood firm.

CHAPTER NINETEEN

The Agency

The soldiers kept our warriors on the move all winter. With game continuing to be scarce, things were difficult. However, Crazy Horse was determined to keep our people free and our Lakota ways alive.

Toward that end he continued to honor his vision of watching over our grandparents' graves. He made sure that the grass and trees that grew from our grandparents' remains were left as our grandparents intended. And he asked our grandparents on the other side for help in keeping our ways alive.

With summer approaching, the soldiers started becoming nervous. The previous summer was still fresh in their memories. They did not want to bury so many of their fellow soldiers ever again. So they sent peace negotiators to try to get our people to give up our fight to maintain our way of life in exchange for presents and food. Bear Coat even sweetened the offer by sending word that there would be a new Northern Agency for Crazy Horse if he surrendered unconditionally.

Crazy Horse scoffed.

An unconditional surrender to Bear Coat would mean our people would have to give up our horses and weapons. It meant they would have to live off whatever the government gave us. That was unacceptable. It was not our Lakota way. Crazy Horse knew that there was a reason why the Creator had us living on our Mother the Earth in the way we did and he would not go against the Creator.

March has always been very cold in our northern plains and 1877 was no exception. During that time, Crazy Horse rode all around our sacred Black Hills continuing to check on our elders' graves. He often stopped to pray, in hopes that the Creator would hear him. It did not take long before the Creator heard his prayer. When he did, the Creator revealed that the graves of Black Buffalo, Walks With Sacred Buffalo, One Horn, and his birth-mother, Rattling Blanket Woman, were all within the Agency borders his uncle Lone Horn had drawn up and sent to the government in 1872 with Black Tongue. In addition to our family's burial grounds, the Creator told him that Lone

Horn had included the grasslands of what is today northeastern Wyoming in his Agency. The grasslands would be large enough for our brother the buffalo to roam. Crazy Horse thanked the Creator.

His uncle had figured out the solution long ago. It had taken an answer to his prayers by the Creator to learn of it. All he had to do now was to make sure it was implemented. His mind was set. He headed back to camp.

While he had been roaming in the Hills, Black Shawl's health had deteriorated. The coughing sickness had seized control of her life. During his absence, Waglula's wife Kills Enemy had taken care of her. This was not the first time the coughing sickness had debilitated her. Each time that it flared up, it was worse than the time before. He had taken her to several different medicine men, but none of them had been able to figure out how to treat the disease.

In addition, it appeared to be contagious. A few weeks after assuming the duties of taking care of Black Shawl, Kills Enemy was stricken by the disease. The urgency to find a medicine that would protect us from the disease became stronger.

Black Shawl's relatives had heard about a white medicine man at the Red Cloud Agency that knew how to prolong the life of those with the coughing disease. The white medicine man, whose name was McGillycuddy, called the sickness tuberculosis. Her relatives told Crazy Horse to bring her to McGillycuddy before it was too late. If he could prolong her life, that would give our own medicine men the time to find her the proper medicine. Crazy Horse did not believe in the white man's medicine, and at the same time, he did not believe in ignoring his wife's relatives' wishes. So he contemplated the unthinkable, a white medicine man helping his wife.

While Crazy Horse was debating whether to allow this, Three Stars sent a message to Waglula, who was camping with the rest of our family at Bear Creek. Three Stars wanted to know what it would take for Crazy Horse to stop fighting the soldiers. Waglula took the message to his son.

Upon receiving the message, Crazy Horse told his father, "Tell Three Stars I want our people to keep their horses. I want them to keep their weapons so we can continue to hunt. And I want the Agency that Lone Horn had set up for our people to become written down in a way that the government will honor, because I want our Nation and our way of life to live forever. Once they agree, then our Nation and the white man's Nation will both have a peace that will last."

Waglula said he would be proud to tell this to Three Stars' messenger. His son's words echoed the heartbeat of our Nation. They were the words of those who wished to maintain our Lakota identity.

That evening they shared a meal and spent time catching up on family news. During this time, Waglula informed his son that Combing had found a wife. Her name was Come After Her and she was already pregnant with Combing's child. Crazy Horse was pleased for his brother. It had been a long time since he had heard news this good.

Once Waglula had departed, Crazy Horse told Black Shawl what they had talked about. She was happy for Combing, but the message he was sending to Three Stars was another matter. Although the sickness had made her feeble, it had not diminished her love for him. "An Agency is where our people and the soldiers spend all their time in one place together. Your vision said that you would be killed in such a place."

Crazy Horse answered with an awkward silence. He had hoped she had forgotten about his vision. He did not want to worry her. She had been there for him when he had been shot. She had grieved with him when they had lost their child. She had been at his side when he said good-bye to his mother at the Greasy Grass. Now she was very sick. It was his turn to take care of her. He would not let her down. Getting her back to an Agency, where she could rest from the constant travel, would be good for her.

Black Shawl already knew what was in his mind. "I will pray that the Creator releases you from your vision," she gasped in between coughs.

As he tucked the buffalo robe around her body, he asked her to pray once she regained her strength.

He left their tipi to pray with the Creator. Being with the Creator always made him happy, and happiness was what he craved now. He knew once he claimed his Agency that his time of walking on this earth would be short. But in his heart he knew our people's lives were more important than his own. The Creator had given his life a purpose, and that was all anyone could ever ask for. It was time.

Once Three Stars received Crazy Horse's answer from Waglula, there was a flurry of messages sent back and forth. Whenever Three Stars went to Washington, Spotted Tail acted as their go-between during these negotiations. He would accept Crazy Horse's messages, quite often brought by Hump Two or another relative, and then have them wired to Three Stars. Whenever Three Stars wired back, he would tell our relative what the message said, and they would carry the message back to Crazy Horse. This went on for a few weeks.

Three Stars ended up promising Crazy Horse and his people that they could keep their horses after a brief period where he would hold them so that he could take back any with the US cavalry brand on them. He also said that after laying down our weapons for a time, those warriors who agreed to become scouts and help keep peace at the Agency would have their weapons returned. He also agreed Crazy Horse would be given his own Agency based on what Lone Horn had drawn up five years ago. Once this was done, Crazy Horse was to go to Washington and meet with the Great White Father.

Although we did not like giving up our horses or our weapons even for a day, the fact that they would be returned, plus we would be allowed to keep our sacred Black Hills, was all that really mattered. Crazy Horse and Three Stars had come to an agreement.

Three Stars suggested that he come in and lay down his arms at the Red Cloud Agency. In Crazy Horse's mind, which Agency he arrived at made no difference. He did not think he would be there for very long before he would be off to his own Agency.

The Red Cloud Agency had a large military presence. Since the government had considered it potentially volatile, they had built several military buildings within the very heart of the Agency. They called these military buildings Camp Robinson.

As the day for Crazy Horse and our warriors' arrival at the Agency neared, the military brought in wagon trains full of rations to issue to them. Upon seeing these new rations, several of those already living at the Agency journeyed out to join Crazy Horse's procession.

On May 6, 1877, just prior to entering the Red Cloud Agency, Crazy Horse and his followers were met by several of the Loafers who had come to escort them into the Agency and help them through the process. Crazy Horse tolerated the Loafers because they knew their way around the Agency. Just before entering, a soldier head man named Clark, whom we called White Hat because of his light-colored, wide-brimmed hat, met Crazy Horse and told him he had come to take our weapons.

Crazy Horse told White Hat that he could not take our weapons, but that our people would lay down our weapons of our own free will. "I wish to make a peace that will last our whole lives and forever," he proclaimed to White Hat.

White Hat told him that once he had laid down his guns, then he must never make war with any nation ever again. Not American. Not Crow. Not Shoshoni. No Nation. Since we were there for peace, Crazy Horse had no trouble agreeing. He laid his rifle at White Hat's feet and the rest of our warriors followed suit. He was allowed to keep a buffalo bone knife.

Once White Hat was satisfied that he had all of our weapons, Crazy Horse and our warriors remounted and rode the rest of the way into the Agency. Nearly all of Crazy Horse's closest relatives, including his father, brothers, and sister, had come into the Spotted Tail Agency three weeks earlier with Touch The Cloud's camp. Our Sacred Calf Pipe Keeper Elk Head had also arrived with Touch The Cloud.

Those who came in with Crazy Horse were mostly our younger warriors. Crazy Horse only had about four hundred and fifty of our people with him that day. About three hundred of them were warriors. Upon being logged into a surrender ledger, Crazy Horse and his followers were issued their rations. However, the surrender ledger has about nine hundred names who surrendered that day. The extra names were some of our more enterprising Loafers who were already drawing rations. They joined in the surrender so that they could share in the new rations being handed out by the soldiers. Many used different names to avoid detection and also to set up an additional issuance of rations for themselves in future months. It was not as fun as stealing horses from the soldiers, but it had its benefits.

Crazy Horse and his warriors set up camp about a half mile northeast of the bluffs just north of Camp Robinson. They called our camp the Lone Horn camp, in honor of Lone Horn for drawing up our new Agency for our people. Crazy Horse set his tipi up on the northern edge of our Lone Horn campsite because Black Shawl was still suffering from the coughing sickness. He knew her disease was contagious and felt by staying on the camp's edge he could limit everyone's exposure.

When he arrived, several of our relatives who had already been living at the Agency came to visit. Initially, there were many feasts and good feelings. The soldier head men greeted him with great respect. They saw him as a worthy adversary and delighted in picking his mind to gain information about their past battles together. Crazy Horse put up many fences between his mind and the soldiers, so the pickings were slim.

One of the first orders of business for Crazy Horse was to take his wife to see the white medicine man McGillycuddy so she could be treated for her coughing sickness. Her response to his remedies was slow but promising. Crazy Horse appreciated McGillycuddy's concern and attentive care of his wife.

As his wife began to show improvement, Crazy Horse started devoting more of his time working to make sure the soldiers did not forget their promise to establish Lone Horn's Agency for our people. He admonished the soldier head men on their frustratingly slow pace at which they were putting our Agency together. He wondered aloud why he had seen no papers from the government certifying our Agency. The Lone Horn Agency was also referred to as the Northern Agency or Crazy Horse's Agency by some with the government.

Living in such close proximity to soldiers was a new experience for him. He had never been around soldiers other than in battle. He could not help but feel the need to challenge them. Each time he went to see the soldier head men, along the way he would often sneak up on the rank and file soldiers and count coup on them with a cherry stick while they were relaxing. The soldiers did not like this, and every time they saw him they tensed up. Even though he was unarmed, we still saw the fear in their eyes.

Crazy Horse signed enlistment papers to become a sergeant in the scouts. He did this to fulfill his promise to Three Stars to be one of those to keep the peace among our people. He wanted to keep part of the bargain so the soldiers could not find an excuse to deny our people the Lone Horn Agency. As a result, the military issued him a pistol. They also issued him a long blue coat and a white military dress shirt to replace his buckskin clothing in order to prove his allegiance to peace. Crazy Horse did, in fact, wear the white shirt; however, he cut the blue coat up and made it into a pair of leggings, which he wore with his buffalo-hide pants.

Crazy Horse was under the impression that once he had stopped fighting the soldiers, the Lone Horn Agency would be imminent. He spent many hours planning for the day when he and his people could move there. He had even pinpointed a sacred place where we could keep our Sacred Calf Pipe. It was just south of what is now Rapid City, South Dakota. But the soldiers continued to be slow to make it happen. He asked White Hat and White Hat's head man Mackenzie why it was taking so long. They told him that he would have to wait for Three Stars to return from Washington before there would be any more progress. They told him that Three Stars was discussing our Agency with their Great White Father. So Crazy Horse continued to practice good faith and waited.

At this time, our people shared the Agencies with our Cheyenne allies. The Cheyenne were led by Crazy Horse's relatives Dull Knife and Little Wolf. They had surrendered back on April 21. Dull Knife and Little Wolf told the soldiers that they wished to stay with our people on our Agency. However, the soldiers had no ears for them. Instead they decided to send them to a place called the Darlington Agency in Oklahoma to be with their Southern Cheyenne brethren who had accepted that Agency in 1869. The military wanted to keep all the Cheyenne together. Dull Knife and Little Wolf bitterly opposed this banishment. The Darlington Agency was far away and on unfamiliar land. They told the soldier head men that they didn't want to go. The soldier head men replied that if they didn't like their new location after a year then they could return north and live among the Lakota. Little Wolf agreed to give it a try. Dull Knife reluctantly went along.

This whole episode made Crazy Horse sad for them. He told the Cheyenne that they were more than welcome to stay at our Agency when the time came. The fact that they only had to stay a year in Oklahoma gave them all hope for a happy reunion.

Near the end of May, Mackenzie was replaced at Camp Robinson by a new head man named Bradley. At the same time, Three Stars returned from Washington. His return gave Crazy Horse renewed hope that our new Agency would soon be a reality. He also hoped that Three Stars would have ears and help his Cheyenne friends stay with the Lakota.

It was not to be.

The Cheyenne were forced to move to Oklahoma two days later. Watching them go broke Crazy Horse's heart and he began to worry that the soldiers may someday do the same to our people. So Crazy Horse renewed his push for our Agency. He pushed the soldiers to turn their promises into reality. He wanted to see the papers that certified our Agency as real. The soldiers always answered that their word was good.

Crazy Horse's constant pressuring of the soldiers over the formation of our Agency soon began to wear thin. Being unable to control his actions and thoughts made them anxious. So the soldiers became obsessed with finding out how to isolate him from the rest of our people.

The atmosphere at the Red Cloud Agency was not very pleasant. Red Cloud hated the fact that Crazy Horse was treated as more important than himself on his own turf. Even Red Cloud's people gave Crazy Horse a hard time. They would tell him that he had been a fool to stay out and fight the past few years because it had gotten him nowhere. At least Red Cloud had made sure his followers received good rations. Now that Crazy Horse was at the Agency, his old ways were worthless. Crazy Horse came to understand that Red Cloud and his fellow Loafers were anything but friends. Jealousy can be a dangerous thing.

In a sudden development, Three Stars pushed Crazy Horse to take his trip to Washington, DC, and meet their Great White Father. Crazy Horse could not believe this request. We were supposed to have our new Agency before he made any trips to Washington. He told Three Stars that he would not go to Washington unless he and our people were allowed to live on our new Agency lands first. He had agreed to certain things in a certain order when he gave up the fight. Changing the order after the fact was something he would not tolerate. He was starting to wonder what was in Three Stars' mind.

Just when he was starting to become convinced that Three Stars was breaking his word, Three Stars approved a buffalo hunt for the fall. It was with the understanding that all our people who wished to live on our new Lone Horn Agency would be able to relocate there after we finished our hunt. This sounded more like what he had agreed to, and he was pleased.

During the first part of July, Three Stars was called away. White Hat was also called away to Fort Laramie at nearly the same time. However, before White Hat left, he and a man named Joe Larrabee brought a young girl named Nellie Larrabee to Crazy Horse's tipi. Joe Larrabee was a white civilian worker at Camp Robinson who had two Cheyenne wives. Nellie Larrabee was one of his nine children. She was sixteen winters at the time. When they arrived, Crazy Horse was not there. He was hunting.

Around the same time, Waglula came up from the Spotted Tail Agency to visit Crazy Horse. He brought his wives, Makah, and Iron Cedar. While he was there, Waglula and our family took a day to go visit another relative. Iron Cedar stayed behind at Crazy Horse's tipi in case a still recovering Black Shawl needed something.

When White Hat and the Larrabees arrived at Crazy Horse's tipi, Iron Cedar was bringing back wood to build a cooking fire. Black Shawl, hearing the activity of visitors, came out to meet them. When they discovered that Crazy Horse wasn't present, they decided to leave Nellie behind with Black Shawl. Nellie had a good heart and told Iron Cedar she would help her take care of Black Shawl.

When Crazy Horse returned and learned that Nellie was willing to help Black Shawl, he did not object. He appreciated the care she gave his wife. However, he did not make Nellie his wife, as the soldiers thought he had.

Being around Crazy Horse made Nellie quite popular with the military head men. Whenever she went to visit her father or go to the fort, she would be quizzed on what Crazy Horse was up to. She had never had this kind of attention before and felt she owed them a reward for the attention they accorded her. So she would tell the soldiers exaggerated stories about Crazy Horse. She exaggerated what went on in meetings with his guests, and the military began to formulate opinions based on her stories. The soldiers seemed to forget that she was a young teenager.

When White Hat returned from Fort Laramie at the end of July, he called a meeting with our head men. During the meeting he read our head men a message from Three Stars that told us to prepare for our buffalo hunt, which would start on August 5. We would be allowed to hunt for forty days. This caused our head men, including Crazy Horse, to burst into wide grins of happiness.

Three Stars' message also asked that our head men appoint eighteen of our members to go to Washington after the hunt on September 15 to tell their Great White Father of our needs. One of our head men, Young Man Afraid Of His Horses, suggested that a feast be held to celebrate all this good news at Crazy Horse's tipi. The agent at the Red Cloud Agency, a man named Irwin, offered three cattle along with some extra coffee and sugar to help make the feast a success. Smiles lit up everywhere except on the faces of Red Cloud and his relatives, who left the meeting in a huff.

Once our head men had returned to their camps, Red Cloud sent two messengers to Agent Irwin. They told the agent that Crazy Horse was a warrior who would turn on him in an instant. They told Irwin that Crazy Horse planned to use the ammunition our warriors were to receive for the hunt to wipe out all the soldiers and any other white people who went along on the hunt. Upon hearing this, Agent Irwin became concerned.

Red Cloud also made sure the same concern was passed to the white people at Spotted Tail's Agency. Eventually they found the ears of Spotted Tail. Both Red Cloud and Spotted Tail did not like the preferential treatment Crazy Horse was getting. Red Cloud wanted to maintain his dominance over his own Agency at all costs, while Spotted

Tail wished to have the largest following of any of our head men in order to increase his clout. Crazy Horse's presence was interfering with both their wishes.

On the day the hunt was to begin, Spotted Tail advised Touch The Cloud not to go because there would probably be trouble. Spotted Tail also contacted White Hat and told him that Crazy Horse planned to use the hunt to leave the Agency and resume hostilities.

It was the same story that Red Cloud's messengers had told Agent Irwin, and the repeated telling had given it an element of credibility.

As a result, White Hat visited Crazy Horse and told him that the hunt was postponed. Crazy Horse could not believe it. He had looked forward to the hunt, as had all of our people, and now it was being postponed at the last minute. White Hat suggested that the hunt might take place after his trip to see the Great White Father.

"We want to go on the hunt," Crazy Horse told White Hat. "I do not need to see any Great White Father. I already have a father and no one comes between myself and our Creator."

Troubled by Crazy Horse's defiant nature, White Hat left. The month of August was an uneasy one. Any hint of trust that had existed between Crazy Horse and the soldiers was deteriorating.

CHAPTER TWENTY

His Final Days

Near the end of August, the Nez Perce Tribe, under the leadership of Chief Joseph, had come to blows with soldiers in the area that is today southeastern Idaho. They were protecting some of their younger warriors from punishment by the soldiers for having been involved in an altercation with white settlers. In order to escape the soldiers' wrath, they attempted to cross the border into Canada. The soldiers pursued them but had not been able to catch them.

Three Stars, who was back East at the time, wired Camp Robinson and told his men there to ready our warriors who had enrolled as scouts so they could help take out the Nez Perce.

As a result of this directive, White Hat called a meeting. He told our head men through his interpreters named Grouard and Garnett that our scouts were needed to help fight Chief Joseph. Crazy Horse had enrolled as a sergeant of the scouts during his first few days at the Agency and had never expected that he would be called upon to fight for the government. He had understood that his responsibility as an army scout was just to keep the peace among our people. He felt he had been deceived.

He still remembered the Nez Perce elder who had come to his uncle Lone Horn asking for shelter. He had seen that these people were not the bad people the soldiers portrayed them to be. In fact, they had a better understanding of our people than the soldiers did.

In addition, there were rumors at the Agency that Sitting Bull was planning to join Chief Joseph. If that happened, we worried that we would have to fight our own people. Our hearts were not with the soldiers on this one.

When it was our time to speak our minds at the meeting, Touch The Cloud spoke first. He told White Hat he was against it. He said that our people had done everything they had been asked to do to keep peace, but now we were being asked to go to war and that was going too far. Many of our head men felt he spoke the truth and voiced their agreement by simply saying "Hau."

Hau, besides being a Lakota greeting, is also a way of saying "I agree" in our language.

Once he had finished, Crazy Horse spoke:

"Three Stars sent word to us that if we came into the Agency we would be treated good and live in peace. We believed him and we came in with our hearts good to everyone. Now you ask us to put blood on our faces at the same time that you ask us to visit your Great White Father in Washington and talk peace. You, White Hat, said to me that when we gave up our guns that we were never to go to war ever again against any nation and we agreed. Now we will keep our word."

Once Crazy Horse had finished speaking, White Hat asked him again if he would help fight the Nez Perce. It was as though White Hat had not listened to a word he had said. This irritated Crazy Horse.

"We will go on our hunt instead!" he answered defiantly.

After hearing his response, White Hat lost his temper and said many things we did not understand. Things became intense. Grouard was the lead interpreter for the soldiers at the time. However, he could not interpret our language when it was spoken too quickly. In the heat of the moment, he became lost in the fast-moving dialogue.

Crazy Horse finally told White Hat that if he agreed to allow our people the hunt that we had been promised, then he would help fight the Nez Perce. White Hat rebuffed Crazy Horse's hunt request and told him that there would not be a hunt this year.

No hunt? Crazy Horse made no effort to hide his disgust.

"If the white man cannot beat his enemies, we can do it for him. But we are tired of war. We came here for peace, but now your Great White Father begs for our help. So we will go north and fight until there is not a Nez Perce left, but we will still have our hunt."

Grouard had remained confused throughout the discussion and ended up giving White Hat a bad interpretation. He told White Hat that Crazy Horse said that "he would go north and fight until not a white man is left."

Chaos erupted.

One of Red Cloud's representatives, named Three Bears, had a slight understanding of the soldiers' language and stood up and began yelling at Crazy Horse. "Do not kill my good friend White Hat! You will have to kill me instead!"

Three Bears' outburst made no sense to Crazy Horse. He had no intention of killing anyone in the room. However, Three Bears, one of Red Cloud's allies, had not said this for Crazy Horse's benefit. We knew that he had said it for White Hat's. It was yet another way to paint Crazy Horse as a bad man to the white people in favor of making Red Cloud look good.

It was all too much for Grouard. He was shaking with anxiety and asked Garnett to take over the interpreting. Garnett agreed and promptly stood next to Crazy Horse. He asked him once again if he would fight with the scouts.

"We will go on our hunt instead," Crazy Horse repeated firmly.

White Hat once again told him that there would be no hunt, at least not as long as the soldiers were at war with the Nez Perce. Tiring of the argument, Crazy Horse turned to our warriors. "These people are afraid to fight their own fights. Let us leave!"

With that, Crazy Horse led our warriors out of the room. Watching nearly all of our warriors leave under his direction made White Hat very nervous, and he went to his head man Bradley and told him that he thought there would be trouble. Bradley responded by sending word to Fort Laramie to send soldiers. He also sent word to Three Stars. Upon receipt of this news, Three Stars returned from the East as quickly as possible.

With the soldiers unsure where our loyalties stood, they decided not to risk having our scouts join their fight after all. The news came as a relief to all of us. So when September began, Touch The Cloud returned to our family camp on the Spotted Tail Agency. A short time afterward, Three Stars arrived from back East. After being briefed, he asked that Crazy Horse and our warriors be stripped of all their weapons. However, he did not want to provoke a fight that would create a lot of bloodshed for his soldiers. So he strategized with the other soldier head men on the best way to do this. They came up with a plan to try to encourage Crazy Horse's followers to abandon him and his village and move across a creek in a show of friendship to the government. That way one side of the creek would be the soldiers' friends and the other side would be those still loyal to Crazy Horse. By reducing the number of warriors in Crazy Horse's village, Three Stars probably thought he was reducing his risk when it came time to collect the weapons. It was a divide and conquer plan.

Toward that end, Three Stars sent Crazy Horse's old friend He Dog and some other warriors to do his dirty work and spread the word of his offer to spare those who left Crazy Horse's village from turning in their weapons. When Crazy Horse saw He Dog in his camp, he asked what he was doing. He Dog told him. Crazy Horse looked at him with curious eyes. He Dog did not want to lose his friendship, but he was also afraid of losing any more of his freedoms to the soldiers.

"Does this mean that we will now be enemies?" He Dog asked.

Crazy Horse replied that the white people were the only ones he knew that made rules for other people that said *If you stay on one side of a line you are safe and if you are on the other side it is okay to kill you.* He told He Dog to camp where he pleased.

As the time approached for when the soldiers were to come to Crazy Horse's village and disarm it, Three Stars must have had a second thought. He sent word that he wanted to talk with Crazy Horse first. Three Stars' change of heart stunned Red Cloud and his followers. They had spent a great deal of time and energy working to isolate and discredit Crazy Horse in the soldiers' minds. Now Three Stars' change of strategy threatened to make it all for naught.

Seeing his influence over his Agency and people diminish with each passing day of Crazy Horse's presence, Red Cloud's anxiety rose and he became desperate. He decided there was only one way to get his influence and power back: he needed to eliminate Crazy Horse.

Toward that end, on the following day, one of Red Cloud's relatives, Woman's Dress made it a point to find Three Stars and tell him that "when Crazy Horse shakes your hand, he's going to stab you with his knife." His words had their desired effect and shook Three Stars up. As a result, Three Stars changed his mind yet again and decided the best thing to do was to capture Crazy Horse and send him away.

On September 4, approximately four hundred soldiers and five hundred of the Loafers went to arrest Crazy Horse at his tipi. White Hat offered $300 and a horse to anybody who brought him in. Red Cloud and the Loafer head man, American Horse, and their bands, along with Crazy Horse's old nemesis No Water, were on hand to help in his arrest. No Water had waited a long time for this moment. He wanted to erase the infamy of their previous encounter. He thought the white man's spirit water had ruined his aim last time, so he boasted to those around him that he would kill Crazy Horse for sure this time.

Since May, Crazy Horse had been waiting for the government papers that would make our Lone Horn Agency a reality. Now with all that had happened, he no longer trusted Three Stars' word. He decided to leave. So Crazy Horse gathered up Black Shawl and together with two of our warriors rode to see his relatives at the Spotted Tail Agency. He left everything he had been given by the government in his tipi, including his ration card.

The Spotted Tail Agency was also where his father, Touch The Cloud, and most of our family members were camped, and it would be good to once again be among those he could trust. With the understanding that his vision was possibly about to be fulfilled, he also wanted to get his wife into our family's caring hands. Once Crazy Horse arrived, he rode into Touch The Cloud's camp amidst our cheers. We were very excited to see him. Touch The Cloud was away at the time.

When we heard that Red Cloud and American Horse's bands were intent on killing him, it made our warriors very angry. They wanted to meet their bands and show them what being a Lakota was all about. We would protect Crazy Horse just as he had protected us his whole life.

Shortly after his arrival, Crazy Horse met with several of our elders and told them one of the main reasons he had left the Red Cloud Agency was because the government had never made our Lone Horn Agency a reality. Hearing this, our elders prayed and found out through their animal helpers and those from the other side that our Lone Horn Agency had indeed been put on the white man's precious paper and was sitting in Washington. This made Crazy Horse happy. He felt a peace permeate his body.

Once some of Spotted Tail's head men heard that Crazy Horse had arrived at their Agency, they rode out to Touch The Cloud's camp to try to send him back to the Red Cloud Agency. When they got there, our relatives and friends would not allow them to get near him.

It became a standoff.

Spotted Tail's head men sent a messenger into our village to tell Crazy Horse that he needed to come to the soldier camp inside the Spotted Tail Agency, which the soldiers called Camp Sheridan, and see the Spotted Tail Agent, Lee.

Now that he had delivered Black Shawl safely to our family, he did not wish to be the cause of any harm to anyone in our camp. So he told the messenger he would go to Camp Sheridan. Our family and friends knew it was a dangerous decision and we told him that if he went, we all wanted to go with him. And so we did.

As we traveled to Camp Sheridan, Spotted Tail's warriors rode all around us to let us know that they would not let Crazy Horse get away. Our warriors, including Crazy Horse's brothers Combing and Bear Pipe, kept a wary eye on the Spotted Tail warriors to make sure they did not take him from us. We felt honored to be able to protect him on the way to the Agent's office. Each of our warriors had a love in their heart for Crazy Horse. He had led us through so many dangers. We held our heads up high on the trip. So did he.

Along the way to the Agent's office, Touch The Cloud arrived to join us. He rode up next to Crazy Horse and they rode silently, side by side, and spoke to each other with their hearts. As we neared the Agent's office, a wagon approached. Our warriors tensed and made sure their weapons were ready. Agent Lee and a few other white men got out of the wagon and walked towards Crazy Horse with their hands stuck out as if to shake his hand. Our warriors were wary and watched to make sure there were no tricks. When they got close enough, Crazy Horse shook their hands. We relaxed once we saw that they meant him no harm.

Agent Lee asked Crazy Horse if he was still coming to his office so they could talk. Crazy Horse told him he was tired of talking but was on his way to his office anyway in order to avoid trouble, which satisfied Lee. So we resumed the trip, this time with Lee and his wagon joining us.

About the same time as Crazy Horse's arrival, Spotted Tail also showed up with a large group of his warriors. At nearly the same time as Crazy Horse's and Spotted Tail's arrivals, No Water led some of Red Cloud's followers into view. When our warriors saw them, their blood ran hot and they wanted to kill these Red Cloud followers. Spotted Tail's warriors rode in between our warriors and theirs to keep us away from each other, but we still tried to get at them anyway. Crazy Horse shouted that he wanted no trouble and so we stopped.

Seeing that our warriors loved Crazy Horse and would still give their lives for him, No Water and his party lost their courage and headed back to the Red Cloud Agency. Without the courage he got from the white man's spirit water, No Water's boast to kill Crazy Horse had become empty.

With the retreat of No Water's party, Spotted Tail turned and rode within a few feet of Crazy Horse and commanded that he go back to Camp Robinson and talk with Three Stars. Crazy Horse stared at him without saying a word. Our warriors did the same. The silence was deafening. Spotted Tail could hear the tension form in our hearts and decided to back away from his demand.

"Every Lakota who comes to this Agency listens to me. You say you want to stay here and live in peace, then you must listen to me. That is the way things are done here. Now will you talk to Agent Lee?"

All eyes turned to Crazy Horse. He quietly got off his horse and peacefully went inside the cabin accompanied by Touch The Cloud, Lee, and some officers. Spotted Tail joined them. Once inside, they asked Crazy Horse what he wanted.

"I want to keep our sacred Black Hills."

A lump formed in Touch The Cloud's throat, he was the only one in the room who truly understood that Crazy Horse had said what was in the hearts of all our people. Lee and the soldiers reacted like it was the opening line of a negotiation. Spotted Tail looked away and pretended not to hear. Crazy Horse went on to tell them about all the troubles he had had at the Red Cloud Agency and asked if he could enroll to be with our family at the Spotted Tail Agency.

"If you let me come here, I will be a peaceful man."

Agent Lee asked several questions of him and found his heart to be good. He told Crazy Horse that he had orders to return him to Camp Robinson, and if he went peacefully, he would try very hard to have Three Stars let him enroll at the Spotted Tail Agency. With that said, Spotted Tail offered him one of his personal horses to ride on the trip back. Crazy Horse reluctantly agreed to return to the Red Cloud Agency.

They then enjoyed a hastily prepared feast and he was told he could spend the night in Touch The Cloud's camp as long as he promised to be back the next morning. He gave his word, and Touch The Cloud added that he and our family's warriors would join him on the return journey. That evening Crazy Horse thought about the vision he had carved on the Owl Rock the previous summer. He knew.

CHAPTER TWENTY-ONE

Joining Those on the Other Side

Crazy Horse had barely slept when morning broke. He had spent the majority of the night praying just outside the village. On his way to his father's tipi for a brief visit, his aunt They Are Afraid Of Her stopped him. She was holding a red blanket.

"Crazy Horse, this was the blanket given to Lone Horn by our enemies to thank us for opening our hearts and saving their weak ones from death."

"I remember."

"Good Looking Woman kept it. When she died it came to me. She wanted it to be yours. Our people know this as a blanket of compassion and peace. One that represents our ability to forgive our enemies and show them our good hearts. Wear it for us."

He thanked her and wrapped himself in it.

"I will wear it with pride."

A healthy meal of buffalo soup was then served and he ate with his cousin Standing Elk.

"I see you are wearing my father's blanket," said Standing Elk.

Crazy Horse nodded. Standing Elk pulled out a holstered revolver and handed it to him.

"Put this under the blanket," advised Standing Elk. Crazy Horse hesitated. "In case of trouble."

Our family was worried and wanted to make sure he had options. After all, the soldiers and Loafers were well armed, and history had proven them to be anything but trustworthy. Crazy Horse tied the holstered revolver around his waist and made sure it was tucked under the blanket. Standing Elk gave a smile of approval.

Touch The Cloud peeked into the tipi and said, "We must go."

Crazy Horse and Standing Elk stood up and prepared to leave. His father gave him one of his horses to ride to the Agent's office. During the night, he had asked one of our young men to take Inyan and hide him in the pines near the Good River because he had a feeling about his future. Our young men did as he requested.

Touch The Cloud, Standing Elk, and some of our family's warriors accompanied Crazy Horse as he headed off to see Agent Lee. Once they arrived, Agent Lee had an ambulance waiting. He offered Crazy Horse a ride in the ambulance to the Red Cloud Agency. Crazy Horse refused. He told Lee that he was not sick and would ride like a warrior. As they took off for Camp Robinson, Touch The Cloud and Crazy Horse rode close to each other. Along the way, Spotted Tail and Red Cloud's warriors joined them and rode on all sides of Crazy Horse and our family's warriors, so our warriors started feeling hemmed in.

Crazy Horse noticed how close these other warriors were, and when the procession stopped for a break, he went to Agent Lee and asked why our warriors had no room. Agent Lee told him that he would protect him in case of trouble and reminded him that if he made it to Camp Robinson without any incidents, he would speak for him to be enrolled at the Spotted Tail Agency. Crazy Horse had given his word that he would come with Lee and he still wanted to enroll at the Spotted Tail Agency so he could stay with his family. So he decided to continue to believe Lee and resumed the journey as though the other warriors did not exist.

As morning pushed into late afternoon, the Red Cloud Agency and Camp Robinson came into view. The scene was tense. Crazy Horse could hear our people arguing from a distance. It made his stomach churn with sadness. He wanted them to stop. Just as Crazy Horse was arriving into the Camp Robinson compound, He Dog came out to greet him with sobering news.

"Look out. Watch your step. You are going into a dangerous place," He Dog warned. Crazy Horse thanked He Dog for his concern, but he could see and hear that for himself. He continued on with Lee's contingent into the Agency.

American Horse and Red Cloud had organized their followers to form a perimeter around Camp Robinson to insure that Crazy Horse could not escape. Some of them were shouting that they wanted Crazy Horse dead. Little Big Man forced his way to Crazy Horse and grabbed him. "Come with me, quitter."

Crazy Horse had cared for our people his entire life. He made sure that they always had food and water. He spent a great deal of time praying to our Creator to make it so. He had been our strongest defender against the white people in order to keep our way of life alive. He lived his life for us. But on this day, our people decided they wanted more. They wanted to see his heart stop beating. He knew that. He knew what was going to happen. He was sad that it had come to this. Many who were there said "he wasn't right" that day. They are right, he was already in mourning for our people.

He had been our greatest hope to find a way of continuing to live in our traditional way of life. He had stayed at the Agency that he so detested to try to reclaim our sacred Black Hills and burial grounds by implementing Lone Horn's dream of an Agency that would encompass all that was Lakota. By killing him, they were about to kill this dream. They were about to kill the Lakota way of life that we had always known.

Little Big Man led Crazy Horse to the Camp adjutant's office. There he was to wait for Bradley to arrive. Touch The Cloud and a few of our warriors joined him in his wait. Crazy Horse also waited to see if Agent Lee would keep his word about speaking to

Three Stars on his behalf. However, Bradley never bothered to show up nor did Lee talk to Three Stars. He was a prisoner, yet nobody had the courage to tell him.

Instead, Lee introduced him to another soldier head man named Kennington. Lee said that Kennington would make sure he did not get hurt. Lee then asked Touch The Cloud and our warriors to come with him so he could talk to them alone. Once Touch The Cloud and our warriors had left the office with Lee, Kennington and Little Big Man motioned Crazy Horse to stand. They flanked his sides along with some of their Indian police and they led him out of the office. They marshaled him along the outskirts of the Camp's parade grounds.

Outside, many of Crazy Horse's followers had just arrived. As soon as they saw him, they recognized his extreme danger. They pushed towards him and cried for him to be rescued. Those loyal to Red Cloud and American Horse intercepted them and drowned their cries for rescue with cries to see him killed.

Our people were on the edge of battle.

Crazy Horse couldn't help but see our people's faces turned towards each other in hate. He knew his time was done on our Mother the Earth, but he did not want to leave his people in this state. As he entered the post guard house, he noticed the solid bars on the windows. As they opened the big wooden door to his right, he saw it was a jail cell with several white prisoners, some manacled and wearing leg irons. He immediately decided that this would not be how everything would end.

"I will not go in there," he said with a clear voice.

Little Big Man and Kennington then tried to force him into the cell. He resisted and broke free. In the process, the red blanket that was draped over his body that represented so much fell to the ground, revealing his revolver. One of the Indian policemen grabbed the revolver from his holster while Little Big Man pulled a knife on him. He snatched the knife out of Little Big Man's hand and bolted out the door. Little Big Man ran after him, finally tackling him and pinning his arms against his body. As they continued to tussle, Crazy Horse yanked one of his arms free and cut Little Big Man on the hand with the knife. Little Big Man cried out in pain and let Crazy Horse go.

Red Cloud and American Horse demanded that their followers "shoot to kill!" American Horse aimed his gun at Crazy Horse but failed to find a clear shot. The Loafer band members surged towards him and hemmed him in.

"Kill the son of a bitch! Kill him!" commanded Kennington as he emerged from the jail house. They acted like a pack of wolves looking to make a kill, growling their hate and bad feelings. Little Big Man once again grabbed him around the waist, and once again Crazy Horse pulled himself free. However, as he yanked out of Little Big Man's grasp, he reeled backwards into the waiting bayonet of a soldier. The soldier stabbed him twice. Crazy Horse collapsed.

The crowd went silent. The anger left their faces. The hearts of even those warriors that had been calling for his death fell to the ground. For the next few moments, our entire Nation became frozen in remorse. Soldiers came running with rifles cocked and ready to fire. Seeing the soldiers drove Crazy Horse's closest family members and friends into action. They rushed to form a circle of protection around him. Touch The Cloud knelt by his side.

Someone sent for the white medicine man McGillycuddy and he came running to tend to Crazy Horse. He examined his wounds. One had punctured his lower back and the other ravaged him just below his rib cage. The wounds were deep and nearly protruded all the way through his body. He knew he could not save him.

He turned to Kennington and told him the wounds were mortal. Kennington did not seem to care and ordered his soldiers to take Crazy Horse back into the jail house. As the soldiers moved toward him, some of our warriors aimed their bows and guns at Kennington's head. Seeing this, the soldiers paused. Realizing that the whole situation could turn even uglier, one of the soldier interpreters named Baptiste Pourier pleaded with Kennington to stop. He suggested that taking Crazy Horse into the adjutant's office would be a safer decision for everyone.

Upon hearing the exchange between Kennington and Pourier, Crazy Horse's supporters took up the cry, "Don't take him into the jail, he is a chief!"

Hearing their words, even Red Cloud and American Horse's followers began to agree. Our entire Nation began to remember who he was. Kennington did not know what to do; he was under orders to put Crazy Horse into the jailhouse. McGillycuddy volunteered to go ask Bradley to remand his order. Kennington acquiesced. McGillycuddy hustled over to Bradley's quarters.

After a short period of time, McGillycuddy came back and said Bradley would not listen. Kennington ordered his soldiers to proceed with taking our dying Crazy Horse to the jailhouse. As the soldiers once again made a move toward Crazy Horse, our entire Nation warned them not to touch him.

"Crazy Horse is a chief and will not be put in the jailhouse!" the Loafer head man American Horse shouted. This caught Kennington's attention. Now he knew that if he put Crazy Horse in jail that he would have no friends at all among our Nation. Not even the Loafers. He valued his life too much to proceed and stopped his men. Our people, no matter how briefly, had united as a Nation once again.

McGillycuddy scurried back to Bradley's quarters. In short order he returned and reported that Bradley had relented and Crazy Horse was to be put in the adjutant's office. Some of the Loafers tried to step forward to carry him; however, our family members Touch The Cloud, Hump Two, and our family's friend Spotted Eagle were the ones who carried him in. McGillycuddy accompanied them and instructed the soldiers to keep everyone else out.

Crazy Horse asked to be laid on the floor so he would be close to our Mother the Earth. McGillycuddy administered morphine to ease his pain while Touch The Cloud stayed close by his side. Not long afterward, Waglula arrived with Red Leggins. His father knelt by his side. Red Leggins stood nearby. "I am here," he informed his son.

Crazy Horse tried to speak when he saw his father, but the words would not come out right. Crazy Horse looked up at him and saw the deep concern in his eyes. He mustered all the strength he had left in his body and addressed his father.

"Father, it is no use to depend on me. I am going to die."

His words made them weep. It was not long afterward that his spirit left for the other side, where he was reunited with his birth mother, his step-mother, and his darling little girl, along with the rest of his family members and siblings who had passed before him. He died during the last few moments of September 5, 1877.

He is now with the Creator.

McGillycuddy asked Waglula if he would like him to take care of his son's body. Waglula told him that it was a father's responsibility to bury his son. With that said, McGillycuddy packed his medical bag and left for the evening. Word of Crazy Horse's death spread quickly.

In the wee hours of September 6, two of our elders arrived in a wagon at the adjutant's office. They came to prepare Crazy Horse for burial. They brought a thick buffalo robe and a large bundle. Inside the bundle was a dead black-tailed deer that had been killed by Hump Two. Once our elders had entered the adjutant's office, Waglula asked the soldiers for some privacy so they could perform a ceremony to send his son to the other side.

The soldiers felt sorry for Waglula and his relatives. They thought it best to leave them alone with the body. So they stood guard right outside the door. Once alone, Waglula and the rest worked quickly in the candlelight. They unwrapped the bundle and cut the deer from head to tail into two pieces. They arranged the sectioned deer on the travois into the shape of a man's body and covered it over with the thick buffalo robe. They tied the robe down with a hemp rope.

After Waglula had cut a piece of his hair and placed it with his son, he took his son's body and folded it into the fetal position and wrapped it to resemble the bundle the two elders had brought in. Touch The Cloud carried the bundle containing the body and placed it back into the wagon in full view of the soldiers standing guard. The deer disguised as his body was carried out on the travois for all to see. The elders even smudged the decoy with burning sage to make sure anyone watching from the shadows would keep their eyes glued to the travois.

Waglula wanted his son to rest in peace. He did not want the soldiers to know where he was buried, because he knew if they did, they would strip his grave for souvenirs. He did not want any of our people to know either, in case any of them came to look for his special medicines that were to be buried with him and take them as their own.

As the morning star began to visit our Mother the Earth, their wagon lumbered back to Waglula's tipi inside Touch The Cloud's camp. Six Indian policemen from the Red Cloud Agency followed them at a distance to see what they were up to. Once Waglula and the wagon arrived, they took the decoy body into his tipi and added additional buffalo robes to it to fill it out more. They left Crazy Horse's body in the wagon.

As the sun began to rise, Waglula, Touch The Cloud, Combing, Bear Pipe, Standing Elk, Charging First, Hump Two, and Black Fox began driving the wagon containing Crazy Horse's body north, along with a second wagon. When the six Indian policemen began to tail them, some of our family members in our village spotted them and rode out to tell them to stop or there would be trouble. The Indian policemen stopped and pretended to retreat to the Red Cloud Agency. They then circled around and followed our family's wagons, spying on them from the ridges.

Our family members in the wagons caught sight of them and purposely led them toward the Good River. Our family members disappeared at dusk into the pines that surrounded the river. The following morning, the Indian policemen went down to the river to pick up the trail and found one set of wagon tracks heading east and another set leading into the Good River without a corresponding set of tracks on the other side of the river. They followed the wagon heading east. Upon catching up to the wagon, they found the wagon empty and being driven by a single driver, Black Fox.

Waglula and the rest of our men had driven the other wagon in the river bed for a long ways. One of our relatives had been waiting in the pines with Inyan and met up with the wagon. They dragged the body on a travois while leading Inyan the rest of the way. Waglula prepared his son's body by taking a small bite of Crazy Horse's owl medicine and blowing it over his son to protect him one last time. It left a glitter on his body and his remains suddenly became heavier. Once they came to his burial place, they dug a hole and buried him. By the time they had put him into the ground, his body had become like stone. They next killed Inyan so Crazy Horse would have his favorite horse to ride when his grandparents, mothers, brothers, sisters, and little girl greeted him on the other side.

Meanwhile, back at our camp, the rest of our family was protecting the black-tail deer body as though it was actually Crazy Horse's. Waglula and the rest of our burial party returned to our village in the wee hours of September 8.

Upon their return, they were confronted about where they had been. They kept silent. Only our immediate family knows where Crazy Horse is buried, and only certain members of our family are chosen from each generation to continue to carry the secret. Someday we hope to bring his body to the Black Hills, our sacred burial grounds, to allow him to rest in the land he had fought so hard to maintain. However that time hasn't arrived yet.

Our family put the decoy body on a scaffold at Camp Sheridan so the soldiers could see it. Nearly our entire Nation mourned his death and came to honor the scaffold. They sent their prayers to his spirit. They brought him wasna and good things to eat for his journey to the other side. Our people were really all torn up.

The soldiers built a wooden coffin and offered it to Waglula. They also brought him the red blanket that had fallen off his son during his murder. Waglula took these and he put the deer's body inside the coffin. He set it back up on the scaffold and then wrapped the red blanket on the outside of the coffin. The soldiers built a fence around the grave to keep the body safe, secure, and under control.

Since the scaffold contained a deer's body, it did not bother him that our old ways and the white people's ways were all mixed together. Had it been Crazy Horse, there would have been no coffin, nor would he have been put on display in a soldier camp. As a final touch, Waglula brought out his big brown horse with the dark mane that Crazy Horse used to ride on hunts and killed it at the base of the scaffold. This created several inquiries from those who had ridden with him about what had happened to Inyan. Wouldn't that have been the horse Crazy Horse would have wanted? We told them that Inyan had been set loose by Waglula to honor his service to his son. Many of them remained skeptical, but we didn't care.

A portion of Crazy Horse's owl medicine was kept and became part of our family's sacred bundle, which was now kept by Waglula. That fall, Waglula and the rest of our family moved up north to our camp at Bear Creek. Kills Enemy was still sick from the coughing sickness, so we tried our best to keep her alive during our move. At about the same time, Bear Pipe's little boy, Comes Home Victorious, died of the whooping cough sickness. It was a painful period for our family; one that we cannot forget easily.

Touch The Cloud also moved north and set up his permanent camp along the north side of the Good River where the present community of Bridger, South Dakota, on the Cheyenne River Reservation is now located. Touch The Cloud wanted to be close to where his father, Lone Horn, was buried. These camps and others in the area were referred to as the northern camps.

With the death of Crazy Horse, his name was passed back to Waglula, who retook the name of Crazy Horse and became known as Old Man Crazy Horse. Sadly, Kills Enemy did not survive the coughing disease and joined Crazy Horse and the rest of our relatives on the other side. Her last request was to lie next to her mother near Iron Cedar Creek. Waglula and Corn honored her request.

CHAPTER TWENTY-TWO

Silence and Misdirection

Reservation life did not fit our people well at all. We were a nomadic people, and these tiny islands of land called reservations that they forced us to live on made us feel like prisoners. We were in unchartered waters. Trying to live in the white man's ways mixed our people up. It would take a strong mind to keep the

The beaded blanket and bridle, given by the Lone Horn family in remembrance of Crazy Horse, which was later stolen. Rider is Violet Roberts at a parade in Faith, SD, in the 1950s. Courtesy Edward Clown family.

flickering flame of our Nation lit. We missed Crazy Horse. The elders asked his father, Old Man Crazy Horse, to be that strong mind as our spokesman for the northern camps. He agreed to take on that role.

In remembrance of Crazy Horse, our elders gave Old Man Crazy Horse a red and white beaded horse blanket with a matching beaded bridle. The surviving members of Lone Horn's family also gave him a beaded blanket and bridle. This set was blue and white. They gave the blanket and bridle to him shortly after Crazy Horse was murdered. These kind of gifts were given to remember those deeply loved ones who passed on. One of the blanket and bridle sets was later sold to a museum in Pierre, South Dakota, in the mid-1960s so the children in our family would have decent clothes to wear. The other set was stolen a short time after the first set was sold.

The government, the military, and their handpicked Indian police were still highly suspicious of our family. They quite often came to visit Old Man Crazy Horse to see what he was up to. We did not trust their visits, and our family members surrounded the area where he lived to redirect anyone away from him that we didn't know or that we knew to be an enemy. These people rarely found Old Man Crazy Horse, and after a while, outsiders never made contact with him. We kept everyone who was not part of our family from knowing any information about us. When we did speak, we quite often gave these strangers decoy information.

Within days of Crazy Horse's murder, Nellie Larrabee and her father dropped by his abandoned tipi to claim all that he had left behind, including his ration card. A few weeks later, Nellie married Albert Greasy Hand. She gave Crazy Horse's ration card to him, and he drew rations with the card as Crazy Horse for six months after Crazy Horse had been killed. We could not believe how dumb the Agency workers seemed to be.

Bear Pipe continued to attempt to carry out his vision of becoming a medicine man. His grandfather Corn did all he could to help. However, fulfilling his vision was elusive and something always seemed to come up that would frustrate his attempts to do so.

The white people had built miles of fences all around us. Sneaking over to steal horses from our traditional enemy the Crow, whose Agency was located about fifty miles west of Billings, Montana, was complicated at best. We could not just make a beeline for our village once we had stolen a horse, but had to stop and cut holes in all of the fences. The whole scenario discouraged us from even trying. On top of that, there was very little to hunt, as the white people had killed over six million buffalo from 1872 until our surrender. Many of those buffalo were killed just for sport. Only a tiny handful of buffalo survived the slaughter.

Black Shawl had moved north with our family and now lived in the same tipi as They Are Afraid Of Her. They stayed together in our family camp.

In November 1877, the government broke their promise to create our Lone Horn Agency. They decided to concentrate on reducing the size of the existing Agencies so they would have more lands available for the white people to use. This just confirmed the fact that we could never look at the government as being an honorable entity to deal with—ever.

Even with all these bad things happening around us, life went on. In early 1878 Combing and Comes After Her experienced the birth of their first child. The baby was a boy and he brought them and us great joy; however, he died almost immediately after birth. Losing children never gets any easier for any of us and we all mourned their baby's passing.

In Oklahoma, Dull Knife, Little Wolf, and our Cheyenne relatives were not faring very well at the Darlington Agency. They had little in common with their Southern Cheyenne brethren. Dull Knife and Little Wolf's people were soon treated as outcasts. Their people died of malaria and measles, two diseases they had never seen in their northern homelands. Approximately one-third of their people perished after relocating to Oklahoma.

In addition, the white Agent who ran the Darlington Agency gave them less than half of the rations they were owed, and Dull Knife and Little Wolf's people began to starve. When the trial year was up, they told the government that they wanted to go home. The government said no. They reminded the government that they had agreed to try it for one year, and if they didn't like it, they could go back. The government told them they had not tried hard enough. After looking into the eyes of their elderly, women, and children dying of disease and starvation, Dull Knife and Little Wolf listened to their hearts and decided to take their people home, back to the north, against the government's wishes.

On the evening of September 9, 1878, Dull Knife, Little Wolf, and our Cheyenne allies and relatives, about three hundred in all, left the Darlington Agency and headed north. They left their tipis up and fires burning to make the soldiers think that they were still at the Agency. Once the soldiers discovered they had left, they sent out thousands of soldiers from the many forts along the way to take them down.

It was scary. They had little ammunition and after a while had to eat their ponies to keep from starving. The soldiers attacked them four different times. Four different times the tiny group was able to beat the soldiers back and keep their women and children safe. Their hunger to go home was strong.

By October, the temperatures were dipping below freezing levels, and they had to slit open some of their ponies and put their children inside the guts to keep them from freezing to death. It was a hard trip. Many of them traveled on foot, wearing tattered clothes that did not shield them from the cold. They traveled this way for over five hundred miles just to be home.

Once they came in sight of the Red Cloud Agency, Dull Knife saw that many of their women and children were incapable of taking any more steps. However, Little Wolf wanted to go farther north and hide in the mountains. Reluctantly, the two leaders split up and Dull Knife and about one hundred fifty of his people journeyed to the Agency to find our family members so they could stay with us.

Some of our Lakota who had become army scouts held a meeting with them while they were still out on the plains and told Dull Knife he should surrender at Fort Robinson. Dull Knife did not want to go there. However, the soldiers sent him reassurances through these scouts that his people would be well fed and that they would seek to get them transferred to the Red Cloud Agency. He decided to trust these reassurances and agreed to come in around late October 1878.

After the Cheyenne arrived at Fort Robinson, the soldiers decided to house them in a barracks, where they were given food and wood to keep their wood stoves burning for heat. After living in the barracks for a little over two months, the army told them the bad news. The government had decided to send them back to Oklahoma. Dull Knife told them he would not go. He said he would rather die. So the army confined the Cheyenne to the barracks and denied them food and fuel for their wood stoves in order to force them to change their minds.

Once again Dull Knife said they would rather die than go back to Oklahoma. So the army cut off their water and put chains across the doors so they could not sneak out and waited for them to capitulate. After two more days of living like that, Dull Knife and every member of his band decided they would rather fight and die before going back to Oklahoma.

When the Cheyenne surrendered, they had kept a few weapons hidden. They had broken the weapons down into pieces and hidden them in the women's clothing. The smaller pieces of guns had been worn by the children as jewelry. On the night of January 9, 1879, they pieced these weapons back together. They ended up with about five rifles and eleven pistols. Staring at certain death, the Cheyenne broke out some windows and escaped from the barracks.

The snow was deep, and the men with the guns kept the soldiers busy while the women and children ran into the night. The soldiers kept coming and soon overwhelmed the Cheyenne trying to keep them at bay. They chased the Cheyenne people and followed their moccasin tracks in the snow. They began gunning down everyone, including the women and children. As Dull Knife and his eight family members ran, his daughter was badly wounded and her husband was killed. His daughter decided to stay by her husband's side and begged her father to take their family and keep going. They kept going. With a heavy heart, he granted her last wish. His daughter died of her wound a short time later.

Dull Knife led his family up into the rocky cliffs so they would leave no footprints in the snow for the soldiers to follow. Many of the rest of the Cheyenne did not take that route. They were gunned down, captured, or seriously injured. The soldiers enlisted some

Dull Knife, 1873. Courtesy Dietmar Schulte-Möhring collection.

of Red Cloud's scouts to help track down some of those who got away. But they never found Dull Knife. He and his family finally made it to our family's camp up at Bear Creek. They hadn't eaten for days. When they finally walked into our village, Dull Knife's daughter Otter Woman Number Two, along with the rest of our family's women, all cried for their horrible losses.

"I have seen how they looked, they were all skin and bones. Even though they were in such a bad way, Dull Knife walked into the camp with his head up strong," Otter Woman Number Two told her son, our great-grandfather Peter Talks, when he was old enough to understand. He passed the story to his daughter, who became our grandmother, Amy Talks Clown.

This is how the story came to us.

When Waglula and the rest of our family saw this, we knew that all we had in this world was each other, and so we held on tight for over a century. Dull Knife ended up staying at our northern camps.

During the spring of 1879, Dull Knife and his family heard that the Creator had helped the white people in the East to open their hearts, and they pressured the military into allowing Dull Knife and his family to stay on their northern lands. So he and his family turned themselves in and were given a place within the Agency.

Little Wolf and the remaining Cheyenne stayed around the Sand Mountains of Nebraska for a few weeks before heading over to their natural home in the Powder River region. After being confronted by the military, they agreed to surrender if they were allowed to stay in the North. The military agreed. On March 27, 1879, Little Wolf's Cheyenne surrendered to Bear Coat at Fort Keogh, which is two miles west of what is today Miles City, Montana.

Eventually, in 1884, a tract of land was set aside for the Northern Cheyenne. They named it the Tongue River Agency in 1886. Today that area in eastern Montana has been renamed the Northern Cheyenne Reservation.

Dull Knife and his eldest wife, White Buffalo Woman, enrolled with our family at what is now the Cheyenne River Agency. They became church members in 1881, and Christianized their names so that they became known as Louis and Louisa Knife.

Meanwhile, back among our Lakota people, the government had developed a cadre of Lakota Loafer head men to rubber stamp their wishes. Sadly, our people were so badly divided that we could no longer trust each other. So our family stopped trusting people outside of our family. Our war of silence had extended to our own people.

Around 1879, one of our elders, Kills At Night, from the Itazipco band and who had spent most of his life protecting our Sacred Calf Pipe Keeper, sent his two sons to mix in with the Loafers to glean any information they could about any new dangers to our people or our Sacred Calf Pipe. They set up their tipis down south. One son went to the Spotted Tail Agency, while the other went to the Red Cloud Agency. They both enrolled for rations under their family name of Kills At Night at the respective Agencies where they were staying. The elder Kills At Night was already enrolled for rations in the Northern Camps at Fort Bennett.

In 1881, the military asked to meet with Old Man Crazy Horse at the Spotted Tail Agency. The younger Kills At Night staying at the Spotted Tail Agency reported unusual soldier activity there and said that it could be a trap. As a result, the elders in the Northern Camps told Old Man Crazy Horse not to go and meet with the military. They told him he would end up either dead or a prisoner. They told him to send someone else.

So he asked a young warrior named Iron Wing to go to the meeting and deliver a letter from him. It was a letter that he had dictated to one of our people who could write the white man's words. Iron Wing was a mixed white and Lakota and knew the white people's language. The letter that Old Man Crazy Horse had prepared for him said he was very ill and could not attend the meeting and that Iron Wing was there in his place.

Iron Wing showed up at the meeting and delivered Old Man Crazy Horse's letter. The soldiers, after reading the letter, showed their disappointment and the meeting was adjourned without allowing Iron Wing an opportunity to speak. When Iron Wing reported to us what had happened, we knew that Old Man Crazy Horse had escaped a trap.

With his health deteriorating, the elder Kills At Night decided to leave our Northern Camps to live with his younger son at the Red Cloud Agency. His younger son had been drawing rations under his father's name, Kills At Night. However, the son's actual name was Undone. Undone had married into the prominent Little Wound family at the Red Cloud Agency. Once the elder Kills At Night arrived, he reclaimed his name from his younger son and began to draw the rations his son had been drawing under that name. That left his rations at Fort Bennett uncollected.

The elder Kills At Night suggested that Old Man Crazy Horse use his name at Fort Bennett to receive rations. That way he would be hard to find. Old Man Crazy Horse thanked Kills At Night, and thus began to receive his rations under the name of his friend Kills At Night.

Meanwhile, anybody who came to the Northern Camp looking for Old Man Crazy Horse was sent away disappointed, or sent to the Red Cloud Agency to talk to Albert Greasy Hand, since he had posed as Crazy Horse after receiving his ration card from Nellie Larrabee. We had them chasing their tails. It made us laugh when we recounted it among ourselves.

In September 1881, Corn and his daughter Iron Between Horns made a visit to the Spotted Tail Agency and camped with the family members who lived down there. The trip was hard on him and he did not want to try to travel back to the Northern Camps until he had recovered, so he planned on staying through the winter. Unfortunately, he ended up leaving for the other side the following month. He was buried in the Little Crow Cemetery in what is today the community of Mission on the Rosebud Reservation in South Dakota.

Bear Pipe's quest to become a strong medicine man had not been going well for a long time, and losing his son and grandfather did nothing to help. He doubted himself, and his ability to follow his vision floundered.

The year 1881 was not good for our family.

The following year, Combing and Comes After Her began their second try at start-ing a family and were successful this time, with the birth of Fremont Frank Combing in 1882. He was the first of our immediate family to be born and survive infancy during our captivity. Little Fremont gave us hope. His Lakota name is lost.

Crazy Horse's sister Iron Cedar and Fights The Thunder's son Old Eagle found each other in 1883 and were married. It was a joyous event and allowed our family to be happy for a time in their happiness. Old Eagle's Agency name was Amos Clown. Old Eagle was a heyoka, and when the Agency interpreter asked him who he was, he told them he was a heyoka. Since there is no word for heyoka in English, they gave him the last name of Clown. They gave Iron Cedar the first name of Julia, so she became known as Julia Clown at the Agency. They set up camp close to They Are Afraid of Her and Black Shawl's tiny cabin made of stucco materials supplied by the government.

In 1886, the elder Kills At Night's heart gave out and he died at the Red Cloud Agency. When word was sent north to inform his relatives, one of the Agents noticed he was still drawing rations at Fort Bennett and decided to ask questions. A messenger was sent to Red Cloud to see what he might know. Red Cloud told the military that he thought the Kills At Night enrollment at Fort Bennett was actually Old Man Crazy Horse. This caused the military to get excited and start poking around our camps.

Our family was able to frustrate the investigation but knew that Old Man Crazy Horse could no longer use the name Kills At Night. So he decided to take the name of his best friend and brother-in-law. He took the name Makuhu, which was his brother-in-law Hump's name in our Lakota language. This is the name he gave the census takers in 1886. However, once he began using it, it became translated differently.

Many of the Natives who did the interpreting at the time were of mixed blood. A large percentage of the interpreters were our Dakota cousins from Minnesota. They spoke and understood our language, but with a decidedly different dialect. Makuhu's name was translated as Breast of Female the first time it showed up on the census. The following year, his name was translated as Female's Breast, and the next year, he was known as Breast of Female once again, even though the name Makuhu was translated as Hump when it belonged to his brother-in-law. From this time on through the rest of his life, he was known to the Agency workers as Breast of Female.

However, the only goal was to bring home rations, and as far as Old Man Crazy Horse was concerned, the government could translate the name any way they wished as long as he could eat and live in peace. It did not bother him that the white people and their interpreters did not know how to translate his name.

CHAPTER TWENTY-THREE

Wounded Knee

By 1889, we had lived under the white man's rule for almost twelve years. They spent that time trying to remake us in their image. The rations they gave us had little to do with our traditional foods. They sent their church people to try to "civilize" us and talk us into giving up our ceremonies and spirituality in favor of theirs. They tried to get us to accept the fact that paper money was more valuable than Our Mother the Earth. They took away our Lakota names in favor of names that had no meaning to us. They discouraged us from using our own language. And they sent our children away to far-off schools so that they would learn to be white people in Lakota bodies.

They Are Afraid Of Her had had enough of this kind of life and left to be with her relatives on the other side. We buried her in the Slim Buttes area so she could be with her little son. Black Shawl, who had lived the last twelve years with They Are Afraid Of Her, decided it was time to rejoin her original family at the Spotted Tail Agency. She told Waglula that she had an aunt who was ill and needed someone to look after her, freeing Waglula from being responsible for Black Shawl's care. Looking after our people was what made her happiest. So she went.

As time went on, it seemed the dark clouds over our lives only became darker. We prayed for a way out of our prison camp atmosphere. We prayed that the white people would go away. When Combing and his wife brought a new son into the world named Charley Combing, it was all the more reason for us to want to live in the old ways so we could pass them along to our newborns and give them a better life. We prayed that our traditional food source, the buffalo, would reappear in big numbers. We prayed for renewed hope. These prayers were prayed on all the Agencies. Even the non-Lakota Natives prayed for this. Unfortunately, Charley Combing died shortly after his birth from another of the white man's diseases.

The intensity of our prayers grew.

During a solar eclipse in 1889, a holy man from the Northern Paiute tribe who lived in what is now western Nevada, named Wovoka, had a vision. In his vision, he visited his deceased ancestors on the other side. There he saw plenty of wild game, and the land was as it had been before the invasion of the whites. His ancestors told him if those living lived a life of universal love, they would be united with all of their friends and family on the other side. Word of his vision spread to all the western tribes, including the Lakota. Two of our in-laws, Short Bull and Kicking Bear, made a trip to Nevada to find out about this vision firsthand.

During Short Bull and Kicking Bear's journey, they stayed at other reservations on their way to Nevada so they would go undetected. After spending some time with Wovoka, they came to understand that if they repeatedly performed a special Spirit Dance, our Mother the Earth would be replenished with buffalo and other wild game, our ancestors would be brought back to life, and the white people would be infected with a disease that would make them disappear from our world. Short Bull and Kicking Bear learned that if they wore a special shirts, the shirts would protect them from any harm or any traces of this disease.

In February of 1890, the government redrew our Agency boundaries once again. The year before, legislation had been passed to reduce the size of our Agencies to make them much smaller. These new boundaries also changed the Agencies into what the government called reservations. The Red Cloud Agency became the Pine Ridge Reservation, the Spotted Tail Agency became the Rosebud Reservation, the land that Sitting Bull's people lived on was made into the Standing Rock Reservation, and the land our family lived on was made into the Cheyenne River Reservation. They cut our rations in half, hoping to force us to give up our culture so we would embrace the white ways. Our children at the far-off schools were forbidden to speak our language or practice our culture under the threat of physical punishment. As these policies began to impact us in a very harsh way, the promises of the Spirit Dance, or Ghost Dance, as it came to be called, began to look good to many of us.

In early fall of 1890, Short Bull and Kicking Bear began to teach the Ghost Dance to many of our people. They and some of our people would sneak away into our sacred Black Hills, where they would teach the dance. During one of these dances, an elder had a vision that a rare root, which grew in the Bighorn Mountains, would be the source of the disease that would wipe out white people. The elder and two of our people took off to the west to find and bring back this root.

During this time, Old Man Crazy Horse and our family stayed in the Bear Creek area and celebrated the marriage of Makah to a woman named Margaret Makes A Noise. Makah's name had also been changed to his childhood nickname, Wolf, by the Agency workers for their records. He was also given the first name of Peter by the Agency workers. From that time forward, he was known in the Agency records as Peter Wolf.

Most of our family did not believe in the Ghost Dance because it was not our Lakota way. However, we did have some relatives who participated.

As many of our people began to participate in the Ghost Dance, their confidence grew. This scared the white people who ran the reservations. Confidence was not something that would be tolerated. So they requested help from the army and the army came.

The Ghost Dance spread mainly in the northern camps, and Kicking Bear began teaching it to the Hunkpapa band near Sitting Bull's cabin, in hopes of getting an endorsement from our most revered living spiritual leader. Sitting Bull did not endorse it; however, he did not condemn it either, thus making the white Agent in charge of overseeing his band, James McLaughlin, extremely nervous. When McLaughlin heard that Sitting Bull was planning on leaving the Standing Rock Reservation to talk to Red Cloud about the Ghost Dance, he ordered Sitting Bull arrested.

On December 15, 1890, the Standing Rock Indian Police, on McLaughlin's orders, showed up to arrest Sitting Bull at his cabin on the Bigger Than It Seems River. However, the arrest did not go smoothly and a skirmish took place. Sitting Bull was killed. The news sent shock waves throughout all of our reservations.

On the Cheyenne River Reservation, the Ghost Dance was traveling from community to community in an attempt by Short Bull and Kicking Bear to introduce it to our people. They first performed it in the community of Whitehorse, which is about thirty miles northeast of Eagle Butte, South Dakota, and then moved it to another community called Cherry Creek, which is about twenty-five miles east of Bridger along the Good River. One Horn's only surviving son, Spotted Elk, who was also known by his nickname Bigfoot, became involved.

At Cherry Creek, our people sent their little ones to the local schoolhouse, where the teacher, Mary Traversie, a mixed Dakota and white woman, would watch over them while their parents participated in the Ghost Dance. Mary later became the wife of Peter Talks and our maternal great-grandmother. She was one of the children who had been sent east and had graduated from the Hampton Normal School in Virginia.

Spotted Elk, undated. Courtesy Donovin Sprague, from the book *Cheyenne River Sioux*.

On December 23, 1890, Spotted Elk led about four hundred of his band across the Good River and onto the Pine Ridge Reservation. Spotted Elk's aunt Wind and his first cousin Frog, along with Frog's wife, accompanied the band. Kicking Bear had gone ahead to catch up with the elder who had gone to bring back the root from the Bighorn Mountains. He also wanted to bring Red Cloud to show him what was happening. They wished to get Red Cloud's Agency, or what is now called the Pine Ridge Reservation, involved in the dance. However, the elder had died on his way to the Bighorn Mountains, so there was no magic root and Kicking Bear failed to win Red Cloud over.

It was the dead of winter and not a good time to travel. The wind chill took the temperatures into the sub-zero range, and Spotted Elk caught pneumonia. Bear Coat's Seventh Cavalry unit was one of the units called onto the reservation when the Agency workers asked for help. Bear Coat stopped Spotted Elk's band on their way to meet Kicking Bear and forced them to camp along Wounded Knee Creek on December 28.

One of the army scouts was an Itazipco relative named Hat. From a neighboring hill, Hat observed Red Cloud and Bear Coat having a discussion. He knew that the Seventh Cavalry had never gotten over their lopsided defeat on the Greasy Grass at the hands of our people, and specifically Crazy Horse. He also understood that if Bear Coat knew that Spotted Elk's band contained several of Crazy Horse's relatives, there was a good chance that he would see this as an opportunity for revenge. Hat could not tell what was said, but he hoped that Red Cloud would not tell him. What followed told us that Red Cloud did indeed tell him.

On December 29, the cavalry surrounded Spotted Elk's camp. Four Hotchkiss artillery pieces, which could fire two-pound explosive shells at a rate of nearly one per second, were pointed at their village. They had our people place their guns into a buckboard, until they had collected nearly every weapon we owned. Once they had collected our weapons, they fired a carnage of bullets indiscriminately into our people's camp.

Spotted Elk was sitting in the box of a buckboard at the time and attempted to stand and ask for a cease-fire when two soldiers fired their rifles into his chest and he slipped to the ground. As he tried to get back up, another soldier fired four bullets into him with his pistol at point-blank range.

Spotted Elk's wife ran and knelt by his side. She was shot three times and killed. His twenty-year-old daughter, Brings White, who was also known to some of us as White Horse Woman, ran to try to save her parents. She was shouting for her father when bullets dropped her just as she reached her Spotted Elk. While her hand was resting on his dead body, a soldier walked over to her and shot her twice in the back of the head, execution style. Spotted Elk's son escaped and was the sole survivor of his immediate family.

About half our camp was killed. The victims were mostly women and children. Lone Horn's widow, Wind, was killed with a blast from one of the Hotchkiss guns. Frog's fifteen-year-old daughter, One Calls, was also a casualty. Frog, his wife, and their twelve-year-old son, Hunts To Death, or as he was known on the ration rolls, Fred Frog, all survived. In their exuberance to kill us, some of the soldiers were killed by their own crossfire.

Upon observing the massacre, Hat threw his blue coat away and rode off toward the Badlands, near what is today the Red Shirt community. He was convinced Red Cloud had told Bear Coat that our family members were among those at the Wounded Knee camp.

The following day the soldiers brought newspaper reporters to see our dead, who were now frozen stiff in the snow. They rearranged our people's bodies to create a new story. They put a white flag in Spotted Elk's hand and took a picture. Then they found a rifle and put it into the arms of one of our elders, as though he had been firing it at the soldiers. The reporters wrote stories and told the American people that Wounded Knee had been a battle, but in reality it was a massacre. The government gave twenty soldiers the Medal of Honor for their role in Wounded Knee, which is three and one-half times the total number of Medal of Honors awarded in the Iraq and Afghan Wars combined during the first full decade of the twenty-first century.

Talks About Him and some of his family had been down at a stream taking care of the horses and were bringing the horses back when the firing started. They watched the massacre from a surrounding ridge. It was traumatic for them. We learned much of the story about the massacre from them.

A mass grave was dug by the military and all our people's bodies were dumped into it. Many of the survivors went back to our northern camps and told the rest of our family what had happened. After Wounded Knee, the government clamped down on our people's movements. We no longer could travel from one reservation to another. We had to have a piece paper from the Agency head man just to visit our relatives a few miles away.

Although most of us did not believe in the powers of the Ghost Dance, we agreed with what it was trying to accomplish. We wanted the nightmare of what the white people were doing to our people and our way of life to end. The dance had given some of our people hope. The massacre killed that hope for many of them. Those of us who wished to live in the old ways went underground and learned to play the white people's game to keep them out of our lives. But we were far less committed to their ways than we led them to believe.

In 1890, Combing and Comes After Her had a daughter. We wondered what kind of world we were bringing our children into.

CHAPTER TWENTY-FOUR

Keeping Quiet

Old Man Crazy Horse and his surviving wife, Red Leggins, continued to live at Bear Creek with their eldest living son, Combing. Combing had divorced Comes After Her and had married Julia Rushes in 1893. Combing brought his daughter from a previous marriage into their union and all five lived together. Combing had built a two-room cabin at Bear Creek. One room housed the wood stove and eating area, while the other room was where the sleeping quarters were. The door was on the south side of the house, with two windows on the east side and two windows facing to the west.

As Old Man Crazy Horse got older, his ability to get around became compromised. Red Leggins and Combing stayed close to make sure he got the best possible care.

Joseph Clown (also known as Peter Clown) and his wife Emeline Did Not Go Home. Photo from the book *Cheyenne River Sioux* by Donovin Sprague. Courtesy Donovin Sprague and Elsie Slides Off.

In 1890 Makah, or Peter Wolf, and Makes A Noise, or Margaret, had their first child, John Wolf. The following year Iron Cedar, or Julia Clown, and Old Eagle, or Amos Clown, had their first child, Moses Clown. Moses was said to have a great resemblance to Old Man Crazy Horse's first son, Crazy Horse. Our family marveled at the similarities. He was given the Lakota name Bear With Horns, after his grandfather Fights The Thunder's brother.

In 1892, Bear Pipe became sick and passed to the other side. His vision to become a strong medicine man went unfulfilled. Of Old Man Crazy Horse's eleven children, he had now outlived all but three.

In 1894, Julia and Amos Clown had another son, named Joseph Clown, who as an adult sometimes went by Peter Clown, and in 1896 they had their first daughter, named Mollie Nellie Clown.

Peter Wolf and his wife had a girl in 1892, named Nancy Wolf, and a second daughter in 1898, named Sally Wolf.

In 1899, Julia and Amos had another daughter, named Lillie Clown. She would be the last member of our family born during Old Man Crazy Horse's life.

On September 7, 1900, the patriarch of our family for so many decades went to join our relatives on the other side. Old Man Crazy Horse was buried at Bear Creek, where he saw so many of us grow up and saw so many of our family members pass to the other side. He was laid to rest on a hilltop, without a marker, next to Sacred Girl. Sacred Girl had been the first of his children that he had buried. We missed him dearly. He left the family's sacred bundle with his eldest living child, Combing. Red Leggins continued to stay with her son and lived her remaining years following the lives of her grandchildren.

She didn't have to wait long for a new life to blossom within her brood. Peter and Margaret had another son later that year, named Joshua Wolf. The following year, Julia and Amos had a third son, named James, and in 1903 Julia and Amos had twin girls, named Lillian and Lillie Elizabeth Clown. The next year, 1904, they had yet another girl, named Louise.

Nellie Wolf was born January 11, 1904, to Peter and Margaret. It was a busy time for new arrivals in our family.

Red Leggins left to join her husband and the rest of her relatives on the other side May 22, 1905, within a few months of the birth of her son Peter's last child, Ida Wolf.

Combing made sure she was buried on the same hill with her husband. Only Combing, Peter Wolf, and Julia Clown were now left from Crazy Horse's immediate family. A new generation needed to be raised. New journeys were about to begin.

However, not all the young ones would live to adulthood. Disease still claimed many. Sally Wolf died in 1907 at the age of eleven, and John and Nancy Wolf died in 1909 while still teenagers.

Among our elders, Dull Knife died in 1908 and was later buried at the Northern Cheyenne Reservation.

Julia and Amos had two more children. In 1908, our grandfather Edward was born and Raymond was their last child, born in 1914. In 1917, Amos and Julia lost one of their twin girls, Lillie Elizabeth, to sickness.

During the very late nineteenth century and early twentieth, we saw the assault on our spirituality and culture build to greater heights. The government teamed up with church groups of many denominations to try to bring our people into the American mainstream. We called them "the Black Robes who take our children" because that's what they did. They took the children to places that were too far for their parents to visit or even check on them. The church people, or Black Robes' slogan became "Kill the Indian to save the man."

The government outlawed our ceremonies, which forced us to carry them out away from the prying eyes of anyone but family and close friends. If we were caught, we would go to jail. When we built our sweat lodges, we had to tear them down immediately after use so that the Reservation police and government agents did not see them. When we did a hemblecha, we quite often dug a trench so that the authorities would not see us pray. Our Sundances were held at secret locations that we had to sneak off to attend, many times in remote areas of the Black Hills.

When our children were taken away by the church people and white educators, they cut their hair and took away their traditional clothing. Our children were punished by white educators for speaking our language by having their mouths washed out with lye soap or worse. Sometimes that punishment was a beating or they went without food. Sometimes they were made to stay in a dark closet for more than a day. These punishments caused many of our children to die while attending these schools. At the Carlisle Industrial School cemetery in Pennsylvania, there are over one hundred seventy-five graves of Native children, many of the white people did not even bother to learn our children's names before they put them into the ground. Their gravestones simply say "Unknown." It was a dark time for our people, one that the Americans of today rarely acknowledge or even know about.

Back on the Reservation, our people's rations were not what they should have been. They barely kept us fed. Meat was nearly non-existent. The cattle we were supposed to get on ration day was ending up at the white people's ranches as part of their herds. Makah knew that our people were not getting what they were promised. But nobody had been willing to speak up.

Of all Old Man Crazy Horse's surviving three children, Makah was the one who always seemed to wear his emotions closest to the surface. He thought about all the wrongs that had been done to us as he and his wife and daughter Nellie drove in his buckboard to the Cherry Creek ration point during January of 1918.

He was irritable, to say the least, once he arrived to pick up his rations. He told the ration workers at Cherry Creek that he was tired of seeing our people robbed of our proper rations and that he was going to find a way to get to Washington to claim his brother Crazy Horse's Agency in the Black Hills, and at the same time expose the corruption on the Reservation. This did not sit well with the Reservation workers. The suspicion that not all of the beef cattle that the government had bought made it to our people was no myth.

On his way back to Bear Creek, four masked white men shot him six times in the chest and killed him near Rudy Creek. Three of the white men wore flour sacks with large eye holes over their heads, while the fourth man wore a bandana over his face, and it was apparent he had a very bushy mustache or beard. Margaret Wolf and Nellie ran into the trees along the dirt road during the attack. The four murderers made sure Makah was dead before they rode off. They allowed his wife and daughter to survive. Makah passed to the other side January 19, 1918. His murderers were never brought to justice.

It was a very difficult two years for Makah's family. His offspring, Ida and Joshua, died in 1919. Only Nellie and her mother survived. Makah's murder had renewed the fear that we were a hunted family.

Julia and Amos Clown's eldest son, Moses, was sent to Haskell Industrial Boarding School in Lawrence, Kansas. In June of 1917, he joined the army, even though as a Lakota he was not considered a US citizen by the government. The government had promised that he and any other Lakota who joined the army would have greater freedoms once their tours of duty were over.

Moses entered his service at Camp Funston, which was about ten miles southwest of Manhattan, Kansas. He was issued a uniform and expected to answer reveille at daybreak. His day consisted of learning to march in unison with his fellow soldiers, learning to use a bayonet, learning to defend himself from gas attacks, and classes in personal hygiene. His day ended at around sunset with the playing of "Taps."

Unfortunately, the government was unprepared for war at the time and had no rifles to issue the men to train with. Instead, they were issued rifle-shaped pieces of wood to use during their training exercises. The Remington and Winchester gun factories had been unable to gear up fast enough to supply all the troops who had joined or who had been drafted into the service at the time. The army's rifle of choice was called the Enfield and was not available in any numbers until the spring of 1918.

Moses was assigned to B Troop Military Police of the 314th Division attached to the 89th Division, which arrived in France by boat in early June of 1918. After two months of training with his newly issued Enfield rifle on the French terrain near Reynel, which is situated between Chaumont and Neufchâteau, he and his unit joined the 1st American Army Unit in Toul, France. He took part in what they called the Battle of Saint-Mihiels from September 12–15, 1918.

He sent us letters and a photograph during his stay in France that our family still cherishes. We also have a second photograph that was sent by the family of one of his fellow soldiers, Irvin Munyon of Lemmon, South Dakota. We are deeply grateful to them for sharing the photo.

The Germans had what many thought to be an impregnable line of fortifications called the Meuse-Argonne line. It was a series of concrete pillbox machine-gun nests looking out over a heavily barb-wired barren field that the allies would have to cross and negotiate through. German artillery lined the area and the Germans had several fall-back positions that were equally difficult to assault. Heavy rains had reduced the barren fields to a deep, suffocating mud that made an advance with any urgency a tough maneuver at best.

Dawn broke for the 89th Division with the roar of a German artillery bombardment on a foggy first of November. Moses' division was supposed to be part of the last great allied offensive of World War I. The American army's entire First American Army was advancing on the German fortifications. The 89th Division was in the center of that line of advance. As it turned out, the German artillery and machine gun fire pounded them so hard that they were the only unit unable to advance.

In attempting to silence the German artillery, the artillery gunmen, in knee-deep mud, tried to drag their 75 mm field guns into position with the help of horses. Within

Left to right: Frank Corn, Bill Redbird, and Moses Clown, about 1918. Courtesy
of Donovin Sprague from his book *Ziebach County 1910-2010*.

Moses Clown 1918. Photo courtesy
Edward Clown family.

Moses Clown and his friend Irvin Munyon 1918.
Courtesy Tom Munyon and the Irvin Munyon Family.

a very short time, about half of the artillery gunners and horses dragging the guns were lying in the quagmire, dead from the bombardment.

Private Moses Clown's 314th unit was called in to help. He and three others from his unit were attempting to swing one of the artillery pieces into place when they were struck with an artillery shell. His leg was blown off and he was instantly killed. World War I ended ten days later, when an Armistice was declared. The timing of his death, so close to the end of the war, seemed like a cruel joke.

Moses Clown's body was not returned to the United States until 1919. Julia Clown became the first Gold Star mother in South Dakota, and with all the attention it brought, the government authorities took another look at her and determined that she was indeed Crazy Horse's sister. We worried what the government might do if they found us. The government's fear of Crazy Horse's legend also seemed to apply to his remaining family members, Julia Clown being one of them. However, our local newspaper wrote up a story about Moses. The story called Moses a hero. It told of how he and his unit had fought to help achieve the ultimate victory of the war and that his remains were finally coming home. He was brought to Dupree, South Dakota, by rail, and a large crowd came out to welcome him home. Under those circumstances, the government decided it was better to leave Julia alone. They couldn't go after the mother of a war hero. That would make them look really bad.

B Troop Military Police of the 314th Division. Moses Clown is in the top row, second from the right, while his friend Irvin Munyon is fourth from the right in the second row from the bottom. Courtesy Tom Munyon and the Irvin Munyon Family.

Our people held a big pow wow in honor of Moses' return, and he was buried in our family cemetery located near our reservation community of Thunder Butte, South Dakota. From that time forward, our relatives and close friends became an even tighter-knit unit and made sure anyone looking for Julia, or Leo Combing for that matter, was directed away from them. They just didn't trust the government at all.

In 1920, the authorities decided they wanted to conduct a probate hearing on Red Leggins death in 1905. Since Combing was the head of the family, he was asked to answer some questions. He did not understand why a hearing was being conducted and did not trust the Reservation workers. The Reservation authorities had already taken half of Old Man Crazy Horse and Red Leggins' allotted six hundred forty acres and given three hundred twenty of them to a white man with the last name of Purdy. They told Red Leggins that she hadn't put the land to good use. We wondered what that meant. The Agency workers said she had not farmed it properly. We always thought that the Creator made that decision. However, when we looked at what the Agency people said, we saw a great deal of land not farmed that was just like hers and was not taken from those that the government said owned it. Of course they were white people, so we understood what was

really happening. We openly wondered if they knew that we were part of the Crazy Horse family and if we would be able to retain any of her land if they found out. So Combing opted on the safe side and denied that Red Leggins was Old Man Crazy Horse's wife. Red Leggins was his and Julia's mother, and the implications of being linked to Crazy Horse still seemed dangerous. So he used the last name his father had used, Makuhu, for the authorities (which they later misinterpreted as Woman's Breast on Red Leggins' probate papers). After all, the dirt on Makah's grave was still fresh after he had told the Reservation authorities he was Crazy Horse's brother. When it came time to question Julia, she told them that she agreed to whatever her brother had told them. Both Combing and Julia just wanted to live their lives in peace and quiet. They were tired of having things taken from them.

Julia Iron Cedar and Amos Old Eagle Clown on the day their son Moses was brought home from Europe, 1919. Courtesy Edward Clown family.

The government also questioned other family members, like Amos Clown's brother Paul Red Bird and one of our in-laws, Moses Straighthead, who had married Mary Marrowbones, one of Little Hawk's nieces. Through the entire ordeal our great grandmother, Mary Traversie Talks, was the interpreter and she helped hold their stories together.

There were six elders who belonged to a warriors' society that were in charge of protecting an Oohenonpa head man named Long Mandan. Long Mandan settled disputes among our people. These society members also helped protect our family from harm, along with our elder treaty signers. They were aware of our Lone Horn's Agency and that the government had promised it to Crazy Horse. Although it had not been officially awarded, they were determined to make sure the government would not get close enough to Crazy Horse's siblings to pressure them into signing it away. They also stayed close to our treaty signers to ensure they didn't get pressured either. Puts On Shoes, who was also known as White Swan or William Swan, was one of the treaty signers who lived among our family. He became a member of this society later in life.

The six elders were all members of the same family. Their names were Little Skunk, Iron Lightning, In The Woods, Counting, Slides Off, and Butcher. They were all first cousins to each other.

CHAPTER TWENTY-FIVE

The Family Sacred Bundle

As Combing aged into his seventies, our family began to think about who in our next generation would hold our family's sacred bundle. Combing's eldest boy, Frank Fremont, had married Jenny Iron Lodge in 1918. She died during childbirth in 1925. Frank Fremont was never right after that. His behavior was such that his father could not entrust our sacred family's bundle to him. Frank died in 1933.

Our family's sacred bundle was just that, sacred. Within the sacred bundle was Crazy Horse's pipe and some of his owl medicine. Amos's father Fights The Thunder's pipe had also become part of it. Our family's sacred bundle needed to be passed to someone who prayed and lived his life in the old ways and who understood what a sacred bundle represented.

About this time our family suffered another blow when Mollie Nellie Butcher left for the other side on November 11, 1930. She was only thirty-four years old. She, like so many of our people, had caught one of the white man's diseases. She was the fourth child that Julia and Amos had lost.

Both Combing and Julia worried about their children. They worried that our Lakota way of life might not survive to our next generation. During the fall of 1932, Combing became sick. He knew his death was near. He requested Julia to visit him one last time and she rushed to her brother's side. Both of them knew that it would be the last time they would see each other in this world and so it was bittersweet. Combing asked her to take our family's sacred bundle and decide who in our family's next generation was most worthy of holding on to it. So she did.

Combing joined his deceased parents, brothers, and sisters on November 3, 1932. Julia was now the last of Old Man Crazy Horse's children to still be alive.

Around 1933, Julia received a letter written in Lakota that had been sent from an Agency called Wounded Knee. Our family knew that there was no Wounded Knee Agency, but we still wanted to know what the letter said. None of our close immediate family could read all that well at that time. Finally, a family friend, William Bourdeaux, stopped by Julia's cabin for a visit and she seized the opportunity to show him the letter because she knew he had good reading skills. He read it to her. The letter said that they had found her brother Crazy Horse's body near Wounded Knee. Bourdeaux later wrote about this in his book *Custer's Conqueror*.

Julia knew that her brother's body was no where near Wounded Knee or even the Pine Ridge Reservation. Our family saw it as ploy to try to lure her into revealing information about herself and our family. So she did not reply.

Julia was our grandmother and passed along everything sacred to us. She passed it on by the way she led her life. She was not interested in being the center of attention. She did not see herself as someone special. She saw herself as part of creation, and as someone who did her best to give our family a future. She did this by giving our family a past and passing our oral history to her children.

Amy Talks Clown, circa 1934.
Courtesy Edward Clown family.

Unfortunately, not all her children had ears for it. But some of them did, like our grandfather Edward. Julia Clown or as she was known in our Lakota community, Iron Cedar, died of heat stroke on July 10, 1936, in 112 degree weather. She was survived by her husband, Amos.

Deciding which of his sons to pass our sacred bundle to, Amos chose our grandfather, Edward. Edward had shown a deep reverence for our Lakota spirituality and way of life. He had listened to his mother and father's oral history and remembered it. He is the reason we know our oral history so well today.

Edward had married Peter Talks' and Mary Traversie Dupris Talks' only child, Amy Talks, in 1934. Amy had been born in 1913.

Mary Traversie Dupris and Peter Talks in front of their cabin, 1950s. Photo courtesy Edward Clown family.

Amy's mother, Mary, had three children from a previous marriage to Edward Dupris, named Doug, Andrew, and Marcella. Peter had worked for Edward Dupris as a ranch hand until Dupris was mortally injured in a farming accident. Peter stayed on the ranch after Edward passed to look after Mary and her children. He and Mary eventually fell in love and married in 1912. Mary's marriage to Peter lasted the rest of her life. She died in 1956.

Amy and Edward built a cabin together in the community of Iron Lightning, South Dakota. It was a log cabin with a stucco exterior. The inside walls were exposed logs. They had two rooms and a wooden plank floor. They rejoiced in the birth of their first child, a boy named Blaine Sr., on July 15, 1934.

Five days after Julia died, Amos had a big giveaway, on July 15, 1936. He also passed our family's sacred bundle to Edward that day. Edward remembered the exact date because it was his first son's second birthday. After everything had been given away, our family burned down Amos and Julia's house so she could have it on the other side. Julia was laid to rest in our family cemetery near her son Moses. Amos, who was going blind at the time, came to live with his daughter Lillian. Lillian was now the wife of James Makes Trouble and had taken his last name as her own.

Passing our family's sacred bundle to Edward was not an easy choice for Amos. However, he felt out of our entire family that Edward was the most spiritually connected to our Lakota ways.

Our family lost Lillian Makes Trouble when she left for the other side on May 19, 1942. After her passing, her daughters Lorraine, Teresa, and Lois took care of Amos.

Mary Traversie Dupris Talks and her grandson Blaine Clown Sr., about 1940. Photo courtesy Edward Clown family.

Amy Talks Clown and Edward Clown, circa 1934. Courtesy Edward Clown family.

Back row left to right: Lester Bernard, Edwina Clown Bernard, Orson Bernard, and Lisa Bernard. Front row: Amy and Edward Clown, 1983. Not pictured, Lee Bernard. Courtesy Edward Clown family.

Our family continued to grow when Edward and Amy had their first daughter, named Edwina, in 1939. She would be the last of their children who would know their Grandfather Amos. As Amos aged his health deteriorated, and on July 22, 1943, he joined Julia on the other side at the age of eighty-one. Amos was buried at our family cemetery with Julia and Moses. Louise now became the only surviving daughter of Amos and Julia.

Three years later, in 1946, Edward and Amy were blessed with a second daughter, named Beverly. Edward made his living from a small ranch that he owned.

During the 1920s and 1930s, the Americans had hired a rock carver to carve the white people's head men's faces onto one of our most sacred mountains in our sacred Black Hills. We called the mountain they defaced the Six Grandfathers. It was painful to watch these white people scar our sacred Black Hills with the faces of their leaders. The anger among our people built to the point that one of our relatives contacted another rock carver, named Korcak Ziolkowski, in 1947, and asked that Crazy Horse's head be carved on a mountain somewhere in the Black Hills just to show that our people had great leaders, too.

Our family was at first honored, even though some of us had misgivings about further defacing our sacred Black Hills. Later in 1947, our family was contacted by Thomas Bob Tail, who was related to Luther Standing Bear. He asked us to come into the Black Hills and pose so Ziolkowski would have the foundation to form a face for his Crazy Horse carving. Joseph, James, and Raymond chose to go. They took a picture of Moses for Ziolkowski to look at.

Edward was suspicious and wondered about the wisdom of allowing a carving of Crazy Horse. He did not think Crazy Horse would have liked it. Crazy Horse was a humble man and loved Creation. So he decided not to go.

Ziolkowski went ahead and made a composite drawing of the rest of the Clown brothers, and when he asked whose nose and chin to use since these features differed on each of their faces, they suggested that Ziolkowski use his own. So it is that Ziolkowski's own nose and chin are part of the carving. He was sworn to secrecy as to the identities of his models because our family was still leery of telling strangers who we were at the time. In 2004, we told this to his widow, Ruth, and she told us she was happy to hear how the face had come about. She told us that Korcak had not told her this nor had she asked him. She and Korcak were not yet together when he met with our relatives. The carving is still highly controversial among our people.

Today we are proud that our grandfather, Crazy Horse, is honored in this way. We are happy that the Crazy Horse Memorial Mountain is building a school for the Native people. However, we take a dim view when those at the Mountain try to tell the history of our family, and specifically Crazy Horse, without consulting us. The knife that is on display in their museum is not our grandfather's and we are disappointed that we were not consulted. The beadwork is wrong and Crazy Horse detested the white man's metal knives. He preferred buffalo bone knives.

A second artifact that is said to have belonged to Crazy Horse is displayed at the Agate Fossil Beds National Monument in Nebraska. It did not belong to him either. It is a whetstone purportedly belonging to Crazy Horse in the James Cook collection. We have examined it and know it was not his.

Back row left to right: Delmar Clown, Delmar Jr., Beverly Clown, and Dardi Clown. Front row: Amy Talks and Edward Clown, 1983. Not pictured, Brandon Clown and Randon Clown. Courtesy Edward Clown family.

Left to right: Edward Clown, Amy Clown, Blaine Clown Sr., Beverly In the Woods Clown, and Ellen Condon In the Woods. Courtesy Edward Clown family.

Thirdly, there are numerous photographs that people say are Crazy Horse. We know there is no legitimate photo of him. He never wanted to have his likeness or shadow stolen by the camera so it could be used by others. Those who say there is a photograph that exists most likely are saying it from behind a cash register.

Edward and Amy's final biological child, Delmar, was born in 1949. In late 1954, Blaine Sr. was sent to Oregon. He had gotten a woman pregnant who was not a good woman and our family wanted to get him away from her. We had some relatives who had moved to the Portland area and they agreed to watch him and keep him out of trouble. In May 1955, he returned to the Reservation or as we call it, the "rez."

Upon his return, he met Beverly In the Woods. She had just given birth earlier that month to a daughter, Charlene, by another man. They dated for the next year and finally married on October 27, 1956. They settled down in Dupree, South Dakota.

The child who Blaine Sr. had conceived with the other woman was born in August, 1955. His name was Floyd Clown. When it was apparent that his mother did not want him, relatives came and got him.

Blaine Sr. and Beverly were already hard pressed financially in trying to take care of her daughter Charlene and themselves. Seeing that their little grandson Floyd's life was at a crossroads, Edward and Amy stepped forward and said they would raise Floyd as their own son. They told Blaine Sr. that he was never to tell Floyd he was his father. They would instead tell little Floyd that Blaine Sr. was his older brother. Blaine Sr. honored this arrangement for the rest of his life.

Blaine Sr. joined the army a short time later to bring home some much needed money for his family. On March 20, 1957, he and Beverly had their first child together, Blaine, Jr. Very soon after giving birth to their first son, Beverly became pregnant again, and

Blaine Clown Sr. served 1957-1959.
Courtesy Edward Clown family.

Edward and Amy Clown in the church.
Courtesy Edward Clown family.

on January 28, 1958, she gave birth to their second son, Doug. The following year they had their third child, Mary Ellen, who died a year later.

Their third son, Don, was born in 1961. They had two more daughters to fill out our family. Doreen was born in 1963 but died two years later, while Sheila, their last child, was born in 1965.

Edward's oldest brother, Joseph, passed to the other side September 7, 1963. Edward and Joseph loved each other, and Edward's heart was heavy when he said good-bye.

Our family's sacred bundle was kept in Edward and Amy's cabin for the next twenty-seven years. Then one summer day in 1966, some of the contents of the cedar chest were removed.

What happened that day is etched deep into the memory of Blaine Sr. and Beverly Clown's second-eldest son, Doug, as though it were yesterday. The cicadas in the fields droned their melodies while a radio played country songs in Edward and Amy's neatly kept cabin far away from the rest of the world.

During the 1950s, Edward had joined the Episcopal Church and became a church lay reader. He still prayed with the pipe, but he also believed in the concept of the Bible. He told our family that he believed there was one Creator for all people regardless of what name they called that Creator. He told us that praying only on Sunday made it simpler to walk a spiritual life.

His wife, Amy, did not attend church, but prayed in traditional Lakota ways. She never criticized his choice to attend and he never criticized her choice not to attend church services. They loved each other for who they were.

However, just because Edward attended church did not mean he had abandoned our Lakota ways. He would spiritually purify our family's sacred bundle from the cedar chest every solstice during a purification ceremony. He also kept the fires going and cooked food at our sacred Sundances. He would load the pipe once a month and pray.

He kept his attendance at traditional Lakota ceremonies secret from those who attended the church since Lakota ceremonies were outlawed at that time. He didn't want to risk anybody within the Christian community knowing, as there was a chance he could be reported to the authorities. It was just the way it was.

None of this made much difference to Edward and Amy's growing brood of grandchildren. Eight-year-old Doug loved spending time with his Grandma Amy. He had told his parents that is where he wanted to be that particular day. So they had dropped Doug off at his grandparents' cabin and took his older siblings and baby brother Don to attend a softball game.

Grandma Amy cooked wonderful things on her gas-bottled stove and loved to share them with her family. She was famous within our family for her soups and baked goods. That day the cabin was filled with the delicious smell of her fresh bread and a boiling pot of white commodity beans with bacon bits.

Grandma Amy always looked forward to seeing her grandchildren, and so Doug's visit made her day. While she cooked, she told him stories stories that were part of our family's oral history. Doug listened spellbound, hanging on each word. But by mid-afternoon there was a sultriness in the air that made Doug sleepy. So he excused himself and slipped into the back bedroom to take a nap.

Suddenly the rumble of an old pickup silenced the cicadas and woke Doug from his nap. It was Grandpa Ed. Doug broke into a wide grin as he headed back to the kitchen to greet him. Grandpa Ed was always a favorite. Doug and the rest of the grandchildren called him Lala Ed. *Lala* is the Lakota word for grandfather. As Lala Ed stepped unevenly into the cabin, Doug noticed that today he was acting different. After Lala Ed sat at the kitchen table, he and Doug exchanged a warm greeting.

Grandma poured Lala Ed a strong cup of coffee. He took a few sips and excused himself and headed to the bathroom. While he was there, Doug heard him open the medicine cabinet and take out some aspirin. He filled a glass with water and swallowed some down before retiring into the bedroom. The house got silent.

"Is something wrong with Lala?" Doug asked. Grandma Amy stopped and thought for a long time.

"He's having a hard time," she finally answered, as she placed a bowl of bean soup in front of Doug. Doug began to eat.

Lala Ed and Grandma Amy never locked the doors of their home. Their doors were always open and they made sure everybody who visited them was fed. On a normal day they fed about twenty-five friends, relatives, or guests. When they bought food, they bought in bulk, and had built a special log house to store it in. And when either of them was asked a question, they always took their time to think before they answered.

When they were alone with their children and grandchildren their guard came down. It was during these times that they passed along our family's oral history. The stories of our ancestors were told, retold, and retold again until their children and grandchildren couldn't help but commit them to memory.

Suddenly the silence in the cabin was broken by Lala Ed springing out of the bedroom and re-entering the kitchen.

"I'm having bad dreams. Really bad dreams," he told his wife. "The medicine's too strong. I need to do something."

Lala Ed looked at Doug. "I need your help." He motioned Doug to follow and together they headed toward the bedroom.

Once they got there, Lala Ed opened the closet door. Coats and jackets on hangers filled the rack. Sitting on the floor of the closet was a large box with a charm quilt covering it. Lala Ed pulled it out of the closet onto the green carpet, which happened to be Grandma Amy's favorite color. He pulled the quilt off to reveal a weathered cedar chest.

"I need you to open it."

Doug had seen the chest before. It was where Lala Ed kept the important family things. It contained Crazy Horse's bundle. Doug opened the cedar chest.

Inside the chest was the Sharp's Breech Loading Rifle that Bear With Horn had given to Crazy Horse during the Fight at the Greasy Grass. There were also the two beaded horse blankets given to Waglula to honor Crazy Horse, along with their matching beaded horse bridles.

Three pipes also sat inside the chest, neatly lined up side by side. All three had their bowls disconnected from their stems with their orifices stuffed with sage, which was the way they were supposed to be kept when not in use. One was Crazy Horse's council pipe that had been given to him during his hemblecha. Another pipe belonged to Fights The Thunder, Lala Ed's grandfather. Both the bowl and the stem were made of red pipestone. The third pipe was a gift from a visiting student from the eastern United States, who had carved a council pipe for Lala Ed.

The student had come to South Dakota in hopes of hearing our old Lakota stories. We did not like telling our stories to those outside of our culture at that time because we were unsure what would do with them. Upon meeting the student, Lala Ed took a liking to him and decided to take him to see our Sacred Calf Pipe Keeper. Once he had met our Pipe Keeper, he asked to hear the story of the Sacred Calf Pipe from him. Our Pipe Keeper told the student it was customary to give an offering before hearing a story. The student had no money and had not come prepared to make an offering. He asked what he should do. The Pipe Keeper told him that he liked his flannel shirt. Without hesitation, the student peeled his shirt off and handed it to the Pipe Keeper. With that the Pipe Keeper began to tell the story.

However, halfway through, the Pipe Keeper stopped. He said he could not finish the story because the flannel shirt was not worth a whole story. The student told him he had nothing more to offer, so the Pipe Keeper left. The student was crestfallen. Seeing his disappointment, Lala Ed finished the story for him. At the story's conclusion appreciation swept over the student's face. He would not forget Lala Ed.

The following Christmas, the third pipe came in the mail. It had a red catlinite bowl with a squirrel hide wrapped by red cloth around a mahogany stem. It was beautiful. It was the student's way of saying thank you. Up until now, Lala Ed had not owned his own personal pipe. But he did now and he had proudly placed it in the cedar chest next to his grandfather and Crazy Horse's pipes.

The cedar trunk also contained Crazy Horse's chokecherry wood spoon and fork stored inside a hide parfleche shaped like a box. The fork was a stick in the shape of a Y, with sharpened points for stabbing meat. Doug also saw two soup bowls made of cottonwood that had belonged to Crazy Horse.

A third soup bowl made from a large knot from a cottonwood with a notch to hang on a belt belonging to another elder, Puts On Shoes, was also inside the cedar chest. Puts On Shoes had died without family, and the Clown family were the friends closest to him at the end so they were given his bowl.

Lying flat in the corner of the chest was a picture of Crazy Horse drawn from Lala Ed's mother Iron Cedar's memory. It had been drawn in 1932 by a passing artist who had met her and Amos on his way to stay with some fellow Mormons in the West. The artist had shown a good heart and gained her trust. He subsequently found out that she knew Crazy Horse. So he asked her to describe him and he drew his picture. When he showed it to her, tears flowed down her cheeks and a lump in her throat made it hard to speak.

"Yes, that's him," she finally said. She had been eleven years old the last time she had seen her brother, but some memories last forever.

At the top of the chest were four medicine bundles, all belonging to Crazy Horse. Three of the medicines were in buffalo leather bags and one was in a buffalo leather pouch to be worn around the neck.

"That medicine's too strong," Lala Ed repeated.

Doug stared at the bundles, wondering their contents.

"Go get some wax paper from Grandma," Lala Ed told Doug.

Doug went into the kitchen and asked Grandma Amy for wax paper. She cut him some and Doug returned with it in hand.

"Spread the wax paper on the bed." Lala Ed instructed.

"On the bed?"

"Yes."

Doug laid the wax paper as neatly as he could on the bed.

"Now take out the medicine bundles," Lala Ed instructed.

Doug looked at him to make sure he had heard correctly.

"You are young and innocent. You are the right one," Lala Ed reassured.

Doug reached in and took out the medicine bundles.

"Empty the medicine out on the wax paper," Lala Ed directed.

Doug emptied them on the wax paper, being careful not to spill any on his grandparents' green bedspread.

"I'm going to bury it and I don't want to get moisture in it," Lala Ed said.

Doug painstakingly rewrapped the medicine in the wax paper and placed it back into one of the buffalo leather bags.

"Bring it along," ordered Lala Ed, as he grabbed a shovel.

As the two of them went out into the summer heat, he called to his wife, "I'm going to bury it in a place that I can see from our bedroom window."

Lala Ed and Doug went a few yards from the cabin and Lala Ed began to dig. Once the hole was dug, he had Doug place the bundle in the hole. Then he covered it. It would be the last time anybody in this world would ever see Crazy Horse's medicine.

By 1965, Ed and Amy's son Delmar was seventeen years old and contemplating a tour in the military. He did not spend time at their cabin as he used to. But Floyd did.

Ten-year-old Floyd loved sports. He was very proficient in basketball and softball. He played them at every opportunity. One day some of his friends told him that Ed and Amy were not his biological parents. They said that his oldest brother Blaine Sr. was his actual biological father. He was stunned. He did not believe them at first, so he asked around to find out if it was true.

He found it was. He wasn't sure how to respond. Should he confront Edward and Amy? Confront Blaine Sr.? Or keep it to himself? He wanted to make the right decision.

Floyd was precious to Ed and Amy. They loved him so much that they did not have the heart to tell him that he was their grandchild. They had gotten used to calling him son. They didn't want him to ever feel rejected by anyone. They wanted his life to be a life of positives.

Floyd finally decided to never tell Ed and Amy that he had learned the true circumstances surrounding his birth. His love was a reflection of their love. He never stopped calling them Mom and Dad.

Meanwhile, Blaine Sr. had stabilized his life and discovered fatherhood within his new family. He studied and became a certified Emergency Medical Technician and eventually got a job as a Community Health Director for the tribe. As a result, he could afford to have vehicles. He acquired ownership of a white four-door Bel Air station wagon and a two-toned green and white Chevy pickup. The chances of getting a job on the rez has never been good. Unemployment has always hovered around seventy to eighty percent, even today. So Blaine Sr. was one of the lucky ones.

Blaine Sr. took after his father. He too became active in the Episcopalian Church. He took on the church role of a Ward Dean. His wife, Beverly, carried a pipe for our family. Her pipe had a bowl that extended above and below its stem to form a T shape. The T shape signified that the owner of the pipe has a family. Those who are alone or single carry a pipe that only extends above the stem in an L shape. Beverly prayed in the traditional Lakota way and, like her mother in-law, Amy, did not attend church.

Blaine Sr. and Beverly lived with their children in the community of Dupree on the west side of the Cheyenne River Reservation. Dupree, like the rest of the rez, was steeped in poverty. Most of the residents collected monthly commodities or rations from the government to keep from starving. But Dupree was also Lakota, where family was more important than money. Poverty did not exist in our people's hearts, only our pocketbooks.

Blaine Sr. and Beverly's children grew up speaking Lakota as their first language. As their children began to attend school, they entered a world dominated by the English language, which presented them with complications. While in the second grade, their son Doug and a friend spoke in Lakota during class. This annoyed the teacher, who happened to be Caucasian. She marched over to both boys and had them hold out their hands. When they did, she whipped their palms with a ruler.

"When you're in class you speak English!" she scolded.

Back row left to right: Don Red Thunder, Blaine Clown Jr., and Doug War Eagle.
Middle row: Charlene Red Thunder and Sheila Clown. Front row: Beverly In
The Woods and Blaine Clown Sr. Courtesy Edward Clown family.

Hurt and angered, Doug immediately turned and walked out of class. Doug had been taught to be proud of who he was, and no teacher was going to take that pride away. When Doug's parents asked him why he had come home during school hours, he told them what had happened.

"I'm never going back," he cried.

After hearing Doug's story, Blaine Sr. became furious. By chance, there was a school board meeting two days later where Blaine Sr. would have an opportunity to let the school officials have a piece of his mind. He went to that meeting. When it came time to hear from the parents, Blaine Sr. stood up and addressed the faculty members, including Doug's teacher.

"I want to protest my son's treatment in the classroom," he stated. "If you're German and you talk the German language in this country, we don't hit you for that. Even if you speak German in a school. So why when my son speaks Lakota is he hit? I think it's prejudice."

The room went quiet. A few moments passed. All eyes slowly turned to Doug's teacher. The silence was deafening. Her face turned pale and she stammered an apology to Blaine Sr. and Doug. Blaine Sr. accepted and let her know he didn't want to hear of anything like that happening again. The teacher resigned later that year. Doug learned a valuable lesson that day from his father: if you stand up for something right, you will win. He never forgot it.

Our parents and grandparents were not the only ones we learned our oral history from. One of our great-grandparents was also there to share. Grandma Amy was very close to her father and our great-grandfather, Peter Talks. She would often visit him. He shared a cabin with Amy's daughter Beverly and her husband, Melvin Bagola. Amy's mother, Mary Talks, had died several years earlier, leaving Peter a widower.

In late August of 1966, Beverly and Melvin needed to get away for a bit. Grandma Amy agreed to take care of her father while they were away. Peter Talks was eighty-two years old at the time and had almost completely lost his sense of sight and smell.

Peter Talks was a character. Grandma Amy's grandchildren had always loved hearing the stories that their great-grandpa Pete would tell. Her grandchildren, Charlene, Blaine Jr., Doug, and Don, referred to him lovingly as Lala Pete. In addition, Lala Pete's younger grandsons Floyd and Delmar also had a keen interest in hearing his stories. They would go out of their way to get Lala Pete coffee or blankets so they might induce him into telling another story.

Sometimes Lala Pete would get devious and begin to tell his stories in the Cheyenne language. Lala Pete's mother, Nancy Otter Woman, had taught her Cheyenne language to him. He knew if he spoke it, it was sure to get a rise out of his daughter Amy. And it did. Amy would get mad and tell him not to talk like that and stick to Lakota or English if he was going to talk to her grandchildren. Lala Pete and her grandchildren would smile at each other and secretly enjoy the drama.

Back row left to right: Gerald Bagola, Beverly Bagola, Julie Bagola. Center: Craig Clown. Front row: Amy and Edward Clown. Not pictured, Lester Clown and Sylvan Larrabee. Courtesy Edward Clown family.

But now Lala Pete was alone and he needed her. So Amy came to take care of him and left her husband, Ed, seventeen-year-old Delmar, and eleven-year-old Floyd back at their cabin.

When August turned to September, it brought the Labor Day Fair to Eagle Butte. There were rides and sweet snacks there, things that were special to a young boy like Floyd. So he and his dad hopped into the truck and went to the fair. Meanwhile, Delmar did what most seventeen-year-old boys do most everywhere: he went cruising with friends. It was one of the few times that the family had left their cabin with nobody there.

While Lala Ed and Floyd were at the fair, Floyd's eldest sister, Edwina, happened to swing by the cabin to see her parents. Once she arrived, she was shocked to find the house empty of everything but the gas-bottled stove. Lala Ed and Grandma Amy had been robbed.

The refrigerator had been dragged into the yard, but the thieves found it too heavy to steal. So it lay in the yard on its side. The rest of the house was completely ransacked. Included in the theft was the family's cedar chest. Our family's sacred bundle was gone.

Only two items from the cedar chest escaped the thieves. One was Crazy Horse's medicine bundles, due to the fact that Lala Ed and Doug had already buried them in the ground. It was as though there had been a premonition. The second item was the red-and-white beaded saddle blanket and bridle made to honor Crazy Horse because it had been sold to a museum in Pierre, South Dakota, to buy the grandkids clothes.

When Edwina came back and brought word to Amy and later to Ed, it broke their hearts. Robbery was an extremely rare occurrence on the rez. It just wasn't done. That's what made it so perplexing.

Later one of their relatives, Mona Red Horse, took Grandma Amy to a ceremony with a medicine man at our rez community of Red Scaffold to try to find out why this had happened. Amy asked the medicine man if the thief had been a relative. To her dismay, the medicine man answered yes.

Delmar Clown at Deer Medicine Rock, 2005. Photo by Mark Frethem.

"I don't want to know anything more," blurted out Grandma Amy. The ceremony ended. She never talked about it ever again. Decades later the words of the medicine man proved to be true.

During the planning of the dedication for the Indian Memorial at the Little Bighorn Battlefield National Monument site, one of our relatives offered the drawing done by the passing Mormon artist of Crazy Horse to put in the park's media guide for the event. It was the same drawing that was in the cedar chest. The relative making the offer was a descendant of one of the relatives we suspected.

During 1967, Lala Pete became gravely ill. While he was left alone, he found a metal pot soaking by the sink. It had a mixture of water and bleach in it. With his sense of sight, smell, and taste no longer working properly, he thought it was soup and drank it. He never recovered. Lala Pete passed to the other side on August 14, 1967, at the age of eighty-three. We mourned him greatly.

Delmar joined the Marines in 1967, and served as an infantryman in Vietnam during 1968. He was severely wounded when one of his fellow Marines, who was walking right behind him on a patrol, stepped on a booby trap. The explosion threw heavy shrapnel into Delmar's legs and hips. He was sent stateside to the Great Lakes Veterans Hospital in Chicago to heal. He was released to go home in 1969.

As a youngster, Delmar had been given the Lakota name Bear With Horns, in honor of his great uncle. Moses Clown had also been given the same name. The name had not proven to be lucky. Our family has now retired it.

Once he got home, Delmar spent time with his younger brother Floyd, who was now a teenager, and convinced him to erase any thoughts of serving in the military. The same year that Delmar came home, James Clown passed to the other side.

CHAPTER TWENTY-SIX

A New Crazy Horse

The beauty of spring's lush green grass had become the last days of summer's prickly straw. Birds began flocking together, an event that told us winter's cold, harsh arrival was imminent. But before summer was gone, there would be one last celebration, one that had a marked history in our family. That celebration would once again be our two-day Labor Day celebration.

The weekend pow wow in Eagle Butte, South Dakota, was a major part of that celebration. This Labor Day would forever be etched into the mind of Lala Ed's eight-year-old grandson Don.

Doug War Eagle dressed for a pow wow, September 8, 1990. Courtesy Edward Clown family.

On the first morning of the Labor Day Pow Wow, young Don awoke in his room, full of expectations. He had entered the pow wow's Junior Boys Feather Fancy Dancing contest. He had been practicing the entire year. It was a chance to win cash. Cash was rare on the Cheyenne River Reservation. Even rarer for eight-year-old boys. In another room of the house, Don's older brothers, eleven-year-old Doug and twelve-year-old Blaine Jr., rolled out of their bunk beds in the bedroom they shared and also excitedly prepared to go to the pow wow.

Quite often Blaine Jr., Doug, and Don spent their Sundays in a white robe as altar boys at Lala Ed's Episcopalian Church. But this Sunday was the first day of the pow wow and none of them would miss it. Even though Doug wasn't interested in entering any of the competitions, he would dance because he liked dancing.

Don shared his room with our family's newest member, his four-year-old sister Sheila. Our fourteen-year-old half-sister Charlene was away at the time. She was spending the weekend in Idaho at a retreat.

As the temperature neared 90 degrees on the last day of August 1969, our family made its way down the dusty dirt road to the pow wow grounds. Our pickup was stocked with supplies for a concession booth our family helped operate for the YMCA on behalf of the Episcopalian Church along with other volunteers. We would sell hot dogs, chips, soft drinks, and such in hopes of raising enough money to help send our reservation youth to summer camp. On this day, our mother, Beverly, wore her best black polyester pantsuit and white blouse.

Lala Ed and Grandma Amy also were skipping church to attend the pow wow. They brought Floyd, who was now fourteen years old. Don's grandparents had even dressed for the occasion. Lala Ed wore his best black Stetson cowboy hat, a neatly pressed blue-plaid western snap shirt, a string tie with a large blue-and-white beaded bolo, and a silver belt buckle, while Grandma Amy wore her pretty dark blue sweater over a light blue plaid dress.

The Eagle Butte Pow Wow grounds consisted of a round grass field with a tall white wooden flag pole dominating the center. The pole was surrounded by a wooden arbor with two rows of wooden bleachers for the spectators. The arbor was painted white. The flag pole flew an American flag.

As our family's arrival became known, we were greeted with heartfelt appreciation. Nearly all those in attendance were in some way either friends or relatives of our family. But there was one who was not. It was a pow wow dancer who called himself Crazy Horse Bison. Prior to the start of the pow wow, Crazy Horse Bison's father asked if he could have the honor of saying the opening prayer. As a visitor to our pow wow he was granted that honor.

As the time approached for the pow wow to start, the organizers of the event asked him to say his prayer. During the prayer, he said that he was a descendant of Crazy Horse and the sixteenth-generation grandson to carry the Crazy Horse name. He claimed to be our Crazy Horse family's present-day spokesman.

It made our family livid.

We knew what this man said was not true. He was actually a descendant of Nellie Larrabee, who had helped Crazy Horse and his wife in their last days. The same Nellie who had given her husband, Albert Greasy Hand, Crazy Horse's ration card after his death so he could pose as Crazy Horse and draw rations. He had liked the extra attention he got by using Crazy Horse's name as his own. This went on for a long time. In fact it went on for so long that the Greasy Hand family had come to believe their own hoax.

Lala Ed vowed that this would not stand. As afternoon turned into early evening, the time neared for the pow wow dancers' grand entry into the pow wow arena. About four hundred to five hundred people had gathered for the spectacle.

Neither Blaine Jr. nor Floyd participated in the pow wow dancing that day. Blaine Jr. had tried dancing but decided it was not for him. Floyd preferred to play sports, but on this day both would lend their support to what was about to happen.

Don and Doug dressed and took their spots in line for the grand entry into the pow wow arena. All in attendance were asked to rise and take off their hats. A special prayer was given by a veteran of US military service. Following the prayer, one of the pow wow drum groups began to beat their drum in a lively fashion and sing a victory song. The crowd stayed standing as a military service veteran with an eagle staff led the procession into the arena and around the giant flagpole in a clockwise direction. Four other veterans followed him; one carried the American flag while another carried the Cheyenne River Sioux Tribal flag. The flag bearers were flanked by the other two veterans, who carried rifles that they would occasionally aim into the sky and fire blanks during the entry.

The adult-male traditional dancers followed the veterans, dancing their way into the arena. They consisted of older men wearing their finest outfits, which were quite often reserved exclusively for this occasion or a Lakota wedding. Their trappings were com-plete with their recognized family beadwork design embroidered into them. They bounced and hopped to the beat of the drum. It was a sight to behold. Crazy Horse Bison was part of this group and our family watched him with jaws tightly clenched.

The Grass Dancers came next. In the old days, the Grass Dancers flattened the grass prior to the pow wow and wore braids of sweetgrass tied to their belts. But things were different and now the Grass Dancers wore multicolored yarn or fringe on their outfits and their goal was to make the fringe move in as many directions as possible during their dance. Near the back of the grand entry procession, Don and Doug nervously awaited their time to enter the arena.

The Fancy Feather Dancer adult-male dancers followed,

Doug War Eagle and Don Thunder with their nephew Derrick In the Woods, 1990. Courtesy Edward Clown family.

wearing larger hip bustles than the Traditional Dancers, and with many more colors. The Fancy Feather Dancers had sleigh bells on their lower legs and shook, ruffled, and displayed fast footwork while trying to make the sleigh bell chiming match the beat of the drums.

Don and Doug stretched their necks to see what was happening ahead of them. They fidgeted a great deal as they waited. Their turn to enter the arena seemed like it would never come.

The women dancers paraded in next, first the female Traditional Dancers in their finest dresses, followed by the female Fancy Shawl Dancers, who wore fringed and colorful shawls spanning their arms from fingertip to fingertip. They twisted and spun as if they were butterflies.

Finally, the junior dancers entered. The fidgeting was over. Don and Doug's turn had arrived. They had survived the butterflies in their stomachs and now their hearts swelled with pride. They were moving into the arena at last. Don wore one eagle bustle and a matching blue vest with white fringe, leggings, and a breechclout. He had blue beaded moccasins and wore a red-dyed headpiece made of deer hair and longer porcupine hair woven to stand upright. Doug wore a single eagle feather hip bustle, a red handkerchief over his tied-back shoulder-length hair, and a white T-shirt with a square apron that doubled as a breechclout. His leggings were dark blue with black, yellow, red, and white beads that stretched down his pants to his white tennis shoes. They danced their hearts outs and did all they could to make our family, parents, and grandparents beam with pride.

Finally, the junior girls completed the grand entry. Once the arena was filled, it became a sea of colors that spun, vibrated, and moved in a mesmerizing fashion. The dancing continued for about twenty minutes, with the pow wow master of ceremonies encouraging our dancers over the public address system. As the grand entry ended, our dancers danced their way out of the arena. Don's father, who had worn his good dark-blue polo shirt, waited for Don with a sense of urgency. After Don had exited the arena, his father told him that he and Lala Ed were going to do something special.

"We will lay a star quilt blanket in the arena. We want you to stand on it. Accept all that is about to happen. I will explain it to you once it is done," he told Don. Don was bewildered by his father's unexpected request and waited for the blanket. The blanket was laid in the center of the arena and young Don stood on it. Next Lala Ed stepped out from the arbor. He stood for all to see with Don's father at his side. The crowd became silent.

"I am giving my grandson a new name. From this day forward he will be known as Tashunke Witko Yamni."

Don wondered if he had heard right. He was puzzled by what was taking place. He knew that Tashunke Witko Yamni was a sacred name. He was being named after his great-great-grandfather Crazy Horse. Yamni in Lakota means "three." He had become Crazy Horse the Third.

An elder named Burdell Blue Arm emerged from the crowd and began the naming ceremony by holding up a spotted eagle feather and singing a four directions song. First he turned with the feather and called to the west that Don would now be known as Tashunke

Witko Yamni. He then turned with the feather and called to the north, then to the east, then to the south, then to the sky, and finally to Mother Earth in the same manner.

Each of the directions had a significance and had their own spirit and animal helpers. It was important that these spirits and animal helpers knew Don's new name so they could help him when he needed it.

Once Burdell had finished addressing all the directions, he tied the eagle feather to Don's head. Burdell then sang a song to honor Don and his new name. Don glanced around the arena, his eyes occasionally stopping and searching Lala Ed's face for clues as to what it all meant. Don's father walked over to him and gently whispered that he needed to dance now. Don obliged with a Sneak Up Dance where he would drop to one knee, peer from side to side, and then dance forward several paces. It was a warrior's dance and one of his favorite. The women trilled. The men whooped. And the drums pulsated rapidly, emphasizing the joy in the community.

Once the song was finished, the drum group broke into a second honoring song and Don was joined in his dancing by Burdell. Within a short time, our entire family joined him in dance. Pride and joy lit our faces. Finally, our entire community formed a circle and danced around him in celebration. Don felt a bit overwhelmed but danced on gamely. When the dance finished, all those in attendance lined up to shake Don's hand in congratulations. He accepted it all with a mixture of pride and bewilderment.

Crazy Horse Bison did not congratulate Don nor did he stay the night. He could see he was not welcome. He would now have to stay away from where our family lived to keep his hoax alive.

With such a short notice, Don's mother and grandmother had to dash home to bring back gifts from their cupboards. When they got back, they laid out pots, pans, towels, and blankets in preparation for a giveaway. Since Don was honored with a new name, a giveaway was in order.

Later that day, Don took second in the Junior Boys Feather Fancy Dancing. He won seventy-five dollars. It was a good day, one nobody in our family wanted to see come to an end.

That evening his father sat Don down to explain why he had been given the name Crazy Horse the Third. He said the man who had called himself Crazy Horse Bison, along with his father, had no business claiming to be part of our family. Lala Ed considered that as an attempt to steal our family's most sacred name. So he gave the name to Don to let those within our circle know that Crazy Horse's family still lived, and that the name was reborn in one of our own.

"You are still young enough to have not been poisoned by the white culture," Blaine Sr. told his son. "So there is still hope for you. That is why you were chosen. We want you to wear the name of Crazy Horse with pride, just as Crazy Horse had worn it when he was alive."

He also told Don not to tell anyone from outside our immediate circle that he was Crazy Horse's relative, to keep it secret. He said our family was still being hunted by the government.

Don did as his father asked. And he and the rest of our family and friends kept the secret for another thirty years.

CHAPTER TWENTY-SEVEN

Learning the Red Road

It had been ninety years since the government, along with church groups, had started pressuring, and in many cases requiring Lakota parents to send their children to boarding schools designed specifically to teach their children the ways of mainstream America. A by-product of that education was to teach their children that our old Lakota ways, their parents' ways, were just plain wrong. These schools were back East where the parents could not have contact with their children during the time they attended.

At the same time the children were being pressured to learn mainstream American ways, police patrolled the reservation looking for those who still practiced Lakota spiritual ceremonies and arrested them. By the late 1960s, this policy had nearly achieved its goal. Our Lakota culture had all but disappeared among our youth.

In the late 1970s, there was talk that the government might lift the ban on our Lakota ceremonies. They seemed to believe that the ban had served its purpose, and now it was time to grant us the same religious freedoms as the rest of their nation. This talk was pleasing to our ears.

Lakota spiritual leader Pete Catches Sr. showed Floyd what to do at a Sundance, 1969. Photo by David W. Zimmerly.

In 1977, Blaine and Beverly's daughter Charlene became the head of the rez's youth program. She felt one of the most important things she could do was to reintroduce our youth to our culture. As a result, she asked a young Lakota man named Jim Marshall to set up a couple of tipis and a sweat lodge in the same way our people did before the times of the rez for our youth to see and feel. He set them up in Ed and Amy's home community of Iron Lightning.

When Charlene had Jim build a sweat lodge without trying to hide it, her uncle Floyd, now a young adult, became interested. Floyd spent a great deal of time visiting with Jim. Jim was still learning our old ways too, so it was an exciting time for them both. Near the end of their visit, Jim invited Floyd to a purification ceremony that he was going to hold in the early morning hours prior to the sun coming up. Floyd accepted and went home to eagerly await the time.

Floyd's life thus far had not been easy. He was now raising a son, Kelly, who was two years old. He had married Kathy Jeffries after he had gotten her pregnant with Kelly. He wanted his child to have two parents. Once she had their son, their union began to crack and only lasted about ninety days. After that she moved to Rapid City, leaving their son with Floyd.

Life was not supposed to be like this. Floyd felt he had done the right thing but still bad things had happened. He felt certain he would end up an alcoholic like so many of his friends on the rez. But instead, he surprised himself and became a responsible father.

He hunted and fished to put food on the table, something he had learned to do as a younger man when he lived with his parents. Sometimes it was delicious deer meat and sometimes it was prairie dog meat, but he always put food on the table for his son. He scrambled and found a job installing heating and cooling systems for the Tribal Housing Authority to make ends meet. In addition, he made sure his ex-wife stayed in his son's life so he would continue to have a mother.

Now he felt his life needed to take new turn. He had attended his father's church quite often but never felt a connection. Life puzzled him. He wanted to find out who he was supposed to be.

Floyd arose at the appointed time of 3:30 am to attend the purification ceremony. The stars of the Milky Way shone brightly that morning. As he arrived, he noticed a roaring fire burning in a shallow dirt pit. It was heating the rocks that would be used in the ceremony. The light from the fire cast dancing shadows on Jim's face as he gave Floyd a hearty welcome. Floyd reciprocated with a smile.

Blankets and carpets covered the sweat lodge to form its skin. The entrance faced to the west. All those that Jim had invited were asked to disrobe and enter the sweat lodge for the ceremony.

The inside of the sweat lodge was dark and its dirt floor was lined with sage. In the center was a pit. Floyd crawled in after Jim and was followed by his cousin Ray Dupris, and then some others. They sat down around the pit. Jim called for the heated rocks. A young man on the outside of the sweat lodge dug into the fire with a pitchfork and pulled out a glowing red-hot rock and placed it in the center pit of the sweat lodge. He did this several more times. The glowing rocks gave a faint light to the sweat lodge's interior. Then the entrance was tightly closed.

Jim poured water on the rocks as they sang the Lakota spiritual songs of our grandfathers. The rocks sizzled and the result was steam. The hot steam penetrated into everyone's very soul. Floyd prayed and felt as one with the universe. He felt a connection to the Creator like he had never felt before. The entrance was opened four times. Sometimes the young man would bring in more hot rocks, and sometimes the tiny group would just catch their breath.

After the entrance door opened for the fourth and final time, they crawled out. As they did, they called out the Lakota phrase *Mitake Oyasin.* Mitake Oyasin means "all my relatives." In our Lakota way, everything has a life, including the animals, the trees, and the rocks. They are all related to one another. Mitake Oyasin is a greeting to everything on and around our Mother the Earth. It is a greeting that recognizes that the two-leggeds and four-leggeds, winged, insects, grass, trees, rocks, stars, and everything else in the universe are related and equal. They are all one with our Mother the Earth, and our Mother the Earth is one with them. Floyd's heart smiled. He had found who he was supposed to be. He was Lakota.

From that time on, Floyd wanted to know as much as he could about the old ways. He decided to hemblecha so he could cry for his vision. Floyd had come to understand that our Mother the Earth was sacred. Every step he took was supposed to be a sacred step. To learn how to take these steps was why he wanted to hemblecha.

His friend Jim took him to a special place on Bear Butte and left him at that place with no food or water, as is required in our Lakota spiritual way. The Creator heard Floyd's cry for a vision and gave him one. The Creator told him to be strong for a Sundance.

In 1978, Floyd followed his vision and traveled to the Standing Rock Reservation to participate in his first Sundance. By coincidence, it was the first year that it was no longer a crime to perform the Sundance ceremony in the United States since the 1890s. An elder Lakota spiritual leader named Pete Catches Sr. was there that year. Pete Sr. was one of the main Lakota spiritual

Pete Catches Sr. at Flag Day Pipe Ceremony, 1969. Photo by David W. Zimmerly.

leaders within our Lakota Nation who had labored hard to reintroduce our Sundance ceremony back to our people.

Pete Sr. had attended Catholic schools as a child. He had experienced a sacred dream when he was young, but ran from his dream to work and attend church in mainstream society, believing the church to be the safe way. As he grew older, his sacred dream grew stronger. He realized that the church and the mainstream society that he knew did not walk with the truth and honesty that was necessary for him to lead the good, clean, spiritual life that he wanted. He felt there was too much hypocrisy. So he returned to the ways of our people and became a medicine man. It was the life that his sacred dream in his youth had told him to live. Now he was finally living it, and in the process he was helping heal our people.

Pete Sr. showed Floyd what he needed to do at the Sundance. He told Floyd that the Sundance is a ceremony of thanksgiving to the Creator for the health and survival of all the people who are of importance to the dancer. During the ceremony, Floyd, along with the other Sundancers, danced around a cottonwood tree while looking at the sun. They did this without food or water for the entire Sundance, which lasted four days.

During the Sundance, Pete Sr. pierced Floyd so he could give his flesh to the Creator. Pete Sr. thrust his pocket knife under and through Floyd's surface flesh on his chest. He then pushed a stick through the cavity and tied a rope to the stick that was attached to our sacred Sundance tree.

Floyd then stood up, danced, and at the end pulled back on the rope until his skin tore and the stick broke free. It was his gift to the Creator. Our flesh is the only thing that belongs to us because the Creator owns everything else. It is all any Lakota has to give to the Creator that is actually his to give.

After the Sundance, one of the other dancers, Rick White, had a vision and Floyd had been part of it. He had seen himself and Floyd performing a hemblecha together in the cold. So after the Sundance, he asked Floyd to hemblecha with him during the winter. Floyd agreed.

The rest of the summer Floyd continued to learn and grow in our Lakota spiritual ways. Two months after his first Sundance, he was helping other Sundancers in the same way Pete Sr. had helped him. Floyd helped at a Sundance upon the request of another Sundance leader named Fools Crow. Fools Crow, like Pete Catches Sr., was one of our Lakota spiritual leaders reintroducing Lakota ways back to our people. Floyd had been chosen to help because he had embraced our ancestors' spiritual ways so completely.

During the Sundance, Fools Crow prayed with a pipe that he said had belonged to Crazy Horse. The pipe looked familiar. Floyd said nothing. It had been over a decade since the cedar chest had been stolen. He couldn't be sure it was the same pipe from the cedar chest, and a Sundance was neither the time nor the place to ask that question, especially of Fools Crow. Fools Crow was as good and as spiritual a man as our Lakota Nation possessed. Pete Catches Sr. and Fools Crow are still remembered today with great reverence.

Floyd's hunger to learn more Lakota spirituality caused him, Jim, Ray, Rick, Gregg Bourland, and other friends to invite Pete Sr. to spend the winter on our Cheyenne River

Reservation where Floyd, Jim, Ray, Rick, and Gregg lived during 1979. By having him spend the winter, they would have the opportunity to continue to learn. Pete Sr. agreed to stay at Carrie Fisherman's place on Ash Creek, south of Dupree.

Pete Sr.'s stay in Dupree was not without hardship. He came down with a fever and his heart beat rapidly. He was taken to a doctor. At the doctor's they discovered that there was a hole in Pete Sr.'s intestine and that it was leaking poison into his body, a condition that if not treated quickly would have led to his death.

It meant an immediate operation.

Pete Sr. was taken to the hospital. Floyd and his friends prayed for him. After a lengthy operation, the doctors patched the hole and the danger passed. Pete Sr. soon recovered and became healthy again. The ordeal brought them all very close together. Pete Sr. could not thank them enough for their thoughts and prayers. Later, at a purification ceremony, Pete Sr. told Floyd, Ray, Jim, Rick, and Gregg to call him grandfather from that time forward. He in turn would call them his grandsons. They were now considered hunka relatives and had become family in a very special way.

A short time later, Pete Sr. left for his home on the Pine Ridge rez. Floyd had learned a great deal from Pete Sr. during his stay, things he would practice the rest of his life. Later in 1979, Floyd found love again and married Karen Little Wounded. They had their first child, and Floyd's second son, Kyle, that same year. The following year they had another son, named P'tan.

On New Year's Day 1981, Floyd made good on his promise to hemblecha with Rick. Pete Sr. took Floyd and Rick to a hill on Ash Creek near Carrie Fisherman's place and left them to hemblecha. It was the dead of winter and they prayed and cried for their vision

Back row left to right: Kelly Clown, Kyle Clown, P'tan Clown, Michael Little Wounded, and Floyd Clown Jr. Front row: Kacie Clown and Floyd Clown. Courtesy Edward Clown family.

for two days and nights. It was a very cold and difficult hemblecha. The ground was hard with frost. Floyd and Rick stuck it out in order to fulfill Rick's vision. Floyd endured this bitter cold to help another. During his hemblecha, the Creator communicated to him and honored him with a Lakota name.

It was a proud moment.

In 1982, Floyd and Karen had their first daughter, Kacie. Floyd's fourth son, Floyd Jr., was born in 1985. And finally in 1988, they adopted Karen's nephew, Michael, as their son.

Floyd continued to Sundance all the way into the early 1990s. He Sundanced for eleven years, and helped other Sundancers to Sundance for fifteen years. In 1994, Floyd acquired his own home on the rez with a yard large enough to build his own sweat lodge. Things couldn't have been better. He had found our Lakota spiritual and cultural way. He had a family. His heart was happy. But unbeknownst to him, this was only the beginning.

In 1980, Don decided to join the Navy and see the world. He had gotten the travel bug from an exchange student program run by the YMCA. When he was a youngster, our family had hosted two exchange students from Japan. The Japanese boys were amazed at how our people shared with each other so freely. They told Don that back in Japan people rarely shared that freely. The following summer his Japanese friends returned the favor by inviting Don to visit Japan and agreeing to host him. He eagerly accepted.

Upon his arrival, his hosts took him on a tour of the country. He was able to visit many of Japan's larger cities, and at each stop he was asked to dance his Lakota dances. Apparently what the Japanese boys had learned about him during their time on the rez had preceded him. He usually chose to perform the Sneak Up Dance and his Japanese audiences would marvel.

Don Red Thunder in the Navy, 1980.
Courtesy Edward Clown family.

Don Red Thunder in Japan. Courtesy
Edward Clown family.

When he came back home, he wanted to live the experience all over again. Since our family did not have the money, the military seemed to be the only option available that would give him the opportunity to travel. So he joined the Navy and went through one of the military's most rigorous training regimens and became a Navy Seal.

During March and April of the following year, 1981, he and the rest of his Seal team, known as Team Seven, parachuted into Cambodia. They went to investigate some intelligence reports indicating the locations of old Vietcong prisoner-of-war camps to see if any Americans were still being held after the Vietnam War. They found the camps completely deserted other than an occasional Cambodian family who had moved in to some of the vacated structures.

Later on that year, Don was injured aboard the Naval ship *USS Garcia* during an exercise. He missed a step going down a ladder during a drill, tearing his knee ligaments and breaking his knee cap. He spent the next eight months trying to heal. When his injury failed to heal properly, he was sent ashore. Six months later, his naval career was over. With his knee permanently injured, he was discharged from the Navy in 1982. He suddenly found himself back on the rez, wondering what to do with his life.

Playing competitive sports had always been one of Don's favorite pastimes, but his loss of mobility due to his injury had put an end to participating in any sport that required putting stress on his knee. So he spent the next few years developing a new set of skills and turned to playing soft tip darts.

As Floyd, Doug, and Don's generation began to have children, we continued to say good-bye to the older ones. It is one of life's never-ending cycles. Raymond left for the other side on March 31, 1981.

Don and Jackie Red Thunder pose on their wedding day with Blaine Sr. and Beverly Clown. Courtesy Edward Clown family.

In the fall of 1983, Don changed his last name to Red Thunder in honor of Amos Clown's paternal grandfather. During that same year, Don attended the United Tribes Technical School in Bismarck, North Dakota, to obtain a certificate qualifying him in food services and as a chef. During this time a young Hunkpapa lady named Jackie Howard caught his eye. She soon became the love of his life and they married June 9, 1984. Don's grandfather Edward officiated at their ceremony in Dupree. When Don married Jackie, she also took the last name Red Thunder and they made their home in Dupree. Don landed his first job working in the Cheyenne River Head Start kitchen and worked there until 1987.

Louise Red Bear died on January 15, 1987, leaving Edward as the sole surviving member of Amos and Julia's offspring.

In 1987, Don was fortunate enough to find a job working at the Indian Health Service in the Food Service Department. Don and Jackie completed their family on June 1, 1988, by adopting Jackie's newborn nephew, Ian, as their son.

In 1992, Don left the Indian Health Service and began to work for his tribe as a Tribal Range Technician. After three months, Don moved to the position of Civil Engineer Technician for the Bureau of Indian Affairs, which he still holds as of this writing. In this capacity, he spends much of his time ensuring that his people's land stays within the Lakota Nation and is not sold off to non-Natives. He also participates in search and rescue operations for the BIA as a chosen representative by his peers and coworkers.

During his first ten years with the BIA, he also spent time as a Wild Land Fire Fighter. He retired from fighting wildfires in 2002. Don, like his brothers and sisters, is fluent in the Lakota language and dedicated to helping keep it alive.

Don, Jackie, and Ian Red Thunder in 2000. Courtesy Edward Clown family.

Doug War Eagle, 2005. Photo by Mark Frethem.

Meanwhile, Don's brother, Doug, decided he wanted to become a healer just as so many members of our family had done before him. Following high school, he began taking a summer program in medicine at the University of North Dakota. However, his request for a Pell Grant was mishandled, thus he had to find work while he reapplied.

He found a job helping to feed the elderly on our rez. Many of our elderly were desperate to pass their stories on while they could, and Doug was more than eager to offer them his ears. In doing so, he heard many of their old stories that few others on or outside our rez had shown any interest in at the time.

Upon his re-acceptance at the University of North Dakota, he continued his pursuit of medicine. However, during his sophomore year he became preoccupied with snagging. Snagging is a modern Native term that refers to dating, or one-night stands. He would take road trips to Minnesota, where the drinking age was only eighteen, as opposed to twenty-one in North Dakota. His new lifestyle sabotaged his studies, and as a result, his grades suffered. He ended up being dropped from college.

Forced to move back to the Cheyenne River rez in 1980, he had the good fortune to find a part-time job archiving as our Cheyenne River Central Records Director. He was charged with registering all tribal documents, including our records used to build genealogies.

Since the job was part-time, he had plenty of free time and decided to take up competitive pow wow dancing. During one of his pow wow competitions he had a mishap. He stepped on something while dancing that sent him into extreme agony. He later learned that an impediment had been thrown out by a disgruntled medicine man into the pow wow arena. It had not been meant for Doug, but the impediment, or bad medicine, did not play favorites. It caused Doug terrific pain, so his father took him to see a close family friend and medicine man named Joe Tiona.

Joe held a ceremony to help Doug. During the ceremony he took out the bad medicine from his foot, which looked like an eagle claw. Doug's pain was immediately relieved and it wasn't long before Doug had healed.

In gratitude for what he had done for his son, Blaine Sr. adopted Joe as a son in a hunka, or making of relatives, ceremony. When Blaine Sr. adopted Joe as a son, Joe, by default, also became a brother to Blaine Sr.'s children.

Without the worries of attending college and dedicating his evenings to his studies, Doug continued to be preoccupied with snagging. In 1984, Doug snagged and ultimately married Jewel Gunderson, and they had a daughter together named Jennifer the following year.

When tribal budget cuts decimated our Central Records Department in 1986, Doug left, and applied for and got into the medical field he had longed for. He became a Medical Records clerk at our Eagle Butte Indian Health Services Clinic.

During this time, Lala Ed was having problems remembering things. He was diagnosed with Alzheimer's disease in 1987 and passed away within a few months of his diagnosis, on August 14, 1987. Losing Lala Ed was tough on our whole family. He had been a pillar of strength for all of us. Now we looked to Blaine Sr. for direction as the male elder member in our family.

Doug and his daughter Jennifer War Eagle. Jennifer passed to the Spirit World
August 10, 2015. She was 30 years old. Photo by Bill Matson.

Doug's marriage to Jewel was not a happy one, and they parted ways in 1989. Doug decided he wanted to leave the bad memories of his marriage behind and moved to Rapid City to take a job as a ward clerk at the Sioux Sans Indian Hospital. For the next seven years, Doug drank heavily. Living in Rapid City became a dark experience. He missed our rez and finally came to the realization that he needed to come home.

Around 1995, Doug began to focus on his most important remaining joy, his ten-year-old daughter, Jennifer. He took a big interest in her pow wow dancing. In Doug's eyes she could do no wrong. He would go to the pow wows to watch her dance. Jennifer told her father she thought her reception would be better if she had a more spiritual last name when she was introduced over the loud speaker at pow wows. She asked her father if she could change her last name to the sacred name of another of our past grandfathers. Doug agreed and decide to join her in the name change. They chose the new last name of War Eagle to honor his great-grandmother Mary Talks' grandfather. War Eagle had been a head man within the Mdewakanton band of the Dakota. It is the last name Doug and Jennifer go by today.

After being approved for ownership of a scattered-site home through public financing on our rez in 1996, Doug was finally able to move back home. Once again he was able to find work at our Eagle Butte Indian Health Services Clinic.

Within a few months of having returned to our rez, Doug was hurt in an automobile accident. A Chevy Suburban rear-ended his Chevy S-10 pickup, leaving him with a case of whiplash and pushing a disc in his back out of place. It caused him a great deal of pain long after the accident. After suffering through his back pains, it seemed life couldn't get any worse. But then it did. Grandma Amy passed to the other side.

During the 1990s, dart tournaments continued to dominate Don's life. In the spring of 1999, his father, Blaine Sr., passed to the other side. It was a sad time. Charlene, Blaine Jr., Doug, Don, and Sheila mourned their father, and at the same time embraced a grieving Floyd openly as their brother.

Don tried to bury his grief by becoming even more ensconced in dart tournaments. He set out to honor his late father by winning the state championship. During the fall of 1999, he teamed with Conrad Clown, Carl Dupree, Dusty Scott, and Milton Jeffries to form a dart team called the Out Rider's Cafe Dart Team. His team entered the South Dakota state tournament, with Don appointed as team captain.

After qualifying for the state tournament by being one of two teams to advance from their regional mini-tournament, they entered the 32-team double-elimination tournament for the state title. On the second day of the tournament, they breezed through undefeated to capture the 2000 South Dakota Soft Tip Dart Tournament A Division State Championship. Don was ecstatic, he had succeeded in honoring his father with a championship.

Later that year, Blaine Sr. came to Don in a dream and told Don to prepare himself. He told him to "stand up and tell the truth." He told him that he needed to tell the world that our Crazy Horse family was alive and well.

Nearly all that had been written about our family and Crazy Horse was wrong. Much of the reason it was wrong was because our family had done everything in their power to make sure that our identity stayed hidden. We did not trust the government or anyone else outside our circle, and neither did our Lakota neighbors. So we and our neighbors told the government and those outside our circle what we thought they would believe. We had done it well. Too well.

It was a big task. Who would believe Don? When a story circulates in the public arena long enough, people come to regard it as truth. The whole idea of telling the truth about our family seemed overwhelming to Don. He thought he would have to do it alone. So Don went to his adopted brother and medicine man, Joe Tiona, to learn why he had been told to do this and how he should go about it. They decided to have a purification ceremony to find the answer.

During the ceremony, Don was told that those on the other side had chosen him because they knew he had the ability to inform the world of our family's existence in modernized ways. Don was also told that his older brother Floyd had spent his entire adult life learning our Lakota ways and he could show him how to get it done. So he went to see Floyd.

"I've been waiting for you for a long time," Floyd replied after hearing Don's plea. They both glowed with a new sense of purpose. The wheels for telling the truth about our family were beginning to turn. It was information that we had for so long denied the world because we were afraid of what might happen. Now we were afraid no more.

Joe has since adopted Don in a hunka ceremony as his son. Joe passed to the other side in 2010.

CHAPTER TWENTY-EIGHT

Standing Up to
Tell the Truth

South Dakota has two seasons, hot and cold. It was the hot season of 2000, and a light breeze helped keep the harsh summer heat nearly bearable.

Doug and Floyd were traveling toward the west when they looked up and saw a Spotted Eagle flying overhead. It flew toward them and then circled back in an easterly direction. Then it came back toward them and circled easterly again. It did this four times, and then flew east for good. The number four has always been sacred in our culture, so they knew the eagle was telling them something.

"Shall we check it out?" asked Floyd.

Doug agreed. So they turned around and followed the eagle.

The eagle led them to the community of Greengrass on the Cheyenne River Reservation. Greengrass is where our Sacred Calf Pipe Keeper watches over our Sacred Calf Pipe. Arvol Looking Horse was our Sacred Calf Pipe Keeper at the time. Once they arrived, they found themselves witnessing an unwrapping ceremony.

The unwrapping ceremony takes place once every seven years. Many of the attendees had planned far in advance to ensure that they had the gas money to attend. There were many of our people there. One of their cousins, Steve Vance, was among them. They all sat around our Sacred Calf Pipe in a circle the shape of a buffalo hoof print with the open side facing east, as was the custom. Many had come to get their personal pipes blessed in the presence of our people's most sacred possession. Floyd and Doug sat down and became part of the hoof print.

After it became apparent that all who had come to get their pipes blessed had done so, Arvol Looking Horse decided it was time to return our Sacred Calf Pipe to its proper place. Arvol and his brother rewrapped the Pipe in new buffalo hides, as was required every seven years. He then turned to whom he considered to be one of our best men there, Dana Dupris, and asked him to pick four good men to carry our Pipe into the hogan. A hogan is the six-sided building that houses our Sacred Calf Pipe.

It was a very great honor to carry the sacred Pipe for our people. Dana chose his three cousins, Floyd, Doug, and Steve. They had not expected this but were honored to accept.

As they approached our Sacred Calf Pipe, a solemn silence filled the air. They circled our Pipe four times and then descended on it. They picked it up with deep reverence and carried it, along with all the burdens, prayers, and blessings that our Pipe represented, back to the hogan. They stopped four times along the way to pray until they placed our Sacred Calf Pipe in its holder inside the hogan.

Doug felt exhilarated. The experience had brought him a new sense of purpose. He felt closer to the Creator. He was not sure whether he had been worthy to have been chosen, but he wanted to be. So following that event, Doug decided to embrace his own personal pipe and pursue the old ways of our Lakota great-grandparents by observing our culture and spiritual ways. At that point he was ready to join Floyd and Don in our quest to spread the news that our Crazy Horse family was still alive.

One of Doug's first prayers upon embracing the culture was to ask for Crazy Horse's sacred pipe to be returned.

Empowered with the fact that Doug had joined them, they knew getting back Crazy Horse's pipe was the most important goal. It was one of the pipes that had been stolen from the cedar chest. To regain it would be a giant step toward helping to heal their family. So they asked our grandfather spirits in a purification ceremony how to get it back. The spirits said that the thief had no use for it and had given it to Fools Crow. They also said that Floyd had seen it. This is the same Fools Crow that Floyd had helped at a Sundance in 1978. Fools Crow had died in 1989. Floyd remembered the pipe and it had indeed fit the description of the one from the cedar chest. Our grandfather spirits told them that Big Nose had it now. Big Nose is what our grandfather spirits called Fools Crow's grandson, Mel Lonehill.

On November 20, 2000, they trekked down to Pine Ridge where Mel lived to ask that the pipe be returned. Since retrieving the pipe was a very sacred endeavor, we took four men to ask for it back. Floyd, Floyd's son Kyle, Doug, and Don made the trip.

Four days prior to their trip Mel had a visit from our grandfather spirits. The spirits had lifted him from his bed and held him against the ceiling. They told him that when our family members came asking for the pipe that belonged to Crazy Horse, he was to give it to them.

His grandfather, Fools Crow, had received our pipe as a gift from one of our rogue relatives. Fools Crow had no idea it had been stolen along with everything else in the cedar chest from Ed and Amy's cabin back in 1966.

Once Floyd, Doug, Don, and Kyle arrived, Mel was waiting with our pipe. Once he handed it over to them, relief and ecstasy consumed the room. Mel told of his experience with the spirits, and the brothers told of theirs in the sweat lodge. On the ride home Floyd, Doug, Don, and Kyle told and retold the story of their meeting with Mel and the recovery of Crazy Horse's pipe with great joy.

A month later, during the winter solstice, they blessed and smudged the pipe for the first time since it had been stolen from them. Doug used the pipe to pray with during his first Sundance and hemblecha at Joe Tiona's Sundance grounds located in the On

Amos Clown's brother Paul Red Bird
with his wife Isabel Her Door. Courtesy
Donovin Sprague and Carlos Red Legs
from the book *Ziebach County 1910-2010*.

the Tree community of the Cheyenne River Reservation in 2001, in which he spent two rounds in the sweat lodge prior to being put in a hole in the ground for a full day, or one red day and one blue day.

Doug went on his second hemblecha the next summer at a place called the Bear's Nose at Bear Butte, which is on the southeast side of the butte. This time he did his hemblecha above the ground.

During his hemblecha, Doug heard a woman singing a prayer with him further down the hill. After he told Floyd and Don this, they all remembered a story told by their late Uncle Raymond about how he had found what he thought was his father, Amos Clown's, sister Noisy's grave near the site that Doug had heard the singing.

Amos Clown had one brother, Paul Red Bird, and two sisters, Lucy (Grows in a Day) Poor Buffalo and Noisy. Noisy had become the woman of the Lakota man Bad War Bonnet, and they along with another Lakota couple, had been hunting game when they were attacked by a group of white men in September 1891. After believing that they had killed both couples, the white men took the couples' wagon of freshly killed meat. However, Noisy survived a severe stomach wound inflicted by the white men and was able to tell the authorities what had happened. Her attackers were tracked down and found in Nebraska. She agreed to testify against them during a government court trial held in October 1891.

During the trial, the white men were found guilty and sentenced to accept a train ticket out of the territory and to never come back. That was their total punishment for murdering our people. Noisy died a few months later due to complications from her stomach wound and was buried next to her husband in the Fort Meade Cemetery.

In 1972, Raymond went to Bear Butte to find his Aunt Noisy's grave. He was unaware she had been buried in the Fort Meade Cemetery less than a mile down the road. When he thought he had found her grave on Bear Butte, he wrote his initials and the year with small rocks on the ground to mark it. The marking read "RC 72."

Floyd, Doug, and Don were aware that Noisy was buried at Fort Meade. Lala Ed had told them. But they wondered why a woman's voice was heard coming from the area of the grave site Uncle Raymond had marked.

After acquiring permission from Jim Jandreau, Bear Butte State Park's Head Ranger, they searched the butte in the general area where Doug had heard the singing to see if they could find the grave site. They found it near a group of Yucca plants. The initials were indeed there, but the 2 in "RC 72" was a bit messed up.

Bear Butte, South Dakota. Photo by Bill Matson.

When embracing and practicing Lakota spirituality in a trusting way, communicating with relatives who have passed over to the other side is natural. Floyd, Doug, and Don wanted to find out who had sung with Doug. Did it indeed come from the person buried in the grave site their Uncle Raymond had found? And if so, who was buried there? So they asked in a purification ceremony and found that it was Good Looking Woman who had sung with Doug.

Floyd, Doug, and Don were amazed. Their bodies tingled all over with good feelings and they revisited Bear Butte and manicured her grave with white gravel and flowers. They rushed back to the sweat lodge to try to see or hear her again and they did. She thanked them for finding her. Her grave had been unattended since 1876.

Floyd, Doug, and Don were determined to tell the world the truth about our family. It would be hard because the world had become accustomed to hearing the manufactured stories about Crazy Horse. Mari Sandoz's novel on Crazy Horse was so well written that for years it was considered non-fiction. Others have written their takes on our family and Crazy Horse. But only we have walked in our family's shoes, and only our family had the internal insight into all the members of our family.

During a ceremony in 2001, Floyd, Doug, and Don were told that those from the other side were going to direct some helpers to help them get our family's story out. They told them that there would be one from the east, three from the south, one from the west, and one from the north. On May 23, 2001, in another purification ceremony, they were told that the helper from the west was on his way. His name was Bill Matson and he was coming from Oregon. He was a documentary film maker for a company called reelcontact.com.

Don Red Thunder, Doug War Eagle, Bill Matson, and Floyd Clown in 2005. Photo by Diana Harvey.

Floyd Clown speaks on behalf of his family at the Little Bighorn Battlefield. Donlan Many Bad Horses, Superintendent Darrell J. Cook, and Kitty Deernose listen. Photo by Mark Frethem.

"Ho-Ka Hey! It is a good day to fight! It is a good day to die! Strong hearts, brave hearts, to the front! Weak hearts and cowards to the rear."
– *Ta Sunke Witko (June 25, 1876)*

"We did not ask you white men to come here. The Great Spirit gave us this country as a home. You had yours...We did not interfere with you... We do not want your civilization!"
– *Ta Sunke Witko*

"My lands are where my dead lie buried."
– *Ta Sunke Witko*

After testing him in a purification ceremony to see if his heart was good, they decided he was indeed the one from the west, and over the next decade they put together four feature-length DVDs on our family's oral history. By 2009, a helper who was supposed to write our family oral history book had not done so, after nearly a decade, so during a long drive back to the rez from a trip to the West Coast, Matson agreed to put our oral history into writing for us. We knew he wasn't a professional writer, but he had been to nearly all the places that were sacred to us. He would know what we were talking about. So we entrusted him to do his best under our watchful guidance.

We are happy that we finally have gotten our oral history into print. It is important that it be so. Our Nation has no future if it does not know its past. We encourage all Lakota families who are willing to show their family trees and accompanying probate papers to tell their family's oral histories, too. We would like to see our people throw off the yoke of those educated in other cultures who claim to have the knowledge to define our people and our people's history.

Ta Sunke Witko (Crazy Horse)
LAKOTA, 1840-1877

In memory of the Lakota Bands of the Great Sioux Nation: Cuthead, Two Kettle, Blackfoot, Minnikojou, Hunkpapa, No Bows, and Flathead. Also the Dakota and Nakota Bands of the Great Sioux Nation, and Cheyenne and Arapaho Nations who fought here with us against the U.S. 7th Cavalry. The battle was fought because the United States wanted the Black Hills and its natural resources.

Ta Sunke Witko fought in this battle to preserve a way of life for the Lakota Oyate. Our Grandfathers protected our Sacred Pipe because it was given to us by the Creator believing that all mankind was given the power of Truth, Justice, and Wisdom. All the warriors at this battle who were killed believed this way. Our Grandfathers say that the Cheyenne and Arapaho came because they had family ties with the Lakota Nation.

Our Grandfather Ta Sunke Witko was a man who prayed with the Sacred Pipe, played with the children, and listened to the elders. He saw that all living things were higher than him because he knew that mankind had the power of choice to do right or wrong, good or bad. Our Grandfathers told us that all mankind were created equal and they represent the earth man with no skin color. In order to heal our Grandmother Earth we must unify through peace.

Pilamaye Le Un Nib'ki
"Thank you, we live."

Ta Sunke Witko Tiwahe
(Family of TA SUNKE WITKO)

In 2003, the National Park Service asked Crazy Horse's family to write a message for the Indian Memorial. Later in 2003, that message was duplicated on an Indian Memorial panel for the public to see. In 2013, the message was rewritten without the family's knowledge or consent. This is the original message as it was meant.

Why probate papers? Family oral histories need to be traceable directly to the families telling them. Otherwise they are not family oral histories. Cut and dried.

Crazy Horse once said that a people without a history are like blades of grass in the wind. We are Lakota. We are a spiritual people, and a spiritual people are never beaten.

Appendix

Probate Papers of Red Leg, or Red Leggins (As We Knew Her)

The testimonies in her probates happened fifteen years after her death. Called to testify were her son Combing, her daughter Iron Cedar (or Julia Clown, as she was known in most reservation records), her daughter-in-law Margaret Wolf, her brother-in-law Paul Red Bird, and an in-law named Moses Straighthead, who had married her cousin Little Hawk's sister's daughter, Mary Marrowbones. The testimonies have been retyped so as to be more legible, however, the original document precedes the transcribed one. They also include testimonies pertaining to Julia Rushes, Combing's second wife.

All of the original documents can be viewed full size at http://reelcontact.com/pages/tashunkewitkotiwahe.

PROPERTY DISPOSED OF BY WILL (Included in property hereinbefore described.)

...te of will ___No will___, 191 Date of departmental approval _____, 191 Serial No. ___

Devisees.	Relationship to Devisee.	Description of Property.
lone		

...MILY OF DECEASED. (Extra sheets may be used for family of deceased heirs, but the word "heir" and his name must appear after the words "Family of Deceased.")
MARRIAGES.

Name of Each Spouse in Sequence.	Marriage.		Date of Death.	Divorces.		Third and Subsequent Re-Marriages. (If white, so state.)
	Date.	Indian custom or by ceremony.	Date.	Indian custom or by court.	
...an Breast	About 1847	Ind.cust.	9/ /00	No divorce		C25.None
...tes marriage of any spouse of deceased—contra.						
...ne						

CHILDREN.

Names.	Sex and Age.	Name of Other Parent.* (If adopted or illegitimate, so state.)	If Dead or Dead, Give Date.
...ll Blanket	F— 26	Woman Breast	1874
...Combing	M— 69	" "	Living
...es Bear Pipe	M— 36	" "	Jan.10,1895
...er Wolf	M— 52	" "	Jan.19, 1916
...ing Home Last	M— 5	" "	About 1870
...amed	F— Infant	" "	About 1850
...a Cedar or			
...Amos Clown	F— 52	" "	Living.

*Under "Additional Information" show facts with regard to failure of illegitimate children and concerning adoptions.

ISSUE OF DECEASED BROTHERS OR SISTERS.

Name of Nephew or Niece.	Sex and Age.	Names of Parents, and How Married.	If Dead or Dead, Give Date.
...igh Horse.	M— Adult	Crazy Horse) Iron Between Eyes) I.C.	Bef.Allmts.
...ame unknown	Unknown	Crazy Horse) Kills Enemy) I.C.	About 1850
" "		" " " "	1850

OTHER LINEAL DESCENDANTS OF DECEDENT. (Identify persons named by allotment number, or by number on annuity on which last paid, describing voucher. Designate parents and grandparents through which they inherit by letters f, m, gf, gm, etc.)

Name of Descendant Who Survived Decedent. (If dead, give date; and give family surviving on extra sheets.)	Age.	Names of Parents and Grandparents of Descendant.
...lone		

GRANDPARENTS OF DECEDENT. (If any are white, so state.)

Names of Father's and Mother's Parents.	Marriage.		Tribe.	If Dead, Give Date.
	Date.	Indian custom or ceremony.		
...ernal gf, Unknown				
...ernal gm, "				
...ternal gf, "				
...ternal gm, "				

COLLATERAL RELATIVES. (Give line of descent from common ancestor of decedent; give names and designate parents and of heirs in line from common ancestor by letters f, m, gf, gm, ggf, ggm, etc. Identify by allotment No. or by number on annuity roll on which last paid.)

Name of Nearest Relative Who Survived Decedent.	If Dead, Give Date; and the Real Heirs of Surviving Family.	How Related to Decedent—Cousin.	Amount of Line from Common Ancestor.
...None			

CHILDREN OF DECEASED CHILDREN.

Name of Grandchildren.	Sex and Age.	Names of Both Parents, How Married— Indian Custom or Ceremony. (If one is white, so state.)	If Grandchild is Dead, Give Date.
All Yellow	F— 1	Stands Straddle)I. C. Shell Blanket)	About 1872
Come Home Victorious	M— 1	James Bear Pipe) I.C. Coming Home Hard Times)Allottee.	Long before
Jennie Wolf	F— 9	Peter Wolf)ceremony Margaret Wolf)	1895
John Wolf	M— 19	Same parents	Jan.,5,1909
Nancy Wolf	F— 17	" "	1909
Nellie Wolf	F— Infant	" "	1893–4
Sallie Wolf	F— 15	" "	June,1907
Ida Wolf	F— 13	" "	1911
Joshua Wolf	M— 19	" "	Jan.,23, 1919
Unnamed	M— 2 days	" "	1903
Nellie Wolf	F— 16	" "	Living

PARENTS OF DECEDENT. (If either is white, or of a different tribe, so state.)

Names.	Allotment.		Marriage.		If Either is Dead, Give Date.	Tribe.
	No.	Date.	Date.	Indian custom or ceremony.		
Father Corn	Unknown		Unknown	Unknown	Unknown	Sioux
Mother Unknown	"		"	"	"	"

BROTHERS AND SISTERS.

Names.	Brother or Sister.	Age.	Name of Common Parent of Half or Whole Blood.	If Brother or Sister is Dead, Give Date.
...ron Between Horns	Sister	Adult		Bef.Allmts.
...ills Enemy	"	"		" "
...ull Head	Brother	"		" "

ADDITIONAL INFORMATION: No homestead rights involved.

_____

_____

_____

_____

CONFLICT between the official record and the testimony. (If any, give description; if no conflict, say "none.") None

_____

I hereby certify that I have made a careful investigation as to the relatives of the decedent; that my report is correct and substantiated by official records and by the testimony taken at a hearing held on ___August 12, 1920,___ under the provisions of the act of June 25, 1910 (36 Stats., 855), and that it appears that at time of the hearing the heirs of the decedent, ___Red Leg,___ and the descent of the estate are as follows:

Heir. ABILITY (Degree of which.)	Relationship to Decedent.	Description of Property. (Give amount of personal property.)	Fractional Share of Descent, Description, or Value.
Leo Combing	Son	See page one	1/3 or 3/9
Iron Cedar or	Dau...		
Mrs.Amos Clown	Dau...		1/3 or 3/9
Margaret Wolf	wife of dec'd son.		1/9
	Dau.of sub.		
Nellie Wolf	dec'd son and sister of sub.dec'd son of sub.dec'd son.		2/9

M.H.Gorman
Examiner of Inheritance.

DATA FOR HEIRSHIP FINDING.

Allottee. Red Leg .... Age 80

Date of death May 22, 1905

Allotment No. 1461 ...... Annuity No. 1154 ...... Vou. 3 ...... 4th Qr. 1905

Description of land ... N/2 Sec. 19, N/2 Sec. 20, T.13 N. R. 23 E. B. H. M.

of S. D. containing 640 acres.

Date of patent ... patent my 6, 1907.

Act under which allotted . March R. 1889 (26 Stat. L., 889)

Father's name ... OATH .... Allotment No. None

Mother's name Unknown .... Allotment No. "

Spouse's name Young Brant .... Allotment No. "

Personal property $40.66 Lease and Interest.

PROBABLE HEIRS.	ADDRESSES.
Leo Combing or known as It Voice or Mrs. Peter Wolf.	Dupree, S. D.
Nellie Wolf.	Dupree, S. D.
Mrs. Clown or Iron Cedar,	Dupree, S. D.

Testimony of Iron Cedar or Mrs. Amos Clown in the heirship cases of Red Leg #1461, and Julia Rushes #1469, deceased Cheyenne River Sioux allottees taken by M. E. Gorman, Examiner of Inheritance pursuant to notice herewith.

Mary Talks, Interpreter.

Q. Give your name, age, tribe and residence. A. Iron Cedar or Mrs. Amos Clown, am 52 years old, Cheyenne River Sioux Tribe and live near Dupree, South Dakota.

Q. Did you know Red Leg and Julia Rushes? A. Yes.

Q. What relation, if any, were they to you? A. Red Leg was my mother and Julia Rushes was my sister-in-law, the wife of my brother, Leo Combing.

Q. Did you hear the testimony given in these cases this morning? A. Yes.

Q. Was that testimony correct as to the family history of Red Leg and Julia Rushes? A. It was all right.

Q. Is there anything that you would like to say in addition to what has been said as to these cases? A. They told it all correct and I am satisfied with what they have said and have nothing to add to it.

Q. Are you interested in these estates? A. I am in the estate of Red Leg, my mother, but am not interested in the estate of my sister-in-law, Julia Rushes.

Leo Combing Testimony in Red Leg and Julia Rushes Probate Hearings

Testimony of Leo Combing in the heirship cases of Red Leg #1461 and Julia Rushes #1469, deceased Cheyenne River Sioux allottees, taken by M. E. Gorman, Examiner of Inheritance pursuant want to motion herewith.

Mary Talks, Interpreter.

Q. Give your name, age, tribe, and residence. A. Leo Combing, am 69 years old, Cheyenne River Sioux Tribe and live near Dupree, South Dakota.

Q. Did you know Red Leg and Julia Rushes? A. Yes.

Q. What relation, if any, were they to you? A. Red Leg was my mother and Julia Rushes was my wife.

Q. What tribe did they belong to? A. Cheyenne River Sioux.

Q. Are they living or dead? A. Both dead.

Q. When did they die? A. Red Leg died May 1905, age 80 years, and Julia Rushes died in January, 1919 (Records show that Red Leg died May 22, 1905, age 80, and Julia Rushes died January 24, 1919, age 69). I think Julia was 70 years old.

Q. Where did they die? A. Red Leg died at Cheyenne Agency, South Dakota. I was there and she died there. Julia Rushes died at my home where I live now on my own allotment on this reservation.

Q. Did either of them live on their own land? A. Neither of them did but Julia's land was near mine but she always lived on my land.

Q. Did either of them make a will? A. Neither of them made a will.

Q. Was Red Leg ever married and if so, how many times? A. She had been married one time only to my father, Woman's Breast.

Q. How and when were they married? A. Indian custom over 70 years ago.

Q. Is Woman's Breast living or dead? A. He died about 20 years ago and was not allotted so far as I know. It was all given to Red Leg and she got 640 acres.

Q. What tribe did he belong to? A. Cheyenne River Sioux.

Q. Did he live with her until he died? A. Yes.

Q. Did she ever live with any man as his wife after he died? A. No she did not.

Q. Was he ever married to any other woman besides Red Leg? A. I do not think so as I never heard of it and I have no half-brothers or half-sisters, all had the same father and mother.

Q. Name the children in order, that Red Leg and Woman's Breast had, and give dates of deaths, ages at time of death. A. They had seven in all and they are as follows:

(1) Shell Blanket, a girl, died before allotments, 46 years ago, age about 26 years.

(2) I, Leo Combing, age 69 years.

(3) James Bear Pipe, died January 10, 1892, age about 38 years.

(4) Peter Wolf, died January 19, 1918, age between 50 and 60.

(5) A boy, Coming Home Last, died about 50 years ago, age 5 years.

(6) Iron Cedar or Mrs. Amos Clown, living, age about 50 years.

(7) Unnamed girl, died in infancy, before I was born, I heard of her but never saw her, and that is all I know about her.

Q. Were these all the children your mother had? A. They were all she ever had.

Q. Did she ever adopt a child? A. No, she never did.

Q. Was Shell Blanket ever married, and if so how many times? A. Yes, she was married one time.

Q. Who was her husband? A. His name was Stands Straddle.

Q. How and when were they married? A. Indian custom nearly 50 years ago.

Q. Is he living or dead? A. He is living.

Q. Did they live together until she died? A. No, They separated Indian custom after they had lived together about three years, that would be about 47 or 48 years ago.

Q. Did she live with any other man as his wife after she separated from him? A. No, she never did.

Q. Did they have any children and is so, how many? A. Yes, they had one.

Q. Was it a boy or a girl? A. It was a girl.

Q. What was her name? A. All Yellow.

Q. Is she living or dead? A. She died before her mother.

Q. How old was she? A. She was a year old.

Q. Was this all the children Shell Blanket ever had? A. It was.

Q. Was James Bear Pipe ever married and if so, how many times? A. He was married only one time to Coming Home Hard Times, still living and married to Victor Ducheneaux.

Q. How and when were they married? A. Indian custom long before allotments.

Q. Did he live with her until he died? A. Yes.

Q. Did he have any children and if so, how many? A. Yes they had one child, boy.

Q. What was his name? A. Comes Home Victorious.

Q. Is he living or dead? A. He is dead.

Q. When did he die? A. He died before his father, less than a year old, long before allotments.

Q. Was this the only child they ever had? A. That was all they ever had.

Q. Did James Bear Pipe ever adopt a child? A. No, he never did.

Q. Then when your mother, Red Leg, died she left just the three children, yourself, Mrs. Clown, and Peter Wolf? A. Yes, they all were living at the time she died.

Q. Has the estate of Peter Wolf been probated? A. His wife told me that it had been probated. (Certified copy testimony in the heirship case of Peter Wolf #662, herewith).

Q. It has been shown that the hearing in the case of Peter Wolf he had a wife and one child living. Are they living now? A. Yes, they are living now.

Q. Who were the father and mother of Red Leg? A. I have heard that her father's name was Corn but I don't know her mother's name and that is all I know about them. I never saw either of them.

Q. What tribe did they belong to? A. Cheyenne River Sioux.

Q. Did she have any brothers and sisters, and if so, name them and tell what you can about them. A. She had two sisters that I saw and I have heard of others but never saw them. One was called Iron Between Horns, and the other was called Kills Enemy. These are all the names I know. She had one brother that died before I was born, when the Indian has some sickness and he was called Bull Head, never married and never had issues. Both sisters died before allotments.

Q. Was Iron Between Horns married, and if so, how many times? A. She was married one time.

Q. Who was her husband? A. Crazy Horse.

Q. Is he living or dead? A. He is dead.

Q. When did he die? A. He died about 40 years ago?

Q. Did they have any children and if so, how many? A. They had one, a boy.

Q. What was his name? A. High Horse.

Q. Is he living or dead? A. He died long ago, before allotments when a young man, killed in an Indian war, and left no issue, there is nothing left of his family at all.

Q. Was Kills Enemy married and if so, how many times? A. She was married to the same as Iron Between Horns, Crazy Horse, by the old Indian custom, and she died first, then Crazy Horse died, and last Iron Between Horns died and all of them died long before allotments.

Q. Did Kills Enemy have any children and if so, how many? A. She had two is what I have heard but they both died before I was born and there is nothing left of her family.

Q. Do you know anything more about the family history of Red Leg? A. That is all I know about it.

Q. You stated that Julia Rushes was your wife, how and when were you married to her? A. I was married by Indian custom when I was 25 years old. (He is now 69 and that would be about 44 years ago).

Q. Did you live with her as her husband from the time you married until she died? A. I did.

Q. Were you ever married before you married her and if so, how many times? A. I was married one time before I married her.

Q. Who was that wife? A. I don't like to say her name, but it was Comes After Her.

Q. How and when were you married to her and did the marriage terminate? A. I married her in Indian custom nearly 50 years ago and threw her away the same way, the way the Indians did in those days, just let her go and get another one. In those days if you get a woman and if her ways were not just what you wanted you would throw her away and that is what I did.

Q. What tribe did she belong to? A. She was a Pine Ridge Sioux.

Q. Did you and Julia have any children and if so, how many? A. No, we never did.

Q. Did she have any child at all? A. No, she never did.

Q. Did you ever adopt a child at all? A. She helped raise a boy of mine, called Fremont Combing. but it was not her son and so she did not really adopt a child at all.

Q. Then she did not have a child of her own at all but simply helped you raise this child. Was that the way it was? A. Yes, that was the way it was.

Q. Who were the father and mother of Julia Rushes? A. I do not know her father and she told me her mother's name but I have forgotten it. I have seen her mother but her father died long ago and I never saw him.

Q. Is her mother living or dead? A. She died in 1876 and her father died long before that.

Q. What tribe did they belong to? A. They were of the Sioux tribe.

Q. Did Julia Rushes have any brothers and sisters and if so, how many, give their names and ages and tell whether they are living or dead, and if dead, give date of death and age at the time of death. A. I have heard about four sisters and one brother, the brother's name was Red Eagle, dead, died before allotments here and he was about 50 to 60 years old, he died on the Rosebud Reservation. Comes Out At Night was the name of one of the sisters and she died at Rosebud after Red Eagle, before Julia Rushes, an old woman when she died, and two of the sisters died long ago and I do not know their names, died long before Julia Rushes grew up when they died but I don't know their ages, and one sister was a twin to Julia Rushes and she died long before Julia and her name was Deer, and she was about 30 years old when she died.

Q. Then when Julia died, her father and mother, brother and sisters all had died before her. Is that correct? A. Yes, that is correct.

Q. At the time Julia died, do you claim to have been her rightful husband? A. I do.

Q. Do you know anything more about the family history of Julia Rushes? A. That is about all I know about it.

Q. Are you interested in these estates? A. I am.

Margaret Wolf Testimony in Red Leg and Julia Rushes Probate Hearings

...timony of Margaret Wolf in the heirship cases of Red Leg #1461, ...1469, deceased Cheyenne River allottees taken by M. F. Crutz... Inheritance pursuant to notice herewith.

Mary Talks Interpreter.

Q. Give your name, age, tribe, and residence. A. Margaret Wolf, am Cheyenne River Sioux Tribe and live at or near Eagle Butte, South Dakota.

Q. Did you know Red Leg and India Rushes? A. Yes, I knew them.

Q. What, if any, relation were they to you? A. Red Leg was my husband's mo... Julia Rushes was the wife of Leo Combing the brother to my deceased husb... Wolf.

Q. Did you hear the testimony given in these cases? A. Yes, I heard it.

Q. Did they give the family history correctly the way you know it? A. They did.

Q. Has the estate of Peter Wolf been probated? A. There was a hearing here a short ti... and we it certified copy of testimony in the heirship case of Peter Wolf who... here in...

Q. Are you willing for the testimony that you gave in that case and that of your witnesses to be copied and used in this case as your testimony for this case? A. Yes, I am willing to that.

Q. Is your daughter Nellie Wolf Hawk Eagle, living? A. Yes, she is home with a small baby

Q. How old is she? A. She is 16 years old

Q. Have you anything else to say about these cases? A. No, I have no more to say.

Q. Are you interested in these estates? A. I am in the estate of Red Leg with my little girl but I am not in the estate of Julia Rushes.

Moses Straighthead Testimony in Red Leg and Julia Rushes Probate Hearings

Testimony of Moses Straighthead in the heirship cases of Red Leg #1461 and Julia Rushes #1469, deceased Cheyenne River Sioux allottees, taken by M. K. Gorman, Examiner of Inheritance, pursuant to notice herewith.

Mary Talks, Interpreter P.

Q. Give your name, age, tribe and residence? A. Moses Straighthead, a m 68 years old, Cheyenne River Sioux tribe and live near Dupree, S. D.

Q. How long have you lived on this reservation? A. I have lived here about 50 years.

Q. Did you know Red Leg and Julia Rushes? A. Yes, I knew them.

Q. What tribe did they belong to? A. Cheyenne River Sioux.

Q. How long did you know them? A. I knew them about 50 years.

Q. Are they living or dead? A. Both dead.

Q. When did they die? A. Red Leg died about 18 years ago and Julia Rushes died about 2 years ago (records show that Red Leg died Nov. 19 1909, age about 80 years, and Julia Rushes died Jan. 21, 1919, age about 60 years)

Q. Where did they die? A. Red Leg died at the Cheyenne River Agency South Dakota, and Julia Rushes died at the home of her husband on her ranch on this reservation on the allotment of her husband.

Q. Did either of these decedents ever live and make their home on their own land? A. As they never did.

Q. Did either of them make a will? A. Not to my knowledge.

Q. Was Red Leg ever married and if so, how many times?

A. She had been married one time to Thunder Hawk, she died before him, about 30 years ago, and all never married again after that until her death.

Q. What tribe did he belong to? A. Cheyenne River Sioux.

Q. Did they live together until he died? A. They did.

Q. Was he married ever married before he married her? A. No.

Q. Did they have any children and if so, how many?

A. They had five that I know.

Q. What are their names, and ages, and dates of deaths of any that are dead

A. They are as follows;
(1) (Emil) Marshal, died before allotments, age about 25 years;
(2) Leo Combing, living, age about 38 years;
(3) James Bear Pipe, died about 27 years ago, age about 35 years;
(4) Peter Wolf, died 2 years ago (Jan. 19, 1919) age about 50;
(5) Iron Cedar or Mrs. Anna Clark, living, age about 55 years.

Q. Were all of these ever born, I have heard that Leo Combing is the only child of those died, but I never knew them as they have died long before then 30 years ago or I would have seen them too.

Q. Were these all the children Red Leg ever had? A. Yes.

Q. Did she ever adopt a child? A. No.

Q. Was Emil Marshal ever married and if so, how many times, to whom, how was and when and how was each marriage terminated?

A. She was married one time, only to friends, (friends), still living.

Q. Do you know anything more about the family of Red Leg?

A. I do not know any more of my own knowledge. What I have told is of my own knowledge, but I have heard that there were five in her family, brothers and sisters but I do not know the others and do not know their families so that I cannot testify to them. I have told all I can tell about her family.

Q. Was Julia Rushes a ver married and if so, how many times, to whom how and when and how was each marriage term instead?

A. She had been married only one time, to Leo Combing, still living, by indian custom about 44 years ago and shelived with him as his wife until she died.

Q. What tribe did she belong to?A. Cheyenne River Sioux.

Q. Was Leo Combing ever married before he married her?A. I know of one time he was before he married her.

Q. Who was his wife?A. Comes After her was her mama.

Q. Is she living or dead?A. She died long age.

Q. Did he live with her from the time he married her until she died?A. No they separated b indian custom long ago, before he married Julia Rushes.

Q. What tribe did she belong to?A. Pine Ridge Sioux.

Q. Did Julia Rushes and Leo Combing have any children? A. No they never had any at all.

Q. Did she ever have a child by any one? A. No she never did.

Q. Did she ever adopt a child?A. Not to my knowledge.

Q. Who were the father and mother of Julia Rushes? A. I do not know them.

Q. Are they living or dead?A. they were dead when I first knew her.

Q. What tribe did they belong to?A. Cheyenne River Sioux.

Q. Did she have any brothers and sisters and if so, name them, and give their ages and dates of deaths of any that are dead?

A. She had one brother named Red Eagle died long before her allotments, age about 50 to 60 years old, he died long before Julia Rushes, and I know one sister, a twin sister to Julia Rushes, named Bear, died long ago, before allotments, long before Julia Rushes, and there were three other sisters that died long before Julia Rushes and I do not know their names, but all of them died long years before Julia Rushes, I do not know of any children from any of these at all.

Q. Then when Julia Rushes died she had a husband, Leo Combing and no issue, no father or mother and no brother or sister living. Is that correct?

A. Yes, that is correct.

Q. Can you tell anything more about the family history of Julia Rushes? A. No I cannot.

Q. Are you interested in these estates? A. No I am not interested.

Witnesses:

Annie P. Gorman, Clerk,

Mary Talks, Interpreter,

Moses Straighthead

Subscribed and sworn to before me this 18th day of Aug, 1920.
M. K. H.

Name, Moses Straighthead,
Age, 68,
Residence, Red Leg,
Tribe, C. R. S.
Address, Dupree, S.D.
Means of knowledge, Knew decedents about 50 years.
Interested in cases, none,
Intelligence and credibility, Good in both respects.

Testimony of Moses Straighthead in the heirship cases of Red Leg #1461 and Julia Rushes #1469, deceased Cheyenne River Sioux allottees, taken by M. E. Gorman, Examiner of Inheritance pursuant want to motion herewith.

Mary Talks, Interpreter.

Q. Give your name, age, tribe, and residence. A. Moses Straighthead, am 65 years old, Cheyenne River Sioux Tribe and live near Dupree, South Dakota.

Q. How long have you lived on this reservation? A. I have lived here about 50 years.

Q. Did you know Red Leg and Julia Rushes? A. Yes, I knew them.

Q. What tribe did they belong to? A. Cheyenne River Sioux.

Q. How long did you know them? A. I knew them about 50 years.

Q. Are they living or dead? A. Both dead.

Q. When did they die? A. Red Leg died about 15 years ago and Julia Rushes died about two years ago (Records show that Red Leg died Mar. 22, 1905, age about 80 years, and Julia Rushes died Jan 24, 1919, age 69 years).

Q. Did either of the deceased ever live and make their homes on their own land? A. No they never did.

Q. Did either of them make a will? A. Not to my knowledge.

Q. Was Red Leg ever married and if so, how many times? A. She had been married one time to Woman's Breast, who died before her, about 20 years ago, and she never married again after that until her death.

Q. What tribe did she belong to? A. Cheyenne River Sioux.

Q. Did they live together until they died? A. They did.

Q. Was Woman's Breast ever married before her? A. No.

Q. Did they have any children and if so, how many? A. They had five that I know of.

Q. What are their names, and ages, and dates of deaths of any that are dead? A. They are as follows:
    (1) Shell Blanket, died before allotments about 40 years ago, age about 28 years.
    (2) Leo Combing, living, age about 69 years.
    (3) James Bear Pipe, died about 27 years ago, about 36 years.
    (4) Peter Wolf, died 2 years ago (Jan. 19, 1918), age about 57.
    (5) Iron Cedar or Mrs. Amos Clown, living, age about 52 years.

These are all of them that I ever saw, I have heard that two died in infancy, long ago, before any of these died, but I never saw them but if they had grown up I would have seen them and they must have died more than 50 years ago or I would have seen them too.

Q. Were these all children Red Leg ever had? A. Yes.

Q. Did she adopt a child? A. No.

Q. Was Shell Blanket ever married and if so, how many times, to whom, and how and when was each marriage terminated. A. She was married one time, only to Stands Straddle, still living, and they separated by Indian custom, long before allotments and before she died and she was never married any more, but died single.

Q. What tribe does Stands Straddle belong to? A. Cheyenne River Sioux.

Q. Did they have any children and if so, how many? A. Yes, they had one child. A girl.

Q. What was her name? A. She was called All Yellow.

Q. Is she living or is she dead? A. Dead.

Q. When did she die? A. She died when she was a year old, before her mother.

Q. Was that all the children she ever had? A. Yes.

Q. Was James Bear Pipe ever married and if so, how many times? A. Yes, he was married one time.

Q. Who was his wife? A. Coming Home Hard times.

Q. How and when were they married? A. Indian custom over 30 years ago.

Q. Is she living or dead? A. Living.

Q. Who is she now? A. She is the wife of Victor Ducheneaux.

Q. Did James Bear Pipe and this woman have any children? A. Yes, they had one child, a boy.

Q. What was his name? A. Kills the Enemy or Comes Home Victorious.

Q. Is he living or dead? A. Dead.

Q. When did he die and how old was he? A. He died long before his father and was about six months old, less than a year.

Q. Was this all the children James Bear Pipe ever had by any woman? A. That was all he ever had.

Q. Was Peter Wolf ever married and if so, how many times? A. He was married one time only.

Q. Who was his wife? A. Margaret Wolf.

Q. How and when were they married? A. By ceremony about 37 years ago.

Q. Is she living or dead? A. Living.

Q. What tribe does she belong to? A. Cheyenne River Sioux.

Q. Has the estate of Peter Wolf been probated? A. I heard it had been probated (Certified copy of testimony in the case of Peter Wolf #662, herewith).

Q. Has Peter Wolf any children living now? A. Yes.

Q. How many? A. One, a daughter.

Q. What is her name? A. Nellie Wolf Hawk Eagle.

Q. How old is she? A. She is about 16 years old.

Q. Did Peter Wolf have any other children living at the time he died? A. He had a son named Joshua Wolf, that died after him, age about 19 years, these were all he had living at the time he died and he has only the one living now.

Q. Then at this time, is there any one left of the family of Red Leg except Leo Combing, son, and Iron Cedar or Mrs. Amos Clown, daughter, and Nellie Wolf Hawk Eagle, granddaughter, and her mother, the wife of her subsequently deceased son, Peter Wolf, and if so tell me what you know of them. A. They are all that is left of her family at this time.

Q. Who were her father and mother? A. I don't know who they were.

Q. Are they living or dead? A. They died long ago, before I knew her.

Q. Do you know anything more about the family of Red Leg? A. I do not know any more to my knowledge. What I have told is of my knowledge, but I have heard that there were five in her family, brothers and sisters but I do not know the others and do not know their families so that I cannot testify to them, I have told all I can tell about her family.

Q. Was Julia Rushes ever married and if so, how many times, to whom, how, and when and how was the marriage terminated? A. She had been married only one time, to Leo Combing, still living, by Indian custom about 44 years ago and she lived with him as his wife until she died.

Q. What tribe does she belong to? A. Cheyenne River Sioux.

Q. Was Leo Combing ever married before he married her? A. I know of one time he was married before he married her.

Q. Who was his wife? A. Comes Home After was her name.

Q. Is she living or dead? A. She died a long time ago.

Q. Did he live with her from the time he married her until she died? A. No. They separated by Indian custom long ago, before he married Julia Rushes.

Q. What tribe did she belong to? A. Pine Ridge Sioux.

Q. Did Julia Rushes and Leo Combing have children? A. No, they never had any at all.

Q. Did she ever have a child by any man? A. No, she never did.

Q. Did she ever adopt a child? A. Not to my knowledge.

Q. Who were the father and mother of Julia Rushes? A. I do not know them.

Q. Are they living or dead? A. They were dead when I first knew her.

Q. What tribe did they belong to? A. Cheyenne River Sioux.

Q. Did she have any brothers and sisters and if so, name them, and give their ages and dates of their deaths of any that are dead. A. She had one brother named Red Eagle died long ago, before allotments, age about 50 to 60 years old, he died before Julia Rushes, and I knew one sister, a twin sister to Julia Rushes, named Deer, died long ago before allotments, long before Julia Rushes, and there were three other sisters that died long before Julia Rushes and I do not know their names, but all of them died years before Julia Rushes, I do not know of any children from any of them.

Q. Can you tell anything more about the family history of Julia Rushes? A. No, I cannot.

Q. Are you interested in these estates? A. No I am not interested.

Paul Red Bird Testimony in Red Leg and Julia Rushes Probate Hearings

Testimony of Paul Red Bird in the heirship cases of Red Leg #1466, and Julia Rushes #1466, deceased Cheyenne River Sioux allottees, taken by M. E. Gorman, Examiner of Inheritance, pursuant to notice herewith.

Mary Talks, interpreter.

Q. Give your name, age, tribe and residence; A. Paul Red Bird, am 50 years old, Cheyenne River Sioux tribe and live near Dupree, S. D.
Q. Have you ever lived on this reservation; A. 50 years.
Q. Did you know Red Leg and Julia Rushes; A. I knew both of them.
Q. How long did you know them; A. I knew them a good many years.
Q. What tribe did they belong to; A. Cheyenne River Sioux.
Q. Are they living or dead; A. Both of them, they are dead, they had Red Leg died about 13 years ago and Julia died over a year ago.
Q. Where did they die; A. Red Leg died at Cherrycreek, South Dakota and Julia died at the home of Lee Combing on Deep Creek on this reservation, in South Dakota.
Q. How old were they; A. Red Leg was about 80 years old, and Julia was about 70 years old.
Q. Did either of them ever live on their own land; A. Neither of them ever lived on their own land.
Q. Did either of them own a will; A. not to my knowledge.
Q. Did either of them have any trust property except their allotments; A. no.
Q. Were they married at the time they died; ...
Q. Has Red Leg ever married and if so how many times; ...
Q. Had Julia been married only one time; ...
Q. Who was her husband; A. Roman Breast.
Q. Did you know him; A. I did.
Q. Is he living or dead; A. He is dead.
Q. When did he die; A. He died about 30 years ago.
Q. Was Julia ever married before he married her; ...
Q. Was he ever married before he married Julia; ...
Q. Was she ever married after he died; ...
Q. Did they have any children; ...
Q. Name them, and give their ages and dates of death if any are dead;

Straddle

They all lived together now but Present Combing did buy a casket for Julia when she died that cost $150., so I heard and he helped to care for her along with the rest of them.
Q. Are his father and mother living; A. Yes.
Q. Then is that all the child she ever did anything for; A. Yes.
Q. Did she adopt him by any court or ceremony; A. There were no...

I certify that the following persons were present at the hearing in the heirship case of Red Leg, deceased Cheyenne River Sioux allottee No. 1461.

...

Examiner of Inheritance.

Testimony of Paul Red Bird in the heirship cases of Red Leg #1461 and Julia Rushes #1469, deceased Cheyenne River Sioux allottees, taken by M. E. Gorman, Examiner of inheritance pursuant want to motion herewith.

Mary Talks, Interpreter.

Q. Give your name, age, tribe, and residence. A. Paul Red Bird, am 59 years old, Cheyenne River Sioux Tribe and live near Dupree, South Dakota.

Q. How long have you lived on this reservation? A. 30 years.

Q. Did you know Red Leg and Julia Rushes? A. I know them both.

Q. How long did you know them? A. I knew them both 39 years.

Q. What tribe did they belong to? A. Cheyenne River Sioux Tribe.

Q. Are they living or dead, and if dead, when did they die? A. Red Leg died about 15 years ago and Julia died over a year ago.

Q. Where did they die? A. Red Leg died at the Cheyenne Agency, South Dakota and Julia died at the home of Leo Combing on Bear Creek on this reservation, in South Dakota.

Q. How old were they? A. Red Leg was about 80 years old, and Julia was about 70 years old.

Q. Did either of them live on their own land? A. Neither of them ever lived on their own land.

Q. Did either of them make a will? A. Not to my knowledge.

Q. Did either of them have any trust property except their allotments at the time they died? A. No, they did not.

Q. Was Red Leg ever married and if so how many times? A. She had been married only one time.

Q. Who was her husband? A. Woman's Breast.

Q. Did you know him? A. I did.

Q. How and when was she married to him? A. Indian custom over 70 years ago.

Q. Is he living or dead? A. He is dead.

Q. When did he die? A. He died about 20 years ago.

Q. What tribe did he belong to? A. Cheyenne River Sioux.

Q. Was he married before he married her? A. He never married before that.

Q. Was she ever married after he died? A. She never was.

Q. Did they have any children and if so, how many? A. I know of four children.

Q. Name, and give their ages and dates of deaths if any are dead. A. They areas follows:
 (1) Leo Combing, living, age about 69 years.
 (2) James Bear Pipe, died in 1892, age about 36 years.
 (3) Peter Wolf, died two years ago (1-19-1918) age about 50 to 60.
 (4) Iron Cedar or Mrs. Amos Clown, living, age about 52 years.
Those are all the ones I ever saw, but I heard of one daughter that married Stands Straddle but I did not know her name, only that there was one daughter that married Stands Straddle.

Q. Are these all you ever heard of? A. These are all I ever heard of, and if there had been any that grew up I would have known them. If that one that married Stands Straddle had lived longer I would have seen her but she died before I knew her family. I am sure that none grew up except the four that I saw and the one that married Stands Straddle.

Q. Was James Bear Pipe ever married and if so how many times? A. He married one time.

Q. Who was his wife? A. Her name was Coming Home Hard Times.

Q. Do you know her? A. I do.

Q. Is she living now? A. Yes, and she is the wife of Victor Ducheneaux.

Q. How and when were Bear Pipe and Coming Home Hard Times married? A. Indian custom long before allotments.

Q. Did they live together until he died? A. They did.

Q. Did they have any children and if so, how many? A. I have heard of one child that died right after birth and that is all the children they ever had. It died before its father, so there is no one left of his family.

Q. Was Peter Wolf ever married and if so, how many times? A. He was married one time to Margaret Wolf, still living.

Q. How and when were they married? A. Ceremony about 37 years ago.

Q. Has the estate of Peter Wolf been probated? A. Yes. (Certified copy of testimony in the case of Peter Wolf #662 herewith).

Q. At the time of the hearing in the case of Peter Wolf and at this time how many of his family were living? A. There is only the wife and one daughter living, and the daughter's name is Nellie Wolf, married to Hawk Eagle, and I hear that she has a child just lately, but they are all there is left of the family of Peter Wolf.

Q. Then at this time there are two children of Red Leg and the wife and one child of a son that died after his mother. Is that correct? A. Yes, that is correct. They are all that is left of her family. All the rest died before her and left no issue.

Q. Do you know anything more about the family history of Red Leg? A. No, I do not.

Q. Was Julia Rushes ever married and if so, how many times, to whom, how, and when and how was each terminated? A. She was married one time only, to Leo Combing, by Indian custom, about or over 50 years ago and he is still living, and he lived with her as her husband until she died.

Q. What tribe does she belong to? A. Cheyenne River Sioux.

Q. Was he ever married before he married Julia? A. I don't know of it if he was.

Q. Did they have any children? A. No, they never did.

Q. Did Julia have a child with any man? A. No, she never did.

Q. Did she ever adopt a child? A. She took care of Fremont Combing, a child of Leo Combing, by another woman, and she helped care for him from the time he was small but they all lived together and his own mother is living now and this boy did something for her when she was old but they all lived together and it is hard to tell what each did for the other. They all live together now but Fremont Combing did buy a coffin for Julia when she died that cost $165, so I heard and he helped to care for her along with the rest of them.

Q. Are his father and mother living? A. Yes.

Q. Then is that all the child she ever did anything for? A. Yes.

Q. Did she adopt him by any court or ceremony? A. There were no courts then and they did not think of it at that time.

Q. Was that about all there was to this adoption? A. She helped to care for him and gave him horses and when he got married she gave him horses and did things like that for him.

Q. Who were the father and mother of Julia Rushes? A. I do not know them.

Q. Are they living or dead? A. They had both died about or over 40 years ago, before I ever knew them and long before Julia.

Q. Did she have any brothers and sisters? A. I never saw any brothers and sisters except Red Eagle, a brother, and I never saw any sisters at all.

Q. Is Red Eagle still living? A. He died long ago, before allotments and long before Julia Rushes.

Q. Did you ever hear of any sisters? A. I have never heard of any sisters and I know if there were any, they must have died long before her as they never came around her in the 39 years that I have known her and I am sure they are all dead before her. That is all I know about her brothers and sisters.

Q. Are you willing to testify that when Julia Rushes died a little over a year ago that she had no brother or sister living? A. I am willing to testify that she had no brother or sister living when she died and they all died long before her.

Q. Are you interested in these estates? A. No.

Probate Papers For Peter Wolf (Makah)

These probate testimonies took place two years after Peter Wolf's assassination. Called to testify were his wife Margaret, Moses Red Bird, who was Paul Red Bird's son, and John Promise, who was minister at the Bear Creek Episcopal Mission in Bear Creek, South Dakota. Margaret was recalled and quizzed on the possibility of Wolf having a second residence. Wolf spent a great deal of time with his relatives, and we believe it was an attempt to find out who those relatives were. The testimonies have been retyped so as to be more legible, however, the original document precedes it. They also include testimonies pertaining to Peter and Margaret's son, Joshua.

Margaret Wolf Testimony in Peter Wolf and Joshua Wolf Probate Hearings

Testimony of Margaret Wolf in the heirship cases of Peter Wolf, No. 662, and Joshua Wolf, No. 2050, of the Cheyenne River Sioux Tribe, taken by M. E. Gorman, Examiner of Inheritance, pursuant to notice herewith.

Q. Give your name, age, tribe, and residence. A. Margaret Wolf, age 56 years, Cheyenne River Sioux and live near Dupree, South Dakota.

Q. Did you know Peter Wolf and Joshua Wolf? A. Yes, Peter Wolf was my husband and Joshua Wolf was my son.

Q. Are they living or dead? A. Both are dead.

Q. When did they die? A. Peter Wolf died January 19, 1918, and Joshua died January 22, 1919.

Q. How old were they? A. Peter was 59 years old when he died, and Joshua was 19 years old when he died.

Q. Where did they die? A. Peter Wolf died on his allotment on this reservation, South Dakota and Joshua died at the same place.

Q. Where was Peter Wolf's permanent home? A. His permanent home was on his allotment where he died and he had lived at that place continuously for 29 years.

Q. Did he have any other home besides that? A. That was all the home he had.

Q. Did he have any personal property? A. No, but he had some I.D. cattle and they had been killed long ago.

Q. Did Joshua Wolf have any personal property? A. No.

Q. Did Peter Wolf make a will? A. No.

Q. Was he ever married and if so, how many times? A. I am the only wife he ever had.

Q. How and when were you and Peter Wolf married? A. July 4, 1886, by ceremony.

Q. Did you live with him as his wife from the time you married him until he died? A. Yes.

Q. Were you ever married before you married him? A. No, I never was.

Q. Did you and Peter Wolf have any children, and if so, how many? A. We had nine children in all.

Q. Beginning with the oldest give the names and ages and tell whether they are living or dead, and if dead give the date of death and age at the time of death. A. They are as follows:

    (1) Jennie Wolf, died 25 years ago, age 8 years.

    (2) John Wolf, died January 3, 1909, age 20 years.

    (3) Nancy Wolf, died January, 1909, age 17

    (4) Nellie Wolf, 1893 or 1894, in infancy.

    (5) Sallie Wolf, died in May, 1907, age 11 years.

    (6) Ida Wolf, died June 11, age 13 years.

    (7) Joshua Wolf, died January 22, 1919, age 19 years.

    (8) Nellie Wolf, living, age 16 years.

    (9) Unnamed boy, born 1903, died 1903, age 2 days. This one was born before Nellie.

Q. Then at this time you have but one child living? A. Yes, I have but the one child, Nellie Wolf, now married to Thomas Hawk Eagle.

Q. Were any of your deceased children married or did any of them have any issue? A. None of them were ever married and none of them ever had any issue.

Q. Did Peter Wolf ever adopt a child? A, No, he never did.

Q. Did he ever have any children by any other woman? A. No, he never did.

Q. Then at this time you and Nellie are all that is left of Peter Wolf's family. Is that correct? A. Yes, that is correct.

Q. Who was Peter Wolf's father and mother? A. His father's name was Woman's Breast and his mother's name was Red Leg.

Q. What tribe did they belong to? A. Cheyenne River Sioux.

Q. Were they allotted? A. His father died before allotments and his mother was allotted.

Q. How and when were they married? A. They were married by Indian custom long before allotments.

Q. Is Red Leg living or dead? A. She died 15 years ago (May 22, 1905).

Q. Did Peter Wolf have any brothers and sisters, and if so, tell all you know about them. A. He had a brother that died long ago, when young, before any allotments, and I don't know his name, and he has a brother named Leo Combing, living, age about 69 years, and a sister named Iron Cedar or Mrs. Amos Clown, living, age about 52 years. These are all I know of them.

Q. Was that brother whose name you do not know ever married, and if so tell what you know of him. A. He had been married but he never had any issue. He was married to the same woman who is now married to Victor Ducheneaux, but I do not know her name. I am sure he never had any issue by her or any other woman. He died long before allotments.

Q. Do you know anything more about the family history of Peter Wolf than you have told? A. I can't go any further back with his family history than I have told.

Q. Are you interested in these estates? A. I am.

Margaret Wolf Recall Testimony, Peter Wolf Probate, as to her Residence

Margaret Wolf is recalled for further questions as to her residence.

Q. Mrs. Wolf, where have you lived since Peter Wolf died? A. I have lived on Peter Wolf's allotment all the time since he died.

Q. Do you make that your permanent home? A. Yes.

Q. Do you claim the right of homestead in Peter Wolf's allotment? A. Yes.

Q. Is there anything else that you wish to say about these cases? A. This is all I have to say.

Moses Red Bird Testimony in Peter Wolf and Joshua Wolf Probate Hearings

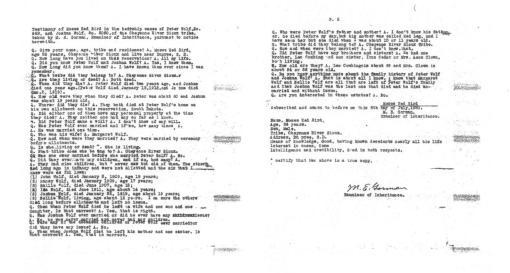

Testimony of Moses Red Bird in the heirship cases of Peter Wolf, No. 662, and Joshua Wolf, No. 2050, of Cheyenne River Sioux Tribe, taken by M. E. Gorman, Examiner of Inheritance, pursuant to notice herewith.

Q. Give your name, age, tribe, and residence. A. Moses Red Bird, age 26 years, Cheyenne River and live near Dupree, South Dakota.

Q. How long have you lived on the reservation? A. All my life.

Q. Did you know Peter Wolf and Joshua Wolf? A. Yes, I knew them.

Q. How long did you know them? A. I have known them ever since I can remember.

Q. What tribe do they belong to? A. Cheyenne River Sioux.

Q. Are they living or dead? A. Both dead.

Q. When did they die? A. Peter Wolf died two years ago, and Joshua died one year ago. (Peter Wolf died January 19, 1918, and Joshua Wolf died January 2, 1919).

Q. How old were they when they died? A. Peter was about 60 and Joshua was about 19 years old.

Q. Where did they die? A. They both died at Peter Wolf's home on his allotment on this reservation, South Dakota.

Q. Did either one of them have any personal property at the time they died? A. They neither one had any so far as I know.

Q. Did Peter Wolf make a will? A. I don't know of any will.

Q. Was Peter Wolf ever married and if so, how many times? A. He was married one time.

Q. Who was his wife? A. Margaret Wolf.

Q. How and when were they married? A. They were married by ceremony before allotments.

Q. Is she living or dead? A. She is living.

Q. What tribe does she belong to? A. Cheyenne River Sioux.

Q. Was she ever married before she married Peter Wolf? A. No.

Q. Did they ever have any children, and if so, how many. A. They had nine children, but I never saw but six of them. The others died long ago in infancy and were not allotted and the six that I knew were as follows:
    (1) John Wolf, died January 3, 1909, age 19 years.
    (2) Nancy Wolf, died January 1909, age 17 years.
    (3) Sallie Wolf, died June 1907, age 12.
    (4) Ida Wolf, died June 1911, age about 14 years.
    (5) Joshua Wolf, died January 22, 1919, age 19 years.
    (6) Nellie Wolf, living, age about 16 years. I am sure the others died long before allotments and left no issue.

Q. Then when Peter Wolf died he left a wife and one son and one daughter. A. Yes, that is right.

Q. Was Joshua Wolf ever married or did he ever have any issue? A. No, he was never married and never had any children.

Q. Were any of the deceased children of Peter Wolf ever married or did they have any issue? A. No.

Q. Then when Joshua Wolf died he left his mother and one sister. Is that correct? A. Yes, that is correct.

Q. Who were Peter Wolf's father and mother? A. I don't know the father, he died before my day, but his mother was called Red Leg, and I have seen her but she died when I was about 10 or 11 years old.

Q. What tribe did they belong to? A. Cheyenne River Sioux.

Q. How and when were they married? A. I don't know that.

Q. Did Peter Wolf have any brothers and sisters? A. He had one brother, Leo Combing, and one sister, Iron Cedar or Mrs. Amos Clown, both living.

Q. How old are they? A. Leo Combing is about 69 years old and Mrs. Clown is about 54 or 55 years old.

Q. Do you know anything more about the family history of Peter Wolf and Joshua Wolf? A. That is about all I know. I know Margaret Wolf and Nellie Wolf are all that are left of Peter Wolf's family and that Joshua Wolf was the last one that died and he died unmarried and without issue.

Q. Are you interested in these estates? A. No.

John Promise Testimony in Peter Wolf and Joshua Wolf Probate Hearings

Testimony of John Promise in the heirship cases of Peter Wolf No. 662, and Joshua Wolf, No. 2050, Deceased Cheyenne River Sioux Allottees, taken by M. E. Gorman, Examiner of Inheritance, pursuant to notice herewith.

Q. Give you name, age, tribe, and residence. A. John Promise, or Once Called, age 53 years, Cheyenne River Sioux and live near Dupree, South Dakota.

Q. How long have you lived on the reservation? A. Fifty years.

Q. Did you know Peter Wolf and Joshua Wolf? A. Yes.

Q. What tribe did they belong to? A. Cheyenne River Sioux Tribe.

Q. Are they living or dead? A. They are both dead.

Q. When did they die? A. Peter Wolf died in January 1918 and Joshua died in January 1919. (Records show that Peter Wolf died January 19, 1918, and Joshua died January 22, 1919).

Q. How old were they when they died? A. Peter was about 59 years old and Joshua was about 19 years old.

Q. Where did they die? A. Peter Wolf died on his own allotment on this reservation and Joshua died there too.

Q. Where did Peter Wolf have his permanent home? A. On his own allotment near Green Grass, where he died.

Q. Did he have any other home besides this one? A. No.

Q. How long had he lived there? A. He lived there about 29 years.

Q. Was that his permanent home all that time? A. Yes.

Q. Did Peter Wolf ever make a will? A. I don't know of any will.

Q. Was Peter Wolf ever married, and if so, how many times? A. He was married only once.

Q. Who was his wife? A. Margaret Wolf.

Q. How and when were they married? A. They were married by ceremony about 34 years ago.

Q. Is Margaret Wolf living or dead? A. She is living.

Q. What tribe does she belong to? A. Cheyenne River Sioux.

Q. Was Margaret Wolf ever married before she married Peter Wolf? A. No.

Q. Did they have any children, and if so, how many? A. They had nine children.

Q. Beginning with the oldest give their names and ages and tell whether they are living or dead and if dead, give date of death and age at time of death. A. They are as follows:
  (1) I don't remember the name of the first one but it was a girl and died before allotments, age about 8 years (Jennie Wolf died 1895, age 8 years).
  (2) John Wolf, died 10 or 11 years ago, age 18 or 19.
  (3) Nancy Wolf, died about the same time that John died, age 17.
  (4) Next was a girl died in infancy, before allotments.

(5) Sallie Wolf, died about 10 or 12 years ago and was about 11.

(6) Ida Wolf, died 9 or 10 years ago, 12 or 13 years old.

(7) Joshua Wolf, died January 22, 1919, age about 19 years, one of the decedents.

(8) Nellie Wolf, living, age about 16 or 17 years.

(9) There was one died in infancy, right after she was born. These are all they ever had.

Q. Did Peter Wolf ever have any children by any other woman besides Margaret Wolf?
A. No.

Q. Did he adopt a child? A. No.

Q. Were any of the deceased children of Peter Wolf ever married or did any of them ever have any children? A. None of them were ever married and none of them had children.

Q. Where does Margaret Wolf live now? A. She lives on her deceased husband's allotment where he died.

Q. Has she made that her home all the time since he died? A. Yes.

Q. Who were Peter Wolf's father and mother? A. His father's name was Woman's Breast and his mother's name I do not remember but I knew her.

Q. How and when were they married? A. I don't know that but it must have been by Indian custom long ago.

Q. What tribe did they belong to? A. Cheyenne River Sioux.

Q. Are they living or dead? A. Both dead.

Q. When did they die? A. His father died before allotments and his mother died after allotments.

Q. Were they allotted? A. His mother was allotted but his father was not.

Q. Did Peter Wolf have any brothers or sisters? A. He has a brother named Leo Combing, living, and a sister, Mrs. Clown or Iron Cedar, living, and he had a brother named Bear Pipe, who died before allotments.

Q. How old are the ones that are living? A. Leo Combing is about 67 or 68 and Mrs. Clown or Iron Cedar is about 52 years old.

Q. How old was Bear Pipe when he died? A. He was about 35 years old when he died and died about 30 years ago.

Q. Did Bear Pipe ever have any children by any woman? A. No, he never did.

Q. Do you know anything more about the family history of Peter Wolf? A. That is about all I know about it. I know that when Peter Wolf died he left a wife, Margaret Wolf and two children, Joshua Wolf and Nellie Wolf, and after Joshua died without being married and without issue and left a mother, Margaret Wolf and a sister, Nellie Wolf.

Q. Are you interested in these estates? A. No.

Q. How long did you know the decedents? A. I knew Peter Wolf about 50 years and Joshua all of his life.

Additional Family Probates

1) Iron Cedar aka Julia Clown

2) Combing aka Leo Combing

3) Old Eagle aka Amos Clown

4) Fights the Thunder

5) Mary Traversie

6) Peter Talks

7) Touch the Cloud

8) Two White Cows or Ida Crow

9) Edward Clown

10) Amy Talks Clown

11) Paul Touch the Cloud

12) Thomas (John) Standing Elk aka Shot at aka Stump

13) Edna Traversie Frazier Swift Horse

14) George Hunter

15) Blaine Edward Clown

UNITED STATES
DEPARTMENT OF THE INTERIOR
OFFICE OF INDIAN AFFAIRS
WASHINGTON

Estate of Iron Cedar or Mrs. Julia Clown

Mr. Paul L. Hallam, Examiner of Inheritance.
Mr. Walter F. Dickens, Supt., Cheyenne River Agency.
Amos Clown, Dupree, S. D.
TOPeter or Joseph Clown, Dupree, S. D.
Edward Clown, Dupree, S. D.
James Clown, Dupree, S.D.
Lillie or Mrs. James Makes Trouble, Dupree, S.D.
Louise or Mrs. Henry Red Bear, Dupree, S.D.
Sam Butcher for Louise or Esther Louise Butcher and Angelica Butcher, Lantry, S.D.

You are hereby notified that the final order was made in the above entitled estate by the Secretary of the Interior, on July 30, 1937 and a copy of said order was mailed to the Superintendent of the Cheyenne River Agency on the _____ day of August, 1937, where it may be inspected.

Under said order the will of December 17, 1928 was approved and heirs determined and the heirs of the estate as follows:

Amos Clown, C.R. #677, widower, ... 2/21
Joseph Peter Clown, C. R. #679, son, ...2/21
Lillie or Mrs. James Makes Trouble, nee Clown C.R.#681, dau . 2/21
James Clown, C. R. #733, son, ... 2/21
Louise or Mrs. Henry Red Bear, nee Clown, C. R. #2005, dau. . 2/21
Edward Clown, C. R. #2061, son, ... 2/21
Raymond Alex Clown, C. R. # 3317, son, ...2/21
Louise or Ethel Louise Butcher, C. R. #4450 (granddaughter representing prior deceased daughter, Mollie or Nellie Butcher, nee Clown), ... 1/21
Angelica or Angelica Methal Clown, C. R. #4697, ditto 1/21
Homestead rights in widower   Original allotment appraised at $1200.00
Cash, securities, etc   None   Inherited lands   "   500.00

Notice is here given that any interested party who was served with notice of the hearing or who was present at the hearing, and who may be dissatisfied with the said decision, and who may desire further proceedings herein, MUST file his petition for rehearing with the Examiner of Inheritance or the Commissioner of Indian Affairs, within sixty (60) days from the date hereof. Under the Rules, petitions filed after that date can not be considered.
Probate fee of $25 to be collected
For details consult Superintendent   Sincerely yours.

No payments made until
sixty days after this
Mailed -   date unless all parties   Acting
                             agree.   Commissioner.

September 8,   1937

(Signed) A. B. Melzner

All of the other facts pertinent to the disposition of decedent's estate are set forth in the accompanying Summary of Report on Heirs of the Examiner of Inheritance and the same have been verified in this office.

Respectfully,

(Signed) A. B. Melzner

7-Lem-23
6-25-24   Acting Commissioner.

The Honorable

The Secretary of the Interior.

Sir:

Submitted herewith are all papers connected with the probate of the estate of Iron Cedar or Mrs. Julia Clown, Allottee #2005 of the Cheyenne River Sioux Indian Tribe in the State of South Dakota, who died on July 10, 1936, at the age of 70 years.

With the record is an instrument executed by the decedent on December 17, 1928, as and for her last will and testament. The testimony of the attesting witnesses shows the decedent to have been of sound and disposing mind and memory at the time of the making and execution of this instrument and not to have been actuated by fraud, duress, undue influence, or coercion. The instrument appears to have been properly executed and attested. It is, therefore, recommended that the aforesaid will receive Departmental approval.

The will makes only a specific devise of a quarter section of decedent's allotment to her son, Joseph or Peter Clown, and the residue of her estate has not been disposed of. It appears, therefore, that a finding of heirship covering said residue, is required. The testimony shows that the decedent left as heirs, her husband, Amos Clown, entitled to 7/21 of her estate; the following children: Joseph or Peter Clown, son; Lillie or Mrs. James Makes Trouble, daughter; James Clown, son; Louise or Mrs. Henry Red Bear, daughter and Edward and Raymond Alex Clown, sons; each entitled to 2/21 of her estate and Ethel (Ethel Louise) Butcher and Methal (Angelica Methal) Butcher, granddaughters, who represent their mother, Nellie or Mollie or Mrs. Sam Butcher, daughter of decedent who died on November 11, 1930; each entitled to 1/21 of decedent's estate.

The NEᵢ of the SWᵢ and lots 3 and 4, containing 152.54 acres, was used by decedent as a home and her widower still resides there; hence, this tract descends subject to the homestead rights of Amos Clown until the same is otherwise disposed of according to law.

UNITED STATES
DEPARTMENT OF THE INTERIOR
OFFICE OF THE SECRETARY
WASHINGTON   2005

ORDER APPROVING WILL AND DETERMINING HEIRS
TO INTESTATE PART OF ESTATE

WHEREAS, Iron Cedar or Mrs. Julia Clown, allottee #2005 of the Cheyenne River Sioux Indian Tribe in the State of South Dakota, died on July 10, 1936 at the age of 70 years;

WHEREAS, a hearing was duly held at the Thunder Butte Station, Dupree, South Dakota, on April 20, 1937, and concluded at Cheyenne Agency, South Dakota, on May 10, 1937, for the purpose of ascertaining the heirs of the decedent and the facts and circumstances surrounding the execution of a certain instrument in writing of date of December 17, 1928, purporting to be the decedent's last will and testament;

WHEREAS, the will contains a specific devise and does not dispose of the residue of decedent's estate;

WHEREAS, the testimony of the attesting witnesses shows the decedent to have been of sound and disposing mind and memory, free from fraud, undue influence, duress or coercion; and this appears to be a proper will to receive Departmental approval;

NOW, THEREFORE, by virtue of the power and authority vested in the Secretary of the Interior by the act of June 25, 1910 (36 Stat. 855-86), as amended by the act of February 14, 1913 (37 Stat. 678), the above mentioned instrument in writing dated December 17, 1928, is hereby approved as the last will and testament of the decedent above named and I hereby find, adjudge, and declare that at the date of the conclusion of the above mentioned hearings the heirs of the decedent entitled to the residue of her estate not disposed of in said will and their respective shares therein, determined in accordance with the first canon of the laws of succession of the State of South Dakota, were, as follows:

Amos Clown, C. R. #677, widower, ... 7/21
Joseph Peter Clown, C. R. #679, son, ... 2/21
Lillie or Mrs. James Makes Trouble, nee Clown,
   C. R. #681, daughter, ... 2/21
James Clown, C. R. #735, son, ... 2/21
Louise or Mrs. Henry Red Bear, nee Clown,
   C. R. #2005, daughter, ... 2/21
Edward Clown, C. R. #2061, son, ... 2/21
Raymond Alex Clown, C. R. #3317, son, ... 2/21
Louise or Ethel Louise Butcher, C. R. #4450,
   granddaughter (representing prior deceased
   daughter, Mollie or Nellie Butcher, nee
   Clown), ... 1/21
Angelica or Angelica Bethel Clown, C. R. #4807,
   granddaughter (representing prior deceased
   daughter, Mollie or Nellie Butcher, nee
   Clown), ... 1/21

The SW¼ of the SW¼ and lots 3 and 4, containing 158.34
acres, used by decedent as a home and her widower still
resides there, hence, this tract descends subject to the homestead rights of Amos Clown until the same is otherwise disposed
of according to law.

The estate of the decedent subject to the jurisdiction of
this Department having been appraised at $1700, a fee of $25
will be collected by the Superintendent or other officer in
charge pursuant to authority found in the act of January 24,
1923 (42 Stat, 1185).

Done at the city of Washington, District of Columbia, and
dated _____ JUL 30 1937 _____

                (Sgd.) Oscar L. Chapman

6-HE-24   Assistant Secretary.

5-107   Sheet 1

UNITED STATES
DEPARTMENT OF THE INTERIOR
OFFICE OF INDIAN AFFAIRS
FIELD SERVICE

Pierre, South Dakota
JUN 24 1937 , 19

SUMMARY OF REPORT ON HEIRS

Estate of __Iron Cedar or Mrs. Julia Clown__, deceased __Cheyenne River Sioux__

Allottee No. __2005__, died __July 10, 1936__, aged __70__ yrs. hearing concluded

at __Cheyenne Agency, S. Dak.__, on May 10, 1937.

Heirs, at the date of hearing, in accordance with the laws of the State of __South Dakota__, in the first canon of descent:

Heir or Devisee	Relationship	Share
Amos Clown, C. R. #677, widower,		7/21
Joseph Peter Clown, C. R. #679, son,		2/21
Lillie or Mrs. James Makes Trouble, nee Clown, C. R. #681, daughter,		2/21
James Clown, C. R. #735, son,		2/21
Louise or Mrs. Henry Red Bear, nee Clown, C. R. #2005, daughter,		2/21
Edward Clown, C. R. #2061, son,		2/21
Raymond Alex Clown, C. R. #3317, son,		2/21
Louise or Ethel Louise Butcher, C. R. #4450, granddaughter representing prior deceased daughter, Mollie or Nellie Butcher, nee Clown,		1/21
Angelica or Angelica Bethel Clown, C. R. #4807, granddaughter, representing prior deceased daughter, Mollie or Nellie Butcher, nee Clown,		1/21

Original allotment, appraised at _____ $ 1200.00

Inherited lands, appraised at _____ 500.00

Cash, securities, or other personal restricted estate appraised at ____ None

Total _____ $ 1700.00

No dower, curtesy, or homestead rights involved.

                        F. L. Hallam, Examiner of Inheritance.

Verified _____ JUL 24 1937 ____, 19____

By _____
          Chief, Probate Division

ESTATE, as far as known, under Government control. (If inherited property is not partitioned, describe all and give proportion. If heirs have not been determined, describe property in which decedent had an apparent interest.)

REAL PROPERTY. (Original and inherited. Describe original on first line.)

No.	Name of Allottee	Description of Land, Date of Trust Patent, and Under Which Allotted	Date	Serial No.
2005	Mrs. Iron Cedar or Julia Clown	N½ of W½ and lots 1, 2, 3, and 4 of Sec. 31 T. 15 N. of R. 31, E. of the S. H. M. in South Dakota, containing 310.49 acres, for which trust patent issued on December 9, 1909, under the act of March 3, 1889 (25 Stat. 888), as amended. The trust period covering this allotment was extended for 10 years by Executive Order dated December 13, 1933. This tract is suitable for farming and grazing and valued at $1200.		
		See Sheet 1-a for inherited interests.		

PERSONAL PROPERTY.

Amount	Source	Where Deposited
None		

PROPERTY DISPOSED OF BY WILL. (Included in property hereinbefore described.)

Date of will _____ 19____ Date of departmental approval _____ 19____ Serial No. ____

Devisee	Relationship to Devisor	Description of Property
Will dated December 17, 1928 accompanies this report.		

                                     Sheet 1-a

INHERITED INTERESTS OF IRON CEDAR OR MRS. JULIA CLOWN,
C. R. #2005

FRACTIONAL SHARE	ESTATE AND APPRAISEMENT	VALUE OF DECEDENT'S SHARE
1/2	Lillie Clown, C. R. #2063 (81846-20), described as the SE¼ of Sec. 6, T. 14 N. of R. 21 E. of the B. H. M. in South Dakota, containing 160 acres, being farming and grazing land valued at $600,	$ 300.00
1/3	By devise, Moses Clown or Running Eagle, C. R. #678 (18705-21), described as the N½ of Sec. 36 T. 16 N. of R. 20 E. of the B. H. M. in South Dakota, containing 160 acres, being farming and grazing land valued at $600,	200.00

TOTAL VALUE OF INHERITED INTERESTS, ... $ 500.00

FAMILY OF DECEASED. (Extra sheets may be used for family of deceased heirs, but the word "heir" and his name must appear after the words "Family of Deceased.")

MARRIAGES.

NAME OR EACH SPOUSE OF DECEASED	Married Date	Married Indian custom or by ceremony	DATE OF DEATH	Divorced Date	Divorced Indian custom or by ceremony	THESE AND ALLOTMENT NO. (If white, so state)
Amos Clown	about 1883	church ceremony	living	not divorced		C.R. #677

Previous marriage of any spouse of deceased—none

CHILDREN.

NAMES	SEX AND AGE	NAME OF OTHER PARENT* (If adopted or illegitimate, so state)	IF CHILD IS DEAD GIVE DATE
Joseph or Peter Clown	M. B.1894	Amos Clown	living
Lillie (Mrs. James) Makes Trouble, nee Clown	F. 38 yrs.	do	do
James Clown	M. 36 yrs.	do	do
Louise (Mrs. Henry) Red Bear, nee Clown	F. 33 yrs.	do	do
Edward Clown	M. 29 yrs.	do	do
Raymond Alex Clown	M. 25 yrs.	do	do
Mollie or Nellie (Mrs. Sam) Butcher	F. B.1895	do	Nov. 11, 1930

"Under "Additional information" show facts with regard to fathers of illegitimate children and concerning adoption.

CHILDREN OF DECEASED CHILDREN.

NAMES OF GRANDCHILDREN	SEX AND AGE	NAMES OF BOTH PARENTS, HOW MARRIED—INDIAN CUSTOM OR CEREMONY (If one is white, so state)	IF GRANDCHILD IS DEAD, GIVE DATE
Louise or Ethel Louise Butcher	F. B.1924	Mollie or Nellie Butcher, m. Sam Butcher, f. Married by ceremony Dec. ?, 1922	living
Angelica or Angeline Nethel Butcher	F. B.1925	do	do

PARENTS OF DECEDENT. (If either is white, or of a different tribe, so state.)

NAMES	Allotment No.	Allotment Date	Married Date	Married Indian custom or ceremony	IF EITHER IS DEAD, GIVE DATE	TRIBE
Father: Woman Breast					long ago	
Mother: Red Legs					do	

OTHER LINEAL DESCENDANTS OF DECEDENT. (Identify persons named by allotment number, or by number on annuity roll on which last paid, describing voucher. Designate parents and grandparents through which heir inherits by letters *f, m, gf, gm, ggf, ggm*, etc.)

NAME OF DESCENDANT WHO SURVIVED DECEDENT (If dead, give date; and give family surviving on extra sheet)	AGE	NAMES OF PARENTS AND GRANDPARENTS OF DESCENDANT
None		

BROTHERS AND SISTERS.

NAMES	BROTHER OR SISTER	AGE	NAME OF COMMON PARENT IF NOT OF WHOLE BLOOD	IF BROTHER OR SISTER IS DEAD, GIVE DATE
Immaterial				

ISSUE OF DECEASED BROTHERS OR SISTERS.

NAME OF NEPHEW OR NIECE	SEX AND AGE	NAMES OF PARENTS, AND HOW MARRIED	IF CHILD IS DEAD, GIVE DATE
Immaterial			

PARENTS OF DECEDENT. (If either is white, or of a different tribe, so state.)

NAMES	Allotment No.	Allotment Date	Married Date	Married Indian custom or ceremony	IF EITHER IS DEAD, GIVE DATE	TRIBE
Father: Woman Breast					long ago	
Mother: Red Legs					do	

OTHER LINEAL DESCENDANTS OF DECEDENT. (Identify persons named by allotment number, or by number on annuity roll on which last paid, describing voucher. Designate parents and grandparents through which heir inherits by letters *f, m, gf, gm, ggf, ggm*, etc.)

NAME OF DESCENDANT WHO SURVIVED DECEDENT (If dead, give date; and give family surviving on extra sheet)	AGE	NAMES OF PARENTS AND GRANDPARENTS OF DESCENDANT
None		

BROTHERS AND SISTERS.

NAMES	BROTHER OR SISTER	AGE	NAME OF COMMON PARENT IF NOT OF WHOLE BLOOD	IF BROTHER OR SISTER IS DEAD, GIVE DATE
Immaterial				

ISSUE OF DECEASED BROTHERS OR SISTERS.

NAME OF NEPHEW OR NIECE	SEX AND AGE	NAMES OF PARENTS, AND HOW MARRIED	IF CHILD IS DEAD, GIVE DATE
Immaterial			

GRANDPARENTS OF DECEDENT. (If any are white, so state.)

NAMES OF FATHER'S AND MOTHER'S PARENTS	Married Date	Married Indian custom or ceremony	TRIBE	IF DEAD, GIVE DATE
Paternal gf, Immaterial				
Paternal gm, "				
Maternal gf, "				
Maternal gm, "				

COLLATERAL RELATIVES. (Give line of descent from common ancestor of decedent; give names and designate parents and grandparents of heir, in line (from common ancestor by letters *f, m, gf, ggm, ggf, ggm*, etc. Identify by allotment No. or by number on annuity roll on which last paid.)

NAME OF NEAREST RELATIVE WHO SURVIVED DECEDENT	IF DEAD, GIVE DATE; AND THE EXTRA SHEETS FOR SURVIVING FAMILY	HOW RELATED TO COMMON DECEDENT	AMOUNT OF LINE FROM COMMON ANCESTOR
Immaterial			

ADDITIONAL INFORMATION: None

CONFLICT between the official record and the testimony. (If any, give description; if no conflict, say "none.")   None

---

ESTATE, so far as known, under Government control. (If inherited property is not partitioned, describe all and give proportion. If heirs have not been determined, describe property in which decedent had an apparent interest.)

REAL PROPERTY. (Original and inherited. Describe original on first line.)

No.	Name of allottee	Description of Land, Date of Trust Patent, And Under Which Allotted	Heirs Found by Department	
			Date	Serial No.
2005	Mrs. Iron Cedar or Julia Clown	N½ of W½ and lots 1, 2, 3, and 4 of Sec. 31 T. 15 N. of R. 21, E. of the B. H. M. in South Dakota, containing 310.48 acres, for which trust patent issued on December 9, 1909, under the act of March 2, 1889 (25 Stat. 888), as amended. The trust period covering this allotment was extended for 10 years by Executive Order dated December 15, 1933. This tract is suitable for farming and grazing and valued at $1200.		

See Sheet 1-a for inherited interests.

PERSONAL PROPERTY.

Amount	Source	Where Deposited
None		

PROPERTY DISPOSED OF BY WILL. (Included in property hereinbefore described.)

Date of will _____ 19___ Date of departmental approval _____ 19___ Serial No. _____

Devisee	Relationship to Devisor	Description of Property

Will dated December 17, 1928 accompanies this report.

UNITED STATES
DEPARTMENT OF THE INTERIOR
OFFICE OF INDIAN AFFAIRS
FIELD SERVICE

Pierre, South Dakota,

April 24, 1934 _____ 19___

SUMMARY OF REPORT ON HEIRS

Estate of Leo Combing, or Combing, _____ deceased Cheyenne River

Allottee No. 1466 ____ died Nov. 3, 1932 ___ aged 65 yrs., hearing XXX concluded at Cherry Creek, South Dakota, on Oct. 23, 1933, original hearing having been held at Eagle Butte, S. D., on Oct. 24, 1933.

Heirs, at the date of hearing, in accordance with the laws of the State of South Dakota.

Heirs Determined	Relationship	Share
Charles Combing, C. R. #1470, son.		1/4
Frances Combing, now Mrs. Joseph New Black Bear, C. R. #1471, daughter.		1/4
Jane Top of Lodge (Jennie Lodge) or Mrs. Frank Combing, C. R. #2021, wife of subsequently deceased son (Frank Combing).		1/4
Angeline White Wing or Mrs. Tincup, C. R. #1472, adopted daughter.		1/4

The Supt. recommends the payment in full of the claim of W. M. Griffiths & Co. (Licensed Indian Trader) of Cherry Creek, S. D., in the amount of $31.50. It appears, also, that decedent's coffin was purchased from the reimbursable fund Int. Chey.Riv.Res. 35 Fund (Support. 1935) this should be repaid.

The trust or restricted estate of the decedent consists of:

Original allotment, appraised at	$3200.00
Inherited lands, appraised at	$2133.35
Cash, securities, or other personal restricted estate appraised at	96.00
Total	$5429.35

No dower, curtesy, or homestead rights involved.

P. L. Hallam
F. L. Hallam _____, Examiner of Inheritances.

Verified _____ 19___

By _____
Chief, Probate Division.

ESTATE, so far as known, under Government control. (If inherited property is not partitioned, describe all and give proportion. If heirs have not been determined, describe property in which decedent had an apparent interest.)

REAL PROPERTY. (Original and inherited. Describe original on first line.)

No.	Name of allottee	Description of Land, Date of Trust Patent, And Under Which Allotted	Heirs Found by Department	
			Date	Serial No.
1466	Combing (Leo)	W½ of Sec. 27, E½ Sec. 28, T. 14 N. of R. 22 E. of the B.H.M., in So. Dak., containing 640 acres for which trust patent issued on Feb. 8, 1909, under act of March 2, 1889 (25 Stat. 888), as amended. The trust period on this tract has been extended ten years by Executive Order dated Dec. 15, 1933. This tract is level to slightly rolling prairie suitable for farming, hay, and grazing and the estimated value is $3200.		

For Inherited Interests, see Sheet 1-a

PERSONAL PROPERTY.

Amount	Source	Where Deposited
96.00	Individual Indian money.	Supervisor, Supt., Cheyenne River Indian Agency, S. D.

PROPERTY DISPOSED OF BY WILL. (Included in property hereinbefore described.)

Date of will _____ 19___ Date of departmental approval _____ 19___ Serial No. _____

Devisee	Relationship to Devisor	Description of Property
No Will involved.		

FAMILY OF DECEASED. (Extra sheets may be used for family of deceased heirs, but the word "heir" and his name must appear after the words "Family of Deceased.")

MARRIAGES.

Name of Each Spouse of Decedent	Married		Divorced		There are Also Children by Deceased	
	Date	Indian custom or by licence	Date of Death	Date	Indian custom or by licence	(If white, so state)
Name unknown, but an Oglala (Pineridge) woman.	Long before allotment	Ind. Cust.	Unknown	Long before allot- ment	Ind. Cust.	Oglala Sioux
Julia Rushes	do.	do.	Jan.24, 1932	Not divorced		Chey.Riv. #1480
Jennie Iron House or Julia Iron Lodge (Plural)	do.	do.	1934	Not divorced		Chey.Riv. #2009

Positive identity of two spouses of decedent unsure

CHILDREN.

Names	Sex and Age	Name of Other Parent (If Adopted or Illegitimate, so state)	If Child is Dead, Give Date
Name Unknown.	M. small child	First wife, an Oglala woman.	Long before decedent.
Name unknown	small child	Jennie Iron House	do.
Frank Combing *	M. born 1890	do.	Sep.30, 1933
Charles Combing	M. " 1892	do.	Living
Frances Combing or Mrs. Joseph New BlackBear, now Mrs. Tincup.	F. " 1895	do.	do.
Angeline White Wing,	F. " 1900	Adopted by decedent and Julia Rushes by Indian Custom in 1907.	do.

* also known as Freemont Combing.

"Under "Additional information" show facts with regard to failure of illegitimate children and concerning adoption.

CHILDREN OF DECEASED CHILDREN.

Names of Grandchildren	Sex and Age	Names of Both Parents, Both Marriages— Indian Custom or Ceremony? (If one is white, so state)	If Grandchild is Dead, Give Date
None survived, although Frank or Freemont Combing had several children from his marriage to Jane Top of Lodge or Jennie Lodge whom he married about 1915 and with whom he lived until his death as shown above. All of these children predeceased allottee without issue.			

PARENTS OF DECEDENT. (If either is white, or of a different tribe, so state.)

Names	Allotment No.	Date	Marriage Date	Indian custom or ceremony	If Either is Dead, Give Date	Tribe
Father: **Not disclosed in evidence.**						
Mother: do.						

OTHER LINEAL DESCENDANTS OF DECEDENT. (Identify persons named by allotment number, or by number on annuity roll on which last paid, describing voucher. Designate parents and grandparents through their inheritance by letters f, m, gf, gm, ggf, ggm, etc.)

Name of Descendant Who Survived Decedent (If dead, give date, and give family surviving on extra sheet)	Age	Names of Parents and Grandparents of Descendant
None.		

BROTHERS AND SISTERS.

Names	Brother or Sister	Age	Name of Common Parent if Not of Whole Blood	If Brother or Sister is Dead, Give Date
Not disclosed in evidence.				

ISSUE OF DECEASED BROTHERS OR SISTERS.

Name of Nephew or Niece	Sex and Age	Names of Parents, and How Married	If Child is Dead, Give Date
Not disclosed in evidence.			

GRANDPARENTS OF DECEDENT. (If any are white, so state.)

Name of Father's and Mother's Parents	Marriage Date	Indian custom or ceremony	Tribe	If Dead, Give Date
Paternal gf. **Unknown.**				
Paternal gm. "				
Maternal gf. "				
Maternal gm. "				

COLLATERAL RELATIVES. (Give line of descent from common ancestor of decedent; give names and designate parents and grandparents of heir, in line from common ancestor by letters f, m, gf, gm, ggf, ggm, etc. Identify by allotment No. or by number on annuity roll on which last paid.)

Name of Nearest Relative Who Survived Decedent	If Dead, Give Date and the Extra Sheets for Surviving Family	How Related to Decedent—Degree	Amount of Loss from Common Ancestor
Unknown.			

ADDITIONAL INFORMATION. **None.**

CONFLICT between the official record and the testimony. (If any, give description; if no conflict, say "none.") **None.**

Docket
21-47

L W

UNITED STATES
DEPARTMENT OF THE INTERIOR
OFFICE OF INDIAN AFFAIRS
FIELD SERVICE
Bismarck, North Dakota

JAN 2333

July 25, 19 47

SUMMARY OF REPORT ON HEIRS

Estate of _____ Amos Clown _____, deceased Cheyenne River Sioux

Allot. No. 677, died July 22, 1943, aged 81, hearing held May 28, 1946

Thunder Butte Substation, Cheyenne River Agency.

Heirs, at the date of hearing, in accordance with the laws of the State of South Dakota:

Heirs or Devisees	Relationship	Share
Peter or Joseph Clown, C.R. al. 679,	son,	6/42
James Clown, C.R. al. 733,	son,	6/42
Lillie Clown or Mrs. Henry Red Bear, C.R. al. 2085,	dau.,	6/42
Louise Clown, C.R. al. 2061,	son,	6/42
Raymond Alex Clown, C.R. al. 3517,	son,	6/42
Louise or Ethel Butcher, C.R. al. 4450, dau. of pre-dec. dau., Mollie Clown Butcher,	gr.-dau.,	3/42
Angelica Mathel Butcher, C.R. al. 4697, " "	gr.-dau.,	3/42
Lorraine Makes Trouble, Standing Rock Sr. 2147, dau. of predec. dau., Mrs. James Makes Trouble,	gr.-dau.,	2/42

The restricted estate of the decedent consists of:

Allotment, appraised at	$ 1920.00
Funds, appraised at	1328.67
Stock, or other personal restricted estate appraised at	365.66
	$ 3614.33

No trustee, or homestead rights involved.

E. J. Welch,
E. J. Welch, Superintendent Examiner of Inheritance.

19

_____
Chief, Probate Division.   [over]

FAMILY OF DECEASED. (Extra sheets may be used for family of deceased heirs, but the word "heir" and his name must appear after the words "Family of Deceased.")

MARRIAGES.

Name of Each Spouse of Deceased	Married Date	Indian custom or by ceremony	Date of Death	Divorced Date	Indian custom or by court	Tribe and Allotment No. (if white, so state)
Iron Cedar	abt.1883	ceremony	7-10-36	Not divorced		C.R. 2005

CHILDREN.

Names	Sex and Age	Name of Other Parent (If adopted or illegitimate, so state)	If Child is Dead, Give Date
Peter or Joseph Clown	m. b. 1894	Iron Cedar	living
Lillie Clown Makes Trouble	f. b. 1879	" "	Living 2-22-42
James Clown	m. b. 1901	" "	living
Louise Clown Red Bear	f. b. 1904	" "	living
Edward Clown	m. b. 1906	" "	living
Mollie(Mollie) Clown	f. b. 1896	" "	1930
Raymond Alex Clown	m. b. 1914	" "	living
Moses Clown	m. b. ----	" "	b.1918
Lillie R. Clown	f. b. ----	" "	1937

CHILDREN OF DECEASED CHILDREN.

Names of Grandchildren	Sex and Age	Names of Both Parents, (For Maternal—Infant Clown on Clown) if one is white so state	If Grandchild is Dead, Give Date
Lorraine Makes Trouble	f. b. 1925	Lillie Clown & Makes Trouble ceremony	living
Esther Makes Trouble	f. b. 2-23-30	" "	living
Lenny Lois Makes Trouble	f. b. 6-4-36	" "	living
Louise or Ethel Butcher	f. b. 1924	Mollie Clown and Samuel Butcher & ceremony	living
Angelica Mathel Butcher	f. b. 1925	" "	living

PARENTS OF DECEDENT. (If either is white, or of a different tribe, so state.)

Names	Allotment No.	Date	Marriage Date	Indian custom or ceremony	If Dead or Living, Give Date	Tribe
Father: Fights The Thunder	541		long ago	evidently I.C.	about 1927	G.R.Sx.
Mother: Thin Out or Rail	Unal		" "	" "	bef. allote.	C.R.Sx.

OTHER LINEAL DESCENDANTS OF DECEDENT. (Identify persons named by allotment number, or by number on annuity roll on which last paid, describing voucher. Designate parents and grandparents through which heir inherits by letters f, m, gf, gm, ggf, ggm, etc.)

Name of Descendant Who Survived Decedent (If dead, give date; and give heirs surviving on this sheet)	Age	Names of Parents and Grandparents of Descendant
Immaterial		

BROTHERS AND SISTERS.

Names	Brother or Sister	Age	Name of Common Parent if None or Whole Blood	If Deceased or Basis if Dead, Give Date
Red Bird or Paul Red Bird	brother	adult	Fights The Thunder	3-4-33
Mrs. Poor Buffalo or Grows In a Day	sister	"	" " "	living

ISSUE OF DECEASED BROTHERS OR SISTERS.

Name of Nephew or Niece	Sex and Age	Name of Parent, and How Married	If Child is Dead, Give Date
Maggie Elk Nation	f. adult	Red Bird & Her Door - core	living
Mrs. Mollie Corn	f. adult	" " " "	d-24-37
George Red Bird	m. adult	" " " "	living
Roger Red Bird	m. adult	" " " "	living
Simon Red Bird	m. adult	" " " "	living
William Red Bird	m. adult	" " " "	living
Anna Red Bird	f. adult	" " " "	living

GRANDPARENTS OF DECEDENT. (If any are white, so state.)

Name of Father's and Mother's Parents	Married Date	Indian custom or ceremony	Tribe	If Dead, Give Date
(Paternal gf. ... Unknown				
(Paternal gm. ... "				
(Maternal gf. ... "				
(Maternal gm. ... "				

COLLATERAL RELATIVES. (Give line of descent from common ancestor of decedent; give names and designate parents and grandparents of heir, in line from common ancestor by letters f, m, gf, gm, ggf, ggm, etc. Identify by allotment No. or by number on annuity roll on which last paid.)

Name of Nearest Relatives Who Survive Decedent	If Dead, Give Date; and The Total Share in Surviving Family	How Related to Decedent-Degree	Ancestry in Line from Common Ancestor
Immaterial			

ADDITIONAL INFORMATION. descent of this estate would be governed by Subsec. 1, Sec. 56.0104, South Dakota Revised Code, 1939

Probate regulations on reopenings and rehearings explained to all persons present at the hearing.

Funeral expenses from relief funds - no claim involved.

The following debts are of record against the estate:

$ 248.79 - Reimbursable indebtedness owing the United States.

$ 92.75 - Department of Social Security, State of South Dakota, covering old age assistance grants made to the decedent/

CONFLICT between the official record and the testimony. (If any, give description; if no conflict, say "none.") None

---

DATA FOR HEIRSHIP FINDING AND FAMILY HISTORY
CONTINUATION SHEET

CHILDREN OF DECEASED BROTHERS AND SISTERS continued:

Name	Sex	Birth	Name of Parents, and How Married	Death/Living	CRU No.
Iola Bernice Clown	F	07-03-26	James Clown & Mary Red Bear	03-21-27	CR-4723
Pearl Jane Clown	F	01-07-28	* * * * & * * * *	infant	DBE
True V. Clown	M	03-22-30	* * * * & Anan Red Bird Living		CR-5220
Reta M. Clown	F	12-04-31	* * * * * * * *	05-10-34	CR-5416
June Clown	M	05-24-33	* * * * * * * *	05-13-34	CR-5649
Alma R. Clown	F	10-07-34	* * * * * * * *	Living	CRU-5842
Betty Lou Clown	F	10-26-36	* * * * * * * *	Living	CRU-6100
Mary M. Clown	F	06-02-38	* * * * * * * *	Living	CRU-6308
Carlin J. Clown	M	03-04-40	* * * * * * * *	Living	CRU-6500
Phoebe L. Clown	F	10-01-41	* * * * * * * *	Living	CRU-6706
Stewart M. Clown	M	03-01-43	* * * * * * * *	12-10-66	CRU-6840
Carol S. Clown	F	08-23-45	* * * * * * * *	Living	CRU-7067
Yvonne Kay Clown	F	06-05-47	* * * * * * * *	Living	CRU-7234
Richard D. Clown	M	11-09-48	* * * * * * * *	Living	CRU-7409
Patricia A. Clown	F	04-25-50	* * * * * * * *	Living	CRU-7572
Roland L. Clown	M	01-04-52	* * * * * * * *	Living	CRU-7636
Louise Ethel Butcher	F	1924	Mollie Clown & Samuel Butcher	Living	CR-4450
Angelica Methel Butcher	F	1925	* * * * * * * *	Living	CR-4697
Dorothy Red Bear	F	07-30-27	Louise Clown & Henry Red Bear	06-29-29	CR-5626
Lila Lee Red Bear	F	11-26-28	* * * * * * * *	Living	CRU-13774
Manuel Joseph Red Bear	M	10-24-33	* * * * * * * *	02-07-84	CR-5627
Wayne Chris Red Bear	M	01-07-37	* * * * * * * *	11-07-54	CRU-5919
Loretta Red Bear	F	11-14-38	* * * * * * * *	Living	CRU-6146
John Red Bear	M	11-14-38	* * * * * * * *	04-30-77	CRU-6349
William I. Red Bear	M	01-13-40	* * * * * * * *	Living	CRU-6451

DATA FOR HEIRSHIP FINDING AND FAMILY HISTORY
CONTINUATION SHEET

CHILDREN OF DECEASED BROTHERS AND SISTERS continued:

Name	Sex	Birth	Name of Parents, and How Married	Death/Living	CRU No.
Rose Ann Red Bear	F	09-16-41	Louise Clown & Andrew Red Bear	Living	CRU-6701
Louis Dale Red Bear	M	04-26-43	* * * * * * * A * * * *	06-23-44	CRU-6856
Mary Jane Red Bear	F	11-30-44	* * * * * * * A * * * *	01-20-45	CRU-6998
Hilmar Henry Red Bear	M	12-10-45	* * * * * * * A * * * *	11-07-63	CRU-7085
Kevin Charles Red Bar	M	07-23-47	* * * * * * * A * * * *	Living	CRU-7247
Zerilda LaRay Clown/Boone	F	11-11-35	Raymond Alex Clown & Sarah Marrowbone	Living	CRU-5986
Arnold Kenneth Clown	M	12-01-36	* * * * * * * A * * * *	Living	CRU-6138
Eldon Kent Clown	M	02-24-38	* * * * * * * A * * * *	Living	CRU-6273
Richard Ronald Clown	M	06-30-39	* * * * * * * A * * * *	05-11-66	CRU-6417
Kermit Delbert Clown	M	01-20-43	* * * * * * * A * * * *	04-17-63	CRU-6832
Imogene Rose Clown	F	01-31-44	* * * * * * * A * * * *	Living	CRU-6929
Lynn Yvette Clown	F	11-13-68	* * * * * * * A & Beatrice Little Dog	Living	CRU-10471

S-106 c

DATA FOR HEIRSHIP FINDING.

Allottee. Fights Thunder .... Age About 67

Date of death May 16, 1916 ....

Allotment No. 541 .... Annuity No. 343 .... Vou. 77 4th Qr. 1919 ....

Description of land W/2 & SE/4, Sec. 36, T. 15 N., and S/2 of NW/4 &
Lots 3 and 4 of Sec. 1, T. 14 N., R. 20 N. of B.H.M. of S.D. 639.79
acres.

Date of patent May 11, 1906 ....

Act under which allotted March 2, 1889(25 Stat. L., 888) ....

Father's name Red Thunder .... Allotment No. None

Mother's name Iron Branch or Melt .... Allotment No. None
(1) Name unknown

Spouse's name (2) Pasala or Plain Cut or Bail or .... Allotment No. "
Rotation,

Personal property. $255. Lease and interest. ....

PROBABLE HEIRS.   ADDRESSES.

Red Bird, or Tail Red Bird,   Dupree, S. D.

Clown or Amos Clown,   "   "   "
Mrs. Poor Buffalo or
Grows in a Day,   "   "   "

S-107, Sheet 1.

CHILDREN OF DECEASED CHILDREN.

NAMES OF GRANDCHILDREN.	SEX AND AGE	NAMES OF BOTH PARENTS, HOW MARRIED—INDIAN CUSTOM OR CEREMONY. (If either is white, or state.)	IF GRANDCHILD IS DEAD, GIVE DATE.
Unnamed	M- Infant	Following or Noise, Bad Boy or War Bonnet)I.C. Bef.Altmts.	
Unnamed	M- "	Same parents.	"
Unnamed	M- "	" "	" "
Unnamed	F- "	" "	" "
		" "	

PARENTS OF DECEDENT. (If either is white, or of a different tribe, so state.)

	ALLOTMENT.		MARRIED.			IF DEAD
NAMES.	No.	Date.	No.	Date.	Indian custom or ceremony.	IF DEAD, GIVE DATE. TRIBE.
Father Red Thunder	None		Bef. Altmts.		I.C.	Bef.Altmts.,F.R.S.
Iron Branch or Melt	None		" "		"	" "

BROTHERS AND SISTERS.

NAMES.	BROTHER OR SISTER.	AGE.	NAME OF COMMON PARENT OR NOT, OR WHOLE BLOOD.	IF BROTHER OR SISTER IS DEAD, GIVE DATE.
Iron Branch	Sister	70		About 1897

ISSUE OF DECEASED BROTHERS OR SISTERS.

NAME OF NEPHEW OR NIECE.	SEX AND AGE.	NAME OF PARENTS, AND HOW MARRIED.	IF CHILD IS DEAD, GIVE DATE.
Running At Him	M- unknown	Six Feet)Iron Branch)I.C.	Unknown
Day	F- "	Same parents.	"
Crane	F- "	" "	"
White Track	F- "	" "	"

OTHER LINEAL DESCENDANTS OF DECEDENT. (Identify persons named by allotment number, or by number on annuity roll on which last paid, describing voucher. Designate parents and grandparents through which heir inherits by letters f, m, gf, gm, pgf, ppo, etc.)

NAME OF DESCENDANT WHO SURVIVED DECEDENT. (If dead, give date, and give family surviving on extra sheets.)	AGE.	NAMES OF PARENTS AND GRANDPARENTS OF DESCENDANT.
None		

GRANDPARENTS OF DECEDENT. (If any are white, so state.)

NAMES OF FATHER'S AND MOTHER'S PARENTS.	MARRIED.		TRIBE.	IF DEAD, GIVE DATE.
	Date.	Indian custom or ceremony.		
Paternal gf. Unknown				
Paternal gm. Unknown				
Maternal gf. Unknown				
Maternal gm. Unknown				

COLLATERAL RELATIVES. (Give line of descent from common ancestor of decedent; give names and designate parents and grandparents of heir in line from common ancestor by letters f, m, gf, gm, pgf, ppo, etc. Identify by allotment No. or by number on annuity roll on which last paid.)

NAMES OF NEAREST COLLATERAL WHO SURVIVED DECEDENT.	IF DEAD, GIVE DATE, AND THE EXTRA SHEETS AND SURVIVING FAMILY.	HOW RELATED TO DECEDENT—DEGREE.	AMOUNT OF LINE FROM COMMON ANCESTOR.
None			

S-107, Sheet 2.

ADDITIONAL INFORMATION: No homestead rights involved.

CONFLICT between the official record and the testimony. (If any, give description; if no conflict, say "none.") None

I hereby certify that I have made a careful investigation as to the relatives of the decedent; that my report is correct and substantiated by official records and by the testimony taken at a hearing held on June 17, 1920 , 19 , under the provisions of the act of June 25, 1910 (36 Stats., 855), and that it appears that at time of the hearing the heirs of the decedent,

Fights Thunder .... and the descent of the estate are as follows:

HEIRS OF DECEDENT. (Designate which.)	RELATIONSHIP TO DECEDENT.	DESCRIPTION OF PROPERTY. (Real estate or personal property.)	PROPORTION TAKEN BY TENANT, DISTRIBUTEE, OR HEIRS.
Tail Red Bird or Red Bird	Son	See page one	1/3
Clown or Amos Clown	Son		1/3
Mrs. Poor Buffalo or Grows in a day,	Dau.		1/3

M. E. Gorman
M. E. Gorman,
Examiner of Inheritance.

(Official designation.)

REPORT ON HEIRSHIP.

(IMPORTANT—See instructions on back of last sheet.)

Cheyenne River _____ AGENCY,

June 17, 1920. ___ 191

Decedent __Fights Thunder__ _____ Tribe __Cheyenne River Sioux__

Allotment No. __541__, Annuity Roll No. __343__, Voucher No. __77__ 4th Qr. 1915

State of domicile at time of death __South Dakota.__, Date of death __May 16, 1915__

Age __About 87__, Location of real property, State of __South Dakota__

ESTATE, so far as known, under Government control. (If inherited property is not partitioned, describe all and give proportion. If heirs have not been determined, describe property in which decedent had an apparent interest.)

REAL PROPERTY. (Original and inherited. Describe original on first line.)

No.	Name of Allottee	Description of Land, Date of Each Patent, and Under Which Allotted.	Heirs Found by Department. Date.	Serial No.
541	Fights Thunder	W/2 & SW/4, Sec. 36, T. 15 N. and S/2 of NW/4 and Lots 3 and 4 of Sec. 1, T. 14 N. R. 20 E. of B.H.M. of S.D. containing 639.79 acres.		
		Trust patent dated May 11, 1905. Allotted under Act of March 2, 1889(25 Stat. L., 888).		
		No apparent and no inherited interests.		

PERSONAL PROPERTY.

Amount.	Source.	Where Deposited.
$353.72	Lease and interest	Depository undesignated.

FAMILY OF DECEASED. (Extra sheets may be used for family of deceased heirs, but the word "heir" and his name must appear after the words "Family of Decedent.")

MARRIAGES.

Name of Each Spouse of Decedent.	Married	Date of Death.	Divorced	From and Against Whom No. (If white, so state.)
	Date.	Indian custom or by whom.		Date.	Indian custom or by whom.	
① Name unknown	Long Bef.Altmts.	I.C.	Bef. Altmts.	No divorce	C.R.S. None
② Masala or Thin Out or Rail or Rotation	" " "	I.C.	" " "	"	None
None known					

CHILDREN.

Name.	Sex and Age.	Name of Other Parent. (If adopted or illegitimate, so state.)	If Child is Dead, Give Date Died.
Red-Bird or Foul Red Bird, Clown or	M- 56	Masala or Thin Out or Rail or Rotation	Living
Amos Clown.	M- 55	" " "	
Hollowing or Noise, Mrs. Poor Buffalo or Grows in a Day	F- 23	" " "	About 1892
	F- 45	" " "	Living
Short Woman or Hohaiin	F- 36	" " "	Bef. Altmts.
Name unknown	Infant	Masala or Thin Out or Rail or Rotation	" "
Name unknown	"	" " "	" "
Name unknown	"	" " "	" "

REPORT ON HEIRSHIP.

(IMPORTANT—See instructions on back of last sheet.)

Cheyenne River, S. D., _____ AGENCY,

May 17, 1916 ___ 191

Decedent __Touch the Cloud__ _____ Tribe __Cheyenne River Sioux__

Pierre Series 369

Allotment No. __373__, Annuity Roll No. ____, Voucher No. ____ Qr. ___

State of domicile at time of death __South Dakota__, Date of death __Sept.5,1905__

Age __66 years__, Location of real property, State of __South Dakota__

ESTATE, so far as known, under Government control. (If inherited property is not partitioned, describe all and give proportion. If heirs have not been determined, describe property in which decedent had an apparent interest.)

REAL PROPERTY. (Original and inherited. Describe original on first line.)

No.	Name of Allottee.	Description of Lands, Date of Each Patent, and Under Which Allotted.	Heirs Found by Department. Date.	Serial No.
373 Pierre 369	Touch the Cloud	SE¼, S½ of NE¼, and the lots 1 and 2 of Sec. 6 and the NE¼ of the NE¼ of Sec. 7 in Tp. 6 N. all in Range 19 E. of the B.H.M., S.D., containing 656.75 acres.		
		Patent issued March 28, 1910.		

PERSONAL PROPERTY.

Amount.	Source.	Where Deposited.
$ None.		

PROPERTY DISPOSED OF BY WILL (included in property hereinbefore described.)

Date of will _____ 191 Date of departmental approval _____ 191 Serial No. _____

Devisee.	Relationship to Devisor.	Description of Property.

Decedent died Sept. 5, 1905, prior to the first will law. No will in legal form. Two separate, alleged wills are made a part of the record. While I am satisfied that John Makes it Long did take some kind of a statement from Touch the Cloud, from an examination of the witnesses, their manner in testifying, and the alleged wills, that these were made under duress and are not such documents as are recommended that they be disapproved.

FAMILY OF DECEASED. (Extra sheets may be used for family of deceased heirs, but the word "heir" and his name must appear after the words "Family of Decedent.")

MARRIAGES.

Name of Each Spouse of Decedent.	Married	Date of Death.	Divorced	From and Against Whom No. (If white, so state.)
	Date.	Indian custom or by whom.		Date.	Indian custom or by whom.	
First wife, name unknown.	not known.		prior to second marriage of which there is now living son born 1859.	Chey.Riv. Sioux.
Womanly	About 1859 by Indian Custom, later church.		not divorced.	
Very Yellow	Plural wife, married after Womanly and was divorced before end of marriage to Womanly.			
Rosie Touch the Cloud	Married in Church, 1864.	For prior marriages of spouses see Additional information.		

CHILDREN.

Name.	Sex and Age.	Name of Other Parent. (If adopted or illegitimate, so state.)	If Child is Dead, Give Date Died.
Unnamed Boy	m (small)	First wife, name unknown.	Long ago, before father.
Struck At,	f (young)	Womanly	Before father.
Amos Charging, First Warrior or Mrs. Hatchet Looks Around	f 55 yr.	do	living
Chief or King Woman, or Mrs. Francis In the Hole.	f 40 yr.	do	living
Killa Mise *	m 3 days		

* This child is made the subject of a separate paragraph in Additional information.

ISSUE OF DECEASED BROTHERS OR SISTERS.

Name of Nephew or Niece.	Sex and Age.	Name of Parents, and How Related.	If Dead or Dead, Give Date.
Not applicable.			

OTHER LINEAL DESCENDANTS OF DECEDENT. (Identify persons issued by allotment number, or by number on annuity roll on which last paid, describing voucher. Designate parents and grandparents through which heir inherits by letters *f, m, gf, gm,* etc.)

Name of Descendant Who Inherits Decedent. (If dead, give date and give family surviving on extra sheets.)	Age.	Name of Parents and Grandparents of Descendant.
None. of dead children.		

GRANDPARENTS OF DECEDENT. (If any are white, so state.)

Names of Father's and Mother's Parents.	Maiden.		Tribe.	If Dead, Give Date.
	Date.	Indian custom or ceremony.		
Paternal gf, Not applicable.				
Paternal gm,				
Maternal gf,				
Maternal gm,				

COLLATERAL RELATIVES. (Give line of descent from common ancestor of decedent; give names and designate parents and grandparents of heir in line from common ancestor by letters *f, m, gf, pm, ggf, ggm,* etc. Identify by allotment No. or by number on annuity roll on which last paid.)

Names of Nearest Relatives Who Survive Decedent.	If Dead, Give Date and His Heirs Being His Surviving Family.	How Related to Decedent—Order.	Amount of Line from Common Ancestor.
Not applicable.			

CHILDREN OF DECEASED CHILDREN.

Name of Grandchildren.	Sex and Age.	Name of Both Parents, How Married—Indian Custom or Ceremony. (If one is white, so state.)	If Grandchild is Dead, Give Date.
None.			

PARENTS OF DECEDENT. (If either is white, or of a different tribe, no status.)

Name.	Allotment.		Marriage.		If Either is Dead, Give Date.	Tribe.
	No.	Roll.	Date.	Indian custom or ceremony.		
Father: Not applicable.						
Mother:						

BROTHERS AND SISTERS.

Name.	Brother or Sister.	Age.	Name of Common Parent of Half or Whole Blood.	If Brother or Sister is Dead, Give Date.
Not applicable.				

ADDITIONAL INFORMATION: There is much testimony pro and con relative to the legitimacy of Rosie Touch the Cloud's child which was born subsequent to the death of Touch the Cloud. The testimony goes both ways. Clayton In the Hole and White Thunder asserted that Rosie Touch the Cloud had been haled before the Indian Court on Charges of immorality. I made a search, however of the Indian Court records and found no entry of that character. I find that there is no proponderance of testimony showing that this child was illegitimate and it must, therefore, be deemed legitimate. The legitimacy of the child, in any event is immaterial, for it died under age (shortly after birth) and consequently could not have been married, etc., so that no right and interest thereupon descended CONFLICT between the official record and the testimony. (If any, give description; if no conflict, say "none.")

The records are silent upon the facts covered under "Additional Information," and otherwise there is no conflict.

I HEREBY CERTIFY that I have made a careful investigation as to the relatives of the decedent; that my report is correct and begun Aug. 15, 1914 and concluded Oct 22, 1914 substantiated by official records and by the testimony taken at a hearing _____, 191__, under the provisions of the act of June 25, 1910 (36 Stats., 855), and that it appears that at time of the hearing the heirs of the decedent,

Touch the Cloud _____ and the descent of the estate are as follows:
(Name of decedent.)

Heirs or Devisees. (Designate which.)	Relationship to Decedent.	Description of Property. (Give element of personal property.)	Proportion Taken by Heirship, Descendant, or Devise.
Rosie Touch The Cloud or HolyWoman wife	See page 1		3/9
Amos Charging First son	son & brother of subsequently deceased son.		2/9
Warrior or Mrs. Hatchet Looks Around	daughter and sister of subsequently deceased son.		2/9
Chief Woman or Mrs. Frances In the Hole (Hold)	do		2/9

This estate descends subject to the homestead rights of the widow. I have requested the farmer in charge of the Cherry Creek District to submit an appraisal and as soon as same is received shall forward it for inclusion in this record.

Paul L. Haclum

Examiner of Inheritances.
(Official designation.)

REPORT ON HEIRSHIP.

(IMPORTANT—See instructions on back of last sheet.)

Cheyenne River AGENCY,

July 8, 1921, 191__

Decedent Mary Traversie, Tribe Cheyenne River Sioux

Allotment No. 497, Annuity Roll No. 1065, Voucher No. 4, 1st Qr., 1910
(Last on which paid.) (Year.)

State of domicile at time of death South Dakota, Date of death May 11, 1909

Age 58, Location of real property, State of South Dakota

ESTATE, as far as known, under Government control. (If inherited property is not partitioned, describe all and give proportion. If heirs have not been determined, describe property in which decedent had an apparent interest.)

REAL PROPERTY. (Original and inherited. Describe original on first line.)

Allotment.			Heirs Found at Installment.	
No.	Name of Allottee.	Description of Land, Date of Trust Patent, and Under Whose Allotted.	Date.	Serial No.
497	Mary Traversie	E/2 of Sec. 7, NE/4 of Sec. 18, NW/4 of Sec. 17, T. 15 N., R. 28 E. N. H. M. of S. B. containing 640 acres.		
		Trust patent issued April 30, 1906. Allotted under Act of March 2, 1889 (25 Stat. L., 888).		
		No apparent and no inherited interests.		

PERSONAL PROPERTY.

Amount.	Source.	Where Deposited.
49.99	Interest	Depository undesignated.

---

242 APPENDIX

PROPERTY DISPOSED OF BY WILL. (Included in property hereinbefore described.)

No will

Date of will ...., 191 Date of departmental approval ...., 191 Serial No. ....

Devisees.	Relationship to Deceased.	Description of Property.
None		

FAMILY OF DECEASED. (Extra sheets may be used for family of deceased heirs, but the word "heir" and his name must appear after the words "Family of Deceased.")

MARRIAGES.

Name of Each Spouse of Decedent.	Married.		Date of Death.	Divorced.		Three and Address (If white, so state.)
	Date.	Indian custom or by ceremony.		Date.	Indian custom or by court.	
Paul Traversie	About 1865	Ceremony	4/11/00	No Divorce		S.R.S.None
None						

CHILDREN.

Name.	Sex and Age.	Name of Other Parent? (If adopted or illegitimate, so state.)	If Child is Dead, Give Date.
Andrew Traversie	M-	Paul Traversie	Living
Mary Dupris Folks	F- 50	" "	"
Edna Swift Horse	F- 46	" "	"
Whitley Traversie	M- 46	" "	"
Edward Traversie	M- 25	" "	7/12/1899
Theophile Traversie	M- 42	" "	Living
Samuel Traversie	M- 40	" "	"
Isabelle Elizabeth LeBeau,	F- 38	" "	"
Thomas Traversie	M- 36	" "	"
Alexander Traversie	M- 34	" "	"
Charles Traversie	M- 1	" "	1889

* "Order" Additional information " show facts with regard to failure of illegitimate children and concerning adoptions.

ISSUE OF DECEASED BROTHERS OR SISTERS.

Name of Nephew or Niece.	Sex and Age.	Names of Parents and when Married.	If Dead, Give Date.
None			

OTHER LINEAL DESCENDANTS OF DECEDENT. (Identify persons named by allotment number, or by number on annuity roll on which last paid, describing voucher. Designate parents and grandparents through which heir inherits by letters f, m, gf, gm, ggf, ggm, etc.)

Names of Descendant Who Survived Decedent. (If dead, give date; and give family surviving on extra sheets.)	Age.	Names of Persons and Grandparents of Descendant.
None		

GRANDPARENTS OF DECEDENT. (If any are white, so state.)

Names of Parents and Minimum Parents.	Married.		Three.	If Dead, Give Date.
	Date.	Indian custom or ceremony.		
Paternal gf, Unknown				
Paternal gm, "				
Maternal gf, "				
Maternal gm, "				

COLLATERAL RELATIVES. (Give line of descent from common ancestor of decedent; give name and designate parents and grandparents of heir in line from common ancestor by letters f, m, gf, gm, ggf, ggm, etc. Identify by allotment No. or by number on annuity roll on which last paid.)

Names of Nearest Relatives Who Survived Decedent.	If Dead, Give Name and Use Extra Sheets for Surviving Family.	How Related to Decedent-Degree.	Ancestry in Line from Common Ancestor.
None			

CHILDREN OF DECEASED CHILDREN.

Name of Grandchildren.	Sex and Age.	Name of Both Parents Now Married—Indian Custom or Ceremony. (If child is white, so state.)	If Grandchild is Dead, Give Date.
None			

PARENTS OF DECEDENT. (If either is white, or of a different tribe, so state.)

Names.	Allotment.		Marriage.		If Either is Dead, Give Date.	Tribe.
	No.	Date.	Date.	Indian custom or ceremony.		
Father: Theophile Brugier	None		Long ago	Ind.cust	1870-80	French
Mother: Dané unknown	None		(dau. of Chief War Eagle)	About 1860	Sioux

BROTHERS AND SISTERS.

Name.	Brother or Sister.	Age.	Name of Common Parent if Son of Whole Blood.	If Brother or Sister is Dead, Give Date.
Eugene Brugier	Brother	70		Living
William Brugier	"	65	Theophile Brugier	"
Samuel Brugier	"	30	" "	"
Julia Conger	sister	75	" "	"

ADDITIONAL INFORMATION: No homestead rights involved.

This hearing was set for June 9, 1931, and continued to July 8, 1931, when the interested parties appeared with their witnesses and case was completed.

CONFLICT between the official record and the testimony. (If any, give description; if no conflict, say "none."). None

I hereby certify that I have made a careful investigation as to the relatives of the decedent; that my report is correct and substantiated by official records and by the testimony taken at a hearing held on July 8, 1931, 191, under the provisions of the act of June 25, 1910 (36 Stats., 855), and that it appears that at time of the hearing the heirs of the decedent, Mary Traversie, and the descent of the estate are as follows:

Heirs or Decedent (Designate Heirs).	Relationship to Decedent.	Description of Property. (Give amount of personal property.)	Proportion Taken by Descent.
Andrew Traversie	Son	See page one	1/9
Mary Dupris Folks	Dau.		1/9
Edna Swift Horse	Dau.		1/9
Whitley Traversie	Son		1/9
Theophile Traversie	Son		1/9
Samuel Traversie	Son		1/9
Isabelle Elizabeth LeBeau,	Dau.		1/9
Thomas Traversie	Son		1/9
Alexander Traversie	Son		1/9

M. S. Gorman

M. S. Gorman,
Examiner of Inheritance.

Sheet 1

UNITED STATES
DEPARTMENT OF THE INTERIOR
OFFICE OF THE SOLICITOR

RECEIVED
OCT 4 67

SUMMARY OF FAMILY HISTORY AND INVENTORY   EXAMINER OF INHERITANCE
BILLINGS, MONTANA

Estate of __Peter Talks__ Tribe __Cheyenne River Sioux__ No. __CR-1579__
MARRIAGES. Born - 1883 - Died - 8/14/67 - 84 years.

Names	Marriage		Date of Death	Divorce		Tribe and Allotment Numbers (If white, so state)
	Date	How		Date	How	
Mary Traversie	12/30/10	Church Ceren.	3-15-56	Never	divorced	CR-2465

CHILDREN. (Show facts regarding illegitimacy and adoption under "Additional Information.")

Names	Sex and Age	Name of Other Parent	Date of Death
CR-3279-Amy Talks	F. B. 11/17/13	Mary Traversie, CR-2465	Living

CHILDREN OF DECEASED CHILDREN.

Names	Sex and Age	Names of Both Parents (If one is white, so state)	Date of Death
None			

PARENTS. (If either is white, so state.)

Names	Marriage		Date of Death	Tribe and Allotment Numbers (If white, so state)
	Date	How		
Father:	Talks About Him	1873	Ind. Cust.	6/1/01	CR Unal.
Mother:	Mrs. Talks About Him	"	"	12/13/21	CR-1577

BROTHERS AND SISTERS.

Names	Sex and Age	Name of Common Parent if Any or Whole Blood	Date of Death
N/A			

CHILDREN OF DECEASED BROTHERS OR SISTERS.

Names	Sex and Age	Names of Both Parents	Date of Death
N/A			

5-107   Sheet 1

UNITED STATES
DEPARTMENT OF THE INTERIOR
OFFICE OF INDIAN AFFAIRS
FIELD SERVICE
Bismarck, North Dakota

March 23 ____, 19 48

SUMMARY OF REPORT ON HEIRS

Estate of __Ida Crow_____, deceased __Cheyenne River Sioux__
Allottee No. __2685__, died __February 21, 1945__, aged __83__, hearing held __November 21, 1946__
at __Cheyenne Agency, S.D.__

Heirs, at the date of hearing, in accordance with the laws of the State of __South Dakota__

Heir or Devisee	Relationship		Share
Louise Gets Off Gilbert, C.R. #1226,	dau.,		6/12
Sam Scott, C.R. #2797,	gr-son,		1/12
Amelia Scott Laundreaux, C.R. #2778,	gr-dau.,		1/12
Grover Scott, C.R. #3171,	gr-son,		1/12
Mildred Scott Philips, C.R. #5688,	gr-dau.,		1/12
Elmer Scott, C.R. #4616,	gr-son,		1/12
Bertha Scott Annis, C.R. #4126,	gr-dau.,		1/12

The trust or restricted estate of the decedent consists of:

Original allotment, appraised at _____ $ __None__
Inherited lands, appraised at _____ __29.38__
Cash, securities, or other personal restricted estate appraised at _____ __00.00__
                                            Total _____ $ __29.38__

No dower, curtesy, or homestead rights involved.

(Signed) E. J. Welch
E. J. Welch _____ Examiner of Inheritance.

Verified _____, 19____
By _____
        Chief, Probate Division.   [over]

FAMILY OF DECEASED. (Extra sheets may be used for family of deceased heirs, but the word "heir" and his name must appear after the words " Family of Deceased.")
MARRIAGES.

Name of Each Spouse of Deceased	Married		Date of Death	Divorce		Tribe and Allotment Numbers (If white, so state)
	Date	Indian Custom or by ceremony		Date	Indian Custom or by court	
Luke Nelson Gets Off	long ago before	I.C.	7-15-1894		Not divorced	C.R.Sx. Unal.
John Crow	1897	cere.	8-9-35		Not divorced	C.R.Sx. 854

CHILDREN.

Names	Sex and Age	Name of Other Parent (If adopted or illegitimate, so state)	Is Child in Trust, Cash, Date
Louise Gets Off	f. b. 1889	Luke Nelson Gets Off	Living
Sophie Gets Off	f. adult	" " "	6-17-35

CHILDREN OF DECEASED CHILDREN.

Names of Grandchildren	Sex and Age	Names of Both Parents, How Married—Indian Custom or Ceremony (If one is white, so state)	Is Grandchild in Trust, Cash Date
Sam Scott	m. b. 1909	Sophia Gets Off and Charles Scott or Summers — cere.	Living
Amelia Scott	f. b. 5-14-05	" " "	Living
Grover Scott	m. b. 1912	" " "	Living
Mildred Scott	f. b. 1916	" " "	Living
Elmer Scott	m. b. 8-2-23	" " "	Living
Bertha Margaret Scott	f. b. 1919	" " "	Living

ESTATE, so far as known, under Government control. (If inherited property is not partitioned, describe all and give proportions. If heirs have not been determined, describe property to which decedent had an apparent interest.)

REAL PROPERTY. (Original and inherited. Describe original on first line.)

Allotment		Description of Lands, Date of Trust Patent, and Under Whom Allotted	Heirs Found by Department	
No.	Name of allottee		Date	Serial No.
2685	Ida Crow	S½ Sec. 14, T. 15 N., R. 30 E., B.H.M., S. Dak., containing 320 acres, conveyed to Cheyenne River Sioux Tribe and no longer held in trust for decedent.		

ALL INHERITED INTEREST ON CHEYENNE RIVER RESERVATION CONVEYED TO CHEYENNE RIVER SIOUX TRIBE.

INHERITED INTERESTS ON SHEET 1-a

PERSONAL PROPERTY.

	Source	Where Deposited
None		

PROPERTY DISPOSED OF BY WILL (Included in property hereinbefore described).

Date of will _____ 19___. Date of departmental approval _____ 19___. Serial No. _____

Devisee	Relationship to Devisee	Description of Property
No will.		

Name	Allotment		Marriage			
	No.	Date	Date	Indian station or ceremony	If Bought in Trad, Give Date	Tribe
Father: One Horn	Unal		No record		Unknown	C.R.Sx.
Mother: Stands On The Ground	"		"	"	"	C.R.Sx.

OTHER LINEAL DESCENDANTS OF DECEDENT. (Identify persons named by allotment number, or by number on annuity roll on which last paid, describing voucher. Designate parents and grandparents through which heir inherits by letters f, m, gf, gm, ggf, ggm, etc.)

Name of Descendant Who Renders Decedent (If dead, give date, and give family surviving or heirs shown)	Age	Name of Parents and Grandparents of Descendant
None		

BROTHERS AND SISTERS.

Name	Registered on Bureau	Age	Name of Common Parent if Not of Whole Blood	If Registered on Rolls at Allot, Give Date
Unknown				

ISSUE OF DECEASED BROTHERS OR SISTERS.

Name of Nephew or Niece	Sex and Age	Names of Parents, and How Marriage	If Dead or Dead, Give Date
Unknown			

NAME OF DECEDENT (Give all names by which decedent was known) Edward Clown

for ___ M ___ or Identification No. ___ 340-A02061 ___   4/4

Date of birth ___ 01-01-08 ___ Certificate attached None Available (Taken from Realty family records)

Death: Date ___ 08-14-87 ___ Place ___ Certificate attached Memory Card

Last Place of Residence ___ Dupree, South Dakota 57623

Death determined to be: ___ X ___ Natural ___ Accidental ___ Violence ___

MARRIAGES

Names	Married Date How	Date of Birth	Date of Death	Divorced Date How	Tribe & Al. / Id. #, or Non-Indian	Deg. of Blood
Amy Talks or Red Leaf		11-17-13	Living	Never Divorced	CR-3279	4/4

CHILDREN (Show facts regarding illegitimacy and adoption under "Additional Information")

Names	Sex	Date of Birth	Name of Other Parent	Date of Death	Tribe & Al. or Ind. #	Deg. of Blood
Blaine Edward Clown	M	07-15-34	Amy Talks or Red Leaf	Living	CRU-5839	4/4
Edwina Valerie Clown	F	01-23-39	" " " " "	Living	CRU-6368	4/4
Beverly Pearl Clown	F	02-27-46	" " " " "	Living	CRU-7104	4/4
Delmar Moses Clown	M	02-25-49	" " " " "	Living	CRU-7382	4/4

CHILDREN OF DECEASED CHILDREN

Names	Sex	Date of Birth	Names of Both Parents	Date of Death	Tribe & Al. or Id. #	Deg. of Blood
None						

SEE ATTACHED PROBATE DOCUMENT OF IDA CROW ALLOTTEE CRA-2685

The following Probate Names and Probate numbers were taken from the Allotment files, filed at the Realty office, Bureau of Indian Affairs, Eagle Butte, SD

NAME	PROBATE NO.
One Horn	Unallotted – CR Sioux
Stands on Ground	Unallotted – CR Sioux
Daughter of Stands on Ground and One Horn	
Ida Crow or Two White Cows	C-43-48
Daughter of Ida Crow and Nelson Gets Off	
Sophia Gets Off (Scott)	5458-57
Children of Sophia Gets Off and Charlie Scott	
Mildred Scott (Phillips)	K-119-
Amelia Scott (Garreau/Laundreau)	RC210Z87
Bertha Scott (Annis)	RC99Z86
Elmer Scott	
Sam Agneau	

DATA FOR HEIRSHIP FINDING AND FAMILY HISTORY

PARENTS

Names	Married Date	How	Date of Birth	Date of Death	Divorced Date	How	Tribe & Al. Id. #, or Non-Indian	Deg. of Blood
Father, Amos Clown	1883	Ceremony	1862	07-22-43	Never Divorced		CR-677	
Mother, Julia Clown or Iron Cedar			1871	07-10-36			CR-2005	4

BROTHERS AND SISTERS

Names	Sex	Date of Birth	If Not of Whole Blood Name of Common Parent	Date of Death	Tribe & Al. or Id. #	Deg. of Blood
Peter or Joseph Clown	M	1894	Iron Cedar	09-03-63	CR-679	4/4
Lillie Clown Makes Trouble	F	1879	" " " "	02-22-42	CR-681	4/4
James Clown	M	1901	" " " "	04-20-69	CR-733	4/4
Mollie Clown	F	1896	" " " "	11-13-30	CR-2005	4/4
Louise Clown	F	1904	" " " "	01-15-87	CR-680	4/4
Raymond Alex Clown	M	1914	" " " "	03-31-81	CR-3317	4/4
Moses Clown	M	unknown	" " " "	1918	Unallotted	

CHILDREN OF DECEASED BROTHERS AND SISTERS

Names	Sex	Date of Birth	Names of Both Parents	Date of Death	Deg. of Blood
Elsie Clown/Slides Off	F	04-10-21	Peter J. Clown & Emily Did Not Go Home	Living	CR-4264	4/4
Orline (Annie) Clown	F	09-25-24	" " " " & " " " "	Living	CR-4729	4/4
Marjorie Clown	F	02-27-30	" " " " & " " " "	Living	CR-5217	4/4
Lucille Clown/Mandan	F	06-07-27	" " " " & " " " "	Living	CR-4954	4/4
Regina Clown/Good Bear	F	11-04-32	" " " " & " " " "	Living	CR-5550	4/4
LaRose Clown	F	1933	" " " " & " " " "	1933	DRE	
Mern Joseph Clown	M	10-11-36	" " " " & " " " "	Living	CRU-6095	4/4
Clifford Clown	M	10-11-38	" " " " & " " " "	10-01-61	CRU-6752	4/4
Lorraine Makes Trouble	F	1923	Lillie Clown & Makes Trouble	1923	SR-2147	
Esther Makes Trouble	F	02-23-30	" " " " & " " " "	Living	CR-5284	4/4
Lois Maks Trouble	F	06-04-36	" " " " & " " " "	Living	CRU-06051	4/4

GRANDPARENTS

Names	Married Date	How	Date of Birth	Date of Death	Divorced Date	How	Tribe & Al. #, or Non-Indian	Deg. of Blood
Paternal gf. Fights The Thunder	Unknown		1828	05-16-16	Never Divorced		CR-541	
Paternal gm. Thin Out or Rail			Unknown	Unknown			Before Allotments	
Maternal gf. Woman Breast	)							
Maternal gm. Red Legs	) Information on maternal grandparents unknown.							

OMB 1074

UNITED STATES DEPARTMENT OF THE INTERIOR
OFFICE OF HEARINGS AND APPEALS
HEARINGS DIVISION

Page 1   4

DATA FOR HEIRSHIP FINDING AND FAMILY HISTORY

NAME OF DECEDENT (Give all names by which decedent was known): **Amy Talks Clown**

Tribe and allottee #: **340A003279**   Deg. of Blood:

Sex **F** or identification No.:

Date of birth: **11-17-13**   Certificate attached:

Death Date: **02-27-96**   Place **IHS-Eagle Butte, SD**   Certificate attached: **Yes**

Last Place of Residence: **Dupree, SD**

Death determined to be: **X**   Married: Accident: Violent:

MARRIAGES

Names	Married Date	How	Date of Birth	Date of Death	Divorced Date	How	Tribe & Al. Non-Indian	Deg. of Blood
Edward Clown	02-27-33		01-01-08	08-14-87	Not Divorced		CRA-2061	

CHILDREN (Show facts regarding illegitimacy and adoption under "Additional Information")

Names	Sex	Date of Birth	Name of Other Parent	Date of Death	Tribe & Al. #, or Id. #	Deg. of Blood
Blaine Edward Clown	M	07-15-34	Edward Clown	living	CRD-5819	
Edwina Valerie Clown	F	01-23-39	same	living	CRU-6368	
Beverly Pearl Clown	F	02-27-46	same	living	CRU-7104	
Delmar Moses Clown	M	02-25-49	same	living	CRD-7382	

CHILDREN OF DECEASED CHILDREN

Names	Sex	Date of Birth	Names of Both Parents	Date of Death	Tribe & Al. #, or Id. #	Deg. of Blood
None.						

DATA FOR HEIRSHIP FINDING AND FAMILY HISTORY

PARENTS

Names	Married Date	How	Date of Birth	Date of Death	Divorced Date	How	Tribe & Al. #, or Non-Indian	Deg. of Blood
Father, Peter Talks	12-30-10		1883	08-14-61	none		CRA-1379	
Mother, Mary Traversie	12-30-10		1871	03-15-56			CRA-2465	

BROTHERS AND SISTERS

Names	Sex	Date of Birth	If Not of Whole Blood Name of Common Parent	Date of Death	Tribe & Al. or Id. #	Deg. of Blood
Andrew Dupris	M	1898	Mary Traversie & Edward	12-09-67	CRA-720	
Marcella Dupris	F	1899	Dupris	01-05-29	CRA-722	
Douglas Dupris	M	1891	same	01-05-23	CRA-721	

CHILDREN OF DECEASED BROTHERS AND SISTERS

Names	Sex	Date of Birth	Names of Both Parents	Date of Death	Tribe & Al. or Id. #	Deg. of Blood
Immaterial.						

GRANDPARENTS

Names	Married Date	How	Date of Birth	Date of Death	Divorced Date	How	Tribe & Al./ #, or Non-Indian	Deg. of Blood
Paternal gf. Talks About Him			1850	06-01-01			CRA-Unal.	
Paternal gm. Otter or Mrs Talks About Him	1873		1856	12-13-21	none		CRA-1577	
Maternal gf. Paul Traversie	About 1866		unknown	04-11-00			CRA-Unal.	
Maternal gm. Mary Brugier			1851	05-11-09	none		CRA-0497	

* U.S. Government Printing Office: 1976-640-097/920 Region 8

1-1001a
(April 1938)   Sheet 2

GRANDPARENTS. (If any are white, so state.)

Names	Married Date	How	Date of Death	Tribe and Allotment Number. (If white, so state)
Paternal gf. Unknown	Unknown		–	–
Paternal gm. "	Prior to		–	–
Maternal gf. Louis Knife	1852	Ind. Cust.	8/10/08	CR-1583
Maternal gm. Louise Knife	"	"	7/8/10	CR-2131

COLLATERAL RELATIVES. (Give line of descent from common ancestor of decedent; give names and designate ents and grandparents of heirs, in line from common ancestor by letters f, m, gf, gm, pgf, pgm, etc.)

Names of Nearest Relatives Who Survived Decedent	If Dead, Give Date, and Use Extra Sheets for Surviving Family	How Related—Degree	A Generation or Lines From Common Ancestor
N/A			

ADDITIONAL INFORMATION. (Discuss all material facts not clearly stated elsewhere herein. Attach extra sheets necessary.)

ddress of probable heir:

w. Amy Talks-Clown – Dupree, South Dakota

REPORT ON HEIRSHIP.

(IMPORTANT—See instructions on back of last sheet.)

CHEYENNE RIVER AGENCY, S. D. AGENCY.

DEC 18 1917

Decedent Paul Touch The Cloud ... Tribe C.R.S.

Allotment No. 1374 ... Annuity Roll No. 2372 ... Voucher No. 35 , 4th Qr.

State of domicile at time of death So. Dak. Date of death 4-24-1907

Age 53 Location of real property, State of So. Dak.

ESTATE, so far as known, under Government control. (If inherited property is not partitioned, describe all and give proportion. If heirs have not been determined, describe property in which decedent had an apparent interest.)

REAL PROPERTY. (Original and inherited. Describe original on first line.)

No.	Name of Allottee	Description of Land, Date of Trust Patent, Act Under Which Allotted	Heirs Found or Determined	Date	Serial No.
1374	Paul Touch The Cloud	Copy from Data for heirship finding			
		Tr. Pat. dated Jan. 30, 1907			
	No apparent + no inherited interests	Allotted under act Mar. 3, 1889 (25Stat. L. 888)			

PERSONAL PROPERTY.

Amount	Source	Where Deposited
None		

ADDITIONAL INFORMATION: No homestead rights involved.

CONFLICT between the official record and the testimony. (If any, give description; if no conflict, say "none.") None

I hereby certify that I have made a careful investigation as to the relatives of the decedent; that my report is correct and substantiated by official records and by the testimony taken at a hearing held on Dec. 18 1917 under the provisions of the act of June 25, 1910 (36 Stat., 855), and that it appears that at time of the hearing the heirs of the decedent Paul Touch the Cloud and the descent of the estate are as follows:

Name and relationship (Designate whole or half blood)	Enjoyment of inheritance	Disposition of property (Give amount of personal property.)	Fractional share inherited
William Chase The Bear	Son		One-ninth
Josephine Touch the Cloud	Dau.		Three-ninths
Rose	Dau.		Three-ninths
Edward Chase The Bear	Son, if any, heirs deprive		One-ninth
Isaac " " "	Same		One-ninth

EXAMINER OF INHERITANCE

CHILDREN OF DECEASED CHILDREN.

Name of Grandchildren	Sex and Age	Name of both parents, now living or dead (If one is white, so state.)	If Grandchild is Dead, give date.
None			

PARENTS OF DECEDENT. (If either is white, or of a different tribe, so state.)

Name	Allotment No.	Date	Patent	Marriage. Indian custom or ceremony	If single or dead, give date.	Tribe.
One Bear of Short Man	None				By. allotte	C.R.D.
Mother (unknown)						

BROTHERS AND SISTERS.

Name	Brother or Sister	Age	Name of common parent, or son of whole blood.	If either is dead, give date.
None known				

DATA FOR HEIRSHIP FINDING.

Allottee Paul Touch The Cloud ... Age 53

Date of death 4-24-1907.

Allotment No. 1374 Annuity No. 2372 Voucher No. 35 4th 1907.

Description of land NE¼, W½ of Lot 2, Lot 3, Sec. 35 ... etc.

Date of patent 1-30-1907.

Act under which allotted March 2, 1889 (25Stat. L. 888)

Father's name One Bear of Short Man ... Allotment No. None

Mother's name Unknown ... Allotment No. "

Spouse's name Comes To Bad ... Allotment No. 2332

Personal property None

PROBABLE HEIRS.

	ADDRESSES.
William Chase The Bear	Dupree, S. D.
Josephine Touch The Cloud	Pierre S. D. Pierre Ind. School.
Rose " " "	" " " "
Edward Chase The Bear	Dupree, S. D.
Isaac Chase The Bear	" "

Probate
5-197
(October 1948)
C-183-54
54-55
ATH

Sheet 1

UNITED STATES
DEPARTMENT OF THE INTERIOR
BUREAU OF INDIAN AFFAIRS
FIELD SERVICE

SUMMARY OF FAMILY HISTORY AND INVENTORY

(Shot At or Stump)
ESTATE OF Thomas (John) Standing Elk/ TRIBE Cheyenne River Sioux No. 1242
MARRIAGES. died November 21, 1951, at 61 yrs.

NAMES	MARRIED		DATE OF DEATH	DIVORCED		TRIBE AND ALLOTMENT NUMBER (If white, so state)
	Date	How		Date	How	
Mary Lulu Fisherman	10-29-22	cere	living	12-10-45	Court	C.R. al. 942
Cecelia Kasto	1-26-46	cere	living	Not divorced		S.R. Uhal.

CHILDREN. (Show facts regarding illegitimacy and adoption under "Additional Information.")

NAMES	SEX AND AGE	NAMES OF OTHER PARENT	DATE OF DEATH
minor			
Several/children died prior to decedent.			

CHILDREN OF DECEASED CHILDREN.

NAMES	SEX AND AGE	NAMES OF BOTH PARENTS (If one is white, so state)	DATE OF DEATH
None			

PARENTS. (If either is white, so state.)

47

NAMES	MARRIED		DATE OF DEATH	TRIBE AND ALLOTMENT NUMBER (If white, so state)
	Date	How		
Father: Matthew Standing Elk	No details known		predec.	C.R. al. 1647
Mother: Susie White Weasel	"	"	predec.	C.R. al. 2376

BROTHERS AND SISTERS.

NAMES	SEX AND AGE	NAME OF COMMON PARENT OF HALF OR WHOLE TRIBE	DATE OF DEATH
Immaterial			

CHILDREN OF DECEASED BROTHERS OR SISTERS.

NAMES	SEX AND AGE	NAMES OF BOTH PARENTS	DATE OF DEATH
Immaterial			

5-197
(October 1948)

Sheet 2   43

GRANDPARENTS. (If any are white, so state.)

NAMES	MARRIED		DATE OF DEATH	TRIBE AND ALLOTMENT NUMBER (If white, so state)
	Date	How		
Paternal gf.	Unknown			
Paternal gm.	"			
Maternal gf.	"			
Maternal gm.	"			

COLLATERAL RELATIVES. (Give line of descent from common ancestor of decedent; give names and designate parents and grandparents of heir, in line from common ancestor by letters f, m, gf, gm, ppf, ppm, etc.)

NAMES OF NEAREST RELATIVES WHO SURVIVED DECEDENT	IF DEAD, GIVE DATE; AND THE HEIRS BESIDE THE SURVIVING FAMILY	HOW RELATED—DEGREE	AGREEMENT IN LINE FROM COMMON ANCESTOR
Immaterial			

ADDITIONAL INFORMATION. (Discuss all material facts not clearly stated elsewhere herein. Attach extra sheets if necessary.)
Descent of this estate is governed by Subsec. 2, Sec. 56.0104, South Dakota Revised Code, 1939.

Probate regulations on reopenings and rehearings explained to all persons present at the hearing.

Decedent's funeral expenses paid by C.R. Tribe - to be repaid.

No will on file.

Claims on file:
$ 187.30 – Cheyenne River Sioux Tribe, Cheyenne Agency, S. Dak., covering payment for casket furnished decedent.
$ 164.85 – Cheyenne River Sioux Tribe, Cheyenne Agency, S. Dak. covering loans made to decedent.
$ 100.00 – Mary L. Standing Elk, 629 Chicago St., Rapid City, S. Dak., covering amount due from decedent for divorce settlement.
$ 100.00 – Minnie Kingman, Cheyenne Agency, S. Dak., covering board furnished decedent for four months during 1951.
$ 252.00 – J. R. Rt Hawk, Howes, S. Dak., covering loans made to decedent over a period of years.
$ 25.00 – R. G. Kandel, Cashier, First State Bank, McLaughlin, S. D., covering loan made to decedent.

Probate
5-8851
(November 1948)
C-190-61
ATH

Sheet 1

UNITED STATES
DEPARTMENT OF THE INTERIOR
OFFICE OF THE SOLICITOR

SUMMARY OF FAMILY HISTORY AND INVENTORY

Horse
ESTATE OF Edna Traversie Frazier Swift/ TRIBE Cheyenne River Sioux No. 2208
MARRIAGES. died January 31, 1957, at 54 yrs.

NAMES	MARRIED		DATE OF DEATH	DIVORCED		TRIBE AND ALLOTMENT NUMBER (If white, so state)
	Date	How		Date	How	
John Frazier (Pro. 14567-17)	11-2-02	cere	10-15-08	Not divorced		C.R. al. 476
George Swift Horse	1-1917	cere	living abt 1948	Court		C.R. al. 501

CHILDREN. (Show facts regarding illegitimacy and adoption under "Additional Information.")

NAMES	SEX AND AGE	NAME OF OTHER PARENT	DATE OF DEATH
Leonard (Sam) Frazier	m. b. 1901	John Frazier	living
Marie Frazier Lamb	f. b. 1905	"	living
William Frazier	m. b. 7-8-25	"	12-23-47
Ernest Frazier	m. b. 1899	"	9-2-46
Leona Swift Horse Cadotte	f. b. 1916	George Swift Horse	living

CHILDREN OF DECEASED CHILDREN.

NAMES	SEX AND AGE	NAMES OF BOTH PARENTS (If one is white, so state)	DATE OF DEATH
Clara Marie Frazier	f. b. 3-27-27	Ernest Frazier and Verna O. Moran	living

UNITED STATES
DEPARTMENT OF THE INTERIOR
Office of the Examiner of Inheritance
Bismarck, North Dakota

Probate
C-130-61

ATH

IN THE MATTER OF THE ESTATE OF:

EDNA TRAVERSIE-FRAZIER-SWIFT HORSE,	Cheyenne River Sioux Allottee No. 2206.	ORDER APPROVING WILL AND DECREE OF DISTRIBUTION.

This case coming on to be heard before the Examiner of Inheritance, Office of the Solicitor, Bismarck, North Dakota, and upon submission of the evidence, the following facts and conclusions of law are presented:

Notices of the hearing on this estate were duly served upon the known heirs, devisees, and other interested persons by mailing a copy of the notice to them at their last known addresses, and by posting the notices at five public places on the Cheyenne River Reservation twenty days in advance of the date of the hearing.

A hearing was duly held at Dupree, South Dakota, on October 24, 1957, for the purpose of ascertaining the heirs at law of the decedent, and the facts and circumstances surrounding the execution of an instrument in writing, dated August 1, 1955, purporting to be her last will and testament.

The evidence adduced at the hearing discloses that the decedent died on January 31, 1957, at the age of 84 years, a resident of the State of South Dakota, leaving surviving her the following heirs at law, determined in accordance with the laws of the State of South Dakota (Subsec. 1, Sec. 56.0104, S. Dak. Rev. Code, 1939), whose respective shares in the estate, had she died intestate, would be:

Leonard (Sam) Frazier, C.R. al. 1979,	son,	1/4
Marie Frazier Lamb, C.R. al. 1978,	dau.,	1/4
Leona Swift Horse Cadotte, C.R. al. 3779,	dau.,	1/4
Clara Marie Frazier, C.R. al. 5105,	gr-dau.,	1/4

By the terms of the decedent's purported last will and testament, she makes a specific devise to her grandson, Emmet Lamb, and leaves the residue of her estate to her children, Marie Frazier Lamb, Leonard (Sam) Frazier, and Leona Swift Cadotte, share and share alike. She also bequeaths the sum of $1.00 to her granddaughter, Marie Clara Frazier, and the sum of $1.00 to Verna O. Moran.

The trust lands of the decedent are situated on the Cheyenne River and Standing Rock Reservations. The Indians of those reservations have voted to accept the provisions of the Act of June 18, 1934 (48 Stat. 984; 25 U.S.C. sec. 464), which act provides that no devise to a person who is not an heir at law of the testator, or a member of the tribe having jurisdiction over the land devised, may be approved.

Order Approving Will in the Estate of
Edna Traversie- Frazier-Swift Horse, C.R. al. 2206
Page 2.

The records disclose that the beneficiaries named in the will are either heirs at law of the decedent or members of the tribe having jurisdiction over the land devised and, therefore, are eligible to take the land devised to them.

The will is not contested and is shown by the accompanying affidavits of the attesting witnesses thereto to have been properly made and executed by the decedent when she was of sound and disposing mind and memory and not actuated thereto by fraud, undue influence, coercion or duress.

NOW, THEREFORE, by virtue of the power and authority vested in the Secretary of the Interior by the Act of June 25, 1910 (36 Stat. 855; 25 U.S.C. sec. 372), as amended by the Act of February 14, 1913 (37 Stat. 678; 25 U.S.C. sec. 373), and the Act of June 18, 1934 (48 Stat. 984; 25 U.S.C. sec. 464), and pursuant to Departmental Regulations of May 29, 1947 (25 CFR 15), delegating probate authority to the Examiners of Inheritance, the within-described written instrument, dated August 1, 1955, is hereby approved as the decedent's last will and testament.

IT IS ORDERED, that the Superintendent will cause to be made a distribution of the trust estate of the decedent in accordance with her last will and testament, subject to the payment of the probate fee and allowed claims, as follows:

Clara Marie Frazier, C.R. al.	The sum of One Dollar ($1.00).
Verna O. Moran, C.R. al.	The sum of One Dollar ($1.00).
Emmet Lamb, C.R. devisee,	All of that part of the decedent's Exchange Assignment No. X-1586, described as W½W½, Sec. 23-15-26 E., B.H.M., S. Dak., containing 160 acres.
Leonard (Sam) Frazier, C.R. al. 1979, 1/3 Marie Frazier Lamb, C.R. al. 1978, 1/3 Leona Swift Horse Cadotte, C.R. al. 3779, 1/3 residuary devisees,	1/2 undivided interest in that part of the allotment of John Frazier, C.R. al. 476, described as W½, N½SE¼, N½S½SE¼, Sec. 24-16-24; SW¼, S½S½NW¼, Sec. 14-15-26 E., B.H.M., S. Dak., containing 640 acres. 1/56 undivided interest in that part of the allotment of Samuel Brugier, Standing Rock Sx. al. 1358, described as Lot 11, Sec. 16-20-23 E., B.H.M., S. Dak., containing 3.05 acres of timberland.

Order Approving Will in the Estate of
Edna Traversie-Frazier-Swift Horse, C.R. al. 2206.
Page 3.

Leonard (Sam) Frazier, C.R. al. 1979, 1/3 Marie Frazier Lamb, C.R. al. 1978, 1/3 Leona S.H. Cadotte, C.R. al. 3779, 1/3 residuary devisees,	All funds to decedent's account at the time of death, if any, subject to the payment of the probate fee and allowed claims. Any and all other trust property, real, personal or mixed, not otherwise disposed of under the terms of the will, if any there be.

The Cheyenne River Sioux Tribe filed a claim against this estate for decedent's funeral expenses in the amount of $578.29; and the Bennett Clarkson Memorial Hospital of Rapid City, South Dakota, filed a claim for expenses of decedent's last illness in the amount of $1137.50. These indebtednesses were incurred, and claims filed therefore, and claims were considered prior to the amendment of the probate regulations which impose limitations on the amounts for funeral and last illness expenses which can be allowed as preferred claims. (25 CFR 15.25 a, 2 & 6). For this reason, both claims will be allowed in full amounts, as filed, as preferred claims.

The following claims are hereby allowed and are to be paid from funds now held or hereafter accruing to the credit of the estate (unless otherwise prohibited by law), in the numerical order listed below, with no preference as to payment of the claims in the same numbered category, and subject to the payment of the probate fee:

1. $ 578.29 - Cheyenne River Sioux Tribe, Eagle Butte, S. Dak., covering decedent's funeral expenses.

   $1137.50 - Bennett Clarkson Memorial Hospital, Rapid City, S. Dak., covering expenses of decedent's last illness.

2. $1312.00 - Department of Public Welfare of South Dakota, Pierre, S. Dak., covering old age assistance grants made to decedent.

The trust estate of the decedent having been appraised at $4,801.08, a probate fee of $50.00, will be collected by the Superintendent or other officer in charge in accordance with authority found in the Act of January 24, 1923 (42 Stat. 1185; 25 U.S.C. sec. 377).

Done at the City of Bismarck, North Dakota, and dated April 13, 1961.

([illegible]) ARTHUR T. HOADLEY

Arthur T. Hoadley
Examiner of Inheritance

5-107 Sheet 1

UNITED STATES
DEPARTMENT OF THE INTERIOR
OFFICE OF INDIAN AFFAIRS
FIELD SERVICE

Pierre, South Dakota
JUN 12 1937, 19

SUMMARY OF REPORT ON HEIRS

Estate of George Hunter deceased Cheyenne River Sioux
Allottee No. 1770, died Jan. 28, 1936, aged 55yrs, hearing held April 13, 1937, at Cherry Creek, S. Dak.

Heirs, at the date of hearing, in accordance with the laws of the State of South Dakota, under the second canon of descent:

30675

HEIR OR DEVISEE	RELATIONSHIP	SHARE
Emily Hunter, nee Yellow Shield, C. R. #1126,	widow, . . .	ALL

Decedent owed a total of $23.36 on reimbursable loans analyzed as $13.92 from Cheyenne River 3% Fund, 1929-1932, and $9.44 Cheyenne River 3% Fund, 1931. It is recommended that the Superintendent be directed to apply to the settlement of these loans such funds as may be, or which may hereafter accrue, to the credit of decedent's estate, after the probate fee hereinafter assessed has first been collected, until said reimbursable indebtedness has been paid in full, this being considered a preferred claim.

It is recommended that the claim of W. M. Griffiths & Co. Licensed Indian Traders of Cherry Creek, S. Dak., in the amount of $33.75, balance due from purchase of tent and clothing, be allowed.

* If more space is necessary to give names of heirs, affix a separate sheet at this point.

The trust or restricted estate of the decedent consists of:

Original allotment, appraised at (Patent in fee.)	$
Inherited lands, appraised at	$ 1628.89
Cash, securities, or other personal restricted estate appraised at	35.31
TOTAL	$ 1664.20

No dower, curtesy, or homestead rights involved.

P. L. Hallam, Examiner of Inheritance.

Verified JUL 8 1937, 19

By [illegible]
Chief, Probate Division.

[OVER]

ESTATE, so far as known, under Government control. (If inherited property is not partitioned, describe all and give proportion. If heirs have not been determined, describe property in which decedent had an apparent interest.)

REAL PROPERTY. (Original and inherited. Describe original on first line.)

No.	Allotment Name of allottee	Description of Land, Date of Trust Patent, and Dates When Allotted	High Fees by Department	
			Date	Serial No.
1770	George Hunter	W½ of Sec. 19, T. 9 N. of R. 20, E. of the B. H., M. in South Dakota, containing 315.96 acres, for which trust patent issued on April 27, 1909, under the act of March 2, 1889 (25 Stat. 888), as amended. Fee patent #742804 (9473D-19) was issued for all of this allotment on May 7, 1920.		
		See Sheet 1-a for inherited interests.		

PERSONAL PROPERTY.

Amount	Source	Where Deposited
$ 35.31	Individual Indian Money, $24.13 of which has accrued since decedent's death.	Supervision, Supt., Cheyenne Agency, South Dakota.

PROPERTY DISPOSED OF BY WILL. (Included in property hereinbefore described.)

Date of will _____ 19___ Date of departmental approval _____ 19___ Serial No. _____

Devisees	Relationship to Devisor	Description of Property
No will involved.		

GRANDPARENTS OF DECENT. (If any are white, so state.)

Names of Parents and Mother's Parents	Married		Tribe	If Dead, Give Date
	Date	Indian custom or ceremony		
(Paternal) gf., Immaterial				
(Paternal) gm., "				
(Maternal) gf., "				
(Maternal) gm., "				

COLLATERAL RELATIVES. (Give line of descent from common ancestor of decedent; give names and designate parents and grandparents of heir, in line from common ancestor by letters f, m, gf, gm, ggf, ggm, etc. Identify by allotment No. or by number on annuity roll on which last paid.)

Names of Nearest Relatives Who Survived Decedent	If Dead, Give Date and Surviving Family	How Related to Decedent—Degree	Amount of Link from Common Ancestor
Immaterial			

ADDITIONAL INFORMATION: None

CONFLICT between the official record and the testimony. (If any, give description; if no conflict, say "none.")

None

FAMILY OF DECEASED. (Extra sheets may be used for family of deceased heirs, but the word "heir" and his name must appear after the words "Family of Deceased.")

MARRIAGES.

Name of Each Spouse of Decedent	Married		Date of Death	Divorced		Where and Allottees No. (If white, so state)
	Date	Indian custom or by ceremony		Date	Indian custom or by ceremony	
Emily Hunter, nee Yellow Shield	1905	church ceremony	living	not divorced		C.R. #1126

CHILDREN.

Names	Sex and Age	Name of Other Parent* (If adopted or illegitimate, so state)	If Child is Dead, Give Date
None			

*Under "Additional information" show facts with regard to fathers of illegitimate children and concerning adoptions.

CHILDREN OF DECEASED CHILDREN.

Names of Grandchildren	Sex and Age	Names of Both Parents, How Married— Indian Custom or Ceremony (If this is which, so state)	If Grandchild is Dead, Give Date
None			

PARENTS OF DECENT. (If either is white, or of a different tribe, so state.)

Names	Allotment			Marriage		If Either is Dead, Give Date	Tribe
	No.	Date	Date	Indian custom or ceremony			
Father: Net Skirt or Charging Hawk	2495					7-18-17	Cheyenne River Sioux
Mother: Four Horses (Her Four Horses)	2986					1-20-18	do

OTHER LINEAL DESCENDANTS OF DECEDENT. (Identify persons named by allotment number, or by number on annuity roll on which last paid, describing voucher. Designate parents and grandparents through which heir inherits by letters f, m, gf, gm, ggf, ggm, etc.)

Name of Descendant Who Survived Decedent (If dead, give date and give family surviving on extra sheets)	Age	Names of Parent and Grandparents of Descendant
None		

BROTHERS AND SISTERS.

Names	Brothers or Sisters	Age	Name of Current Parent if Not of Whole None	If Brothers or Sisters is Dead, Give Date
Immaterial				

ISSUE OF DECEASED BROTHERS OR SISTERS.

Name of Nephew or Niece	Sex and Age	Names of Parents, and How Married	If Child is Dead, Give Date
Immaterial			

UNITED STATES DEPARTMENT OF THE INTERIOR
OFFICE OF HEARINGS AND APPEALS
HEARINGS DIVISION
Court International Building
2550 University Avenue West, Suite 416N
St. Paul, Minnesota 55114
Telephone: (651) 917-0172

PROBATE NO:
IP TC 320 G 99

NOTICE
TO ALL PERSONS HAVING AN INTEREST IN THE
SUBJECT MATTER OF THIS PROCEEDING

NOTICE IS GIVEN that on **OCT 3 1 2000** a decision was entered in the Estate of Blaine Edward Clown, a Cheyenne River Sioux Indian, 340U-005819. A copy is attached to this Notice.

This decision becomes final sixty (60) days from the date of mailing of this notice unless within such period a written petition for rehearing shall have been filed with the Superintendent by an aggrieved party in accordance with the provisions of 43 C.F.R. §4.241.

The petition for rehearing must be under oath and must give a concise but complete statement of the grounds upon which it is based. If it is based upon newly discovered evidence, it shall be accompanied by the affidavits of witnesses stating fully what the new testimony is to be. The petition shall include the petitioner's justifiable excuses for the failure to discover and present that evidence, tendered as new, at the hearings held prior to the issuance of the decision.

No claim shall be paid and no distribution shall be made during the pendency of proceedings following the filing of a petition for rehearing, except as specifically authorized by the Administrative Law Judge.

Distribution of the estate and payment of claims will be made by the Superintendent, Bureau of Indian Affairs, Cheyenne River Agency, P.O. BOX.325, EAGLE BUTTE, SD 57625 For information contact the Superintendent's office, attention: REALTY.

PARTICULAR NOTICE IS GIVEN TO THE PARTIES IN INTEREST HERE NAMED:

ABERDEEN AREA OFC, BIA, LAND TITLES & RECORDS OFC, 115 4TH AVE SE, ABERDEEN, SD 57401
SUPERINTENDENT, CHEYENNE RIVER AGENCY, P.O. BOX 325, EAGLE BUTTE, SD 57625
SUPERINTENDENT, STANDING ROCK AGENCY, P.O. BOX 8, FORT YATES, ND 58534
OFFICE OF TRUST FUND MGMT, ATTN: AREA TRUST FUNDS ACCOUNTANT, 115 4TH AVE SE,
   MC 590, ABERDEEN, SD 57401
MRS. BEVERLY CLOWN P.O. BOX 151   DUPREE, SD 57623
BLAINE CLOWN JR.   DUPREE, SD 57623
DONALD RED THUNDER P.O. BOX 313   EAGLE BUTTE, SD 57625
SHEILA RED THUNDER P.O. BOX 1588   EAGLE BUTTE, SD 57625
FLOYD G. CLOWN P.O. BOX 1303   EAGLE BUTTE, SD 57625
DOUGLAS CLOWN WAR EAGLE, P.O. BOX 459, DUPREE, SD 57623
CHARLENE RED THUNDER   P.O. BOX 55, BEMIDJI, MN 56619
1ST FINANCIAL BANK USA P.O. BOX 98   DUPREE, SD 57623
CHEYENNE RIVER SIOUX TRIBE LOAN PROGRAM P.O. BOX 590 EAGLE BUTTE, SD 57625

Dated and mailed: **OCT 3 1 2000**

By _Barbara Gottke_

Marcel S. Greenia
Marcel S. Greenia
Administrative Law Judge

INDIAN PROBATE NO.
IP TC 320 G 99

UNITED STATES DEPARTMENT OF THE INTERIOR
OFFICE OF HEARINGS AND APPEALS
HEARINGS DIVISION

IN THE MATTER OF THE ESTATE OF)	ORDER DETERMINING
BLAINE EDWARD CLOWN,)	HEIRS AND DECREE OF
340U-005819)	DISTRIBUTION
DECEASED CHEYENNE RIVER SIOUX INDIAN)	

This is a proceeding to determine the heirs and to settle the estate of Blaine Edward Clown. It is conducted pursuant to the power and authority vested in the Secretary of the Interior as delegated to the undersigned (43 C.F.R. §4.1).

Upon receipt of the notice of death, a hearing was duly noticed and held at Eagle Butte, South Dakota, on 04/14/2000, and the record thereafter closed.

FINDINGS OF FACT AND CONCLUSIONS OF LAW, based upon the evidence, are as follows:

1. Vital Statistics. The decedent was born 07/15/1934 and died of natural causes at Rapid City, South Dakota, on 04/04/1999, a domiciliary of the State of South Dakota.

2. Family History. The decedent's only marriage was to Beverly M. In The Woods Clown, which ended by the decedent's death. The decedent and Beverly had six children; namely, Blaine, Douglas, Mary Ellen, Donald, Doreen and Sheila. Mary Ellen and Doreen died as infants prior to the decedent's death, and the other four children survive the decedent. The decedent was also the father of one other child; namely, Floyd, and he survives the decedent. The decedent acknowledged Floyd as his own by signing a Paternity Affidavit on 05/20/1956. The decedent did not adopt any children and none of his children were adopted by other parents.

In finding Floyd Gene Clown to be an heir of the decedent, the provisions of Section 5 of the Act of February 28, 1891, are applicable. That Act provides that for the purpose of determining the descent of land to the heirs of any deceased Indian, every Indian child, shall for such purpose be deemed the legitimate issue of his or her father. Estate of Francis Sears, IA-1397 (May 27, 1965).

3. Restricted or Trust Assets. At the date of death, the decedent was the owner of trust or restricted property, real and/or personal, located on the Cheyenne River and Standing Rock Reservations listed on the inventories attached, and other reporting documents. There is a cash balance, plus accruing interest, in the decedent's Individual Indian Money Account.

Page 2

Estate of Blaine Edward Clown
IP TC 320 G 99

4. Claims. A claim was filed against the decedent's estate by the 1st Financial Bank USA, P.O. Box 98, Dupree, South Dakota 57623, on 05/11/1999, in the amount of $5,596.52, for a loan made to the decedent on 10/11/1975. Pursuant to S.D. Codified Laws Ann. § 15-2-8, the six-year statute of limitations has expired. Therefore, this claim is disallowed.

A claim was filed against the decedent's estate by the Cheyenne River Sioux Tribe located in Eagle Butte, South Dakota 57625, on 05/11/1999, in the amount of $21,793.48, for a loan made to the decedent on 03/25/1977. Because this claim was subsequently cancelled by the Cheyenne River Tribal Resolution and written-off by the Council, this claim is disallowed.

5. Will. No Last Will and Testament was submitted for probate in this estate, and there is no substantial evidence to conclude that the decedent executed a Will.

6. Heirs. At death, the decedent was survived by heirs at law whose respective names, enrollment numbers, birth dates, relationships, and interests in the estate under the statutes of descent of the State of South Dakota [S.D. Codified Laws Ann. § 29A-2-102(2) (1995)] and The Standing Rock Act of June 17, 1980, Pub. L. No. 96-274, Sec. 3(a)(1), 94 Stat. 537 (1980) are as stated in paragraph A below.

WHEREFORE, IT IS ORDERED AND DECREED:

A. Trust real property located on the Standing Rock Reservation in the State of South Dakota, including any income accrued after the decedent's death, shall pass to:

Beverly M. In The Woods Clown, 340U-6189	06/09/1937	spouse	½ or	5/10
Blaine Edward Clown Jr., 340U-8143	03/20/1957	son		1/10
Douglas Andrew Clown, 340U-8435	01/28/1958	son		1/10
Donald Peter Red Thunder, 340U-9205	12/21/1961	son		1/10
Sheila Ann Red Thunder, 340U-9934	06/13/1965	daughter		1/10
Floyd Gene Clown, 340U-8208	08/23/1955	son		1/10

All other trust property located in the State of South Dakota (**with the above exception**), including any income accrued after the decedent's death, and trust personalty in the decedent's Individual Indian Money account, which passes under the laws of the State of domicile of decedent, shall pass to:

Beverly M. In The Woods Clown, 340U-6189	06/09/1937	spouse	all

B. The Superintendent or other officer in charge distribute the estate to the heirs as stated in paragraph A above.

Page 3

Estate of Blaine Edward Clown
IP TC 320 G 99

C. The distribution of interests remaining in trust or in restricted status is to be made subject to the burden of payment of allowed claims as stated in paragraph 4 above.

THIS DECISION IS FINAL FOR THE DEPARTMENT UNLESS A PETITION FOR REHEARING IS TIMELY FILED IN ACCORDANCE WITH 43 C.F.R. §4.241 WITHIN 60 DAYS FROM THE DATE HEREOF AS SET FORTH IN THE NOTICE ATTACHED HERETO, OR UNLESS A PETITION FOR REOPENING IS FILED PURSUANT TO 43 C.F.R. §4.242. NO CLAIMS SHALL BE PAID AND NO DISTRIBUTION SHALL BE MADE DURING THE PENDENCY OF PROCEEDINGS FOLLOWING THE FILING OF A PETITION OF REHEARING, EXCEPT AS SPECIFICALLY AUTHORIZED BY THE ADMINISTRATIVE LAW JUDGE.

Done at St. Paul, Minnesota, on:

OCT 3 1 2000
Date

Marcel S. Greenia
Marcel S. Greenia, Administrative Law Judge
Court International Building
2550 University Avenue West, Suite 416N
St. Paul, Minnesota 55114

Attachments

vlj

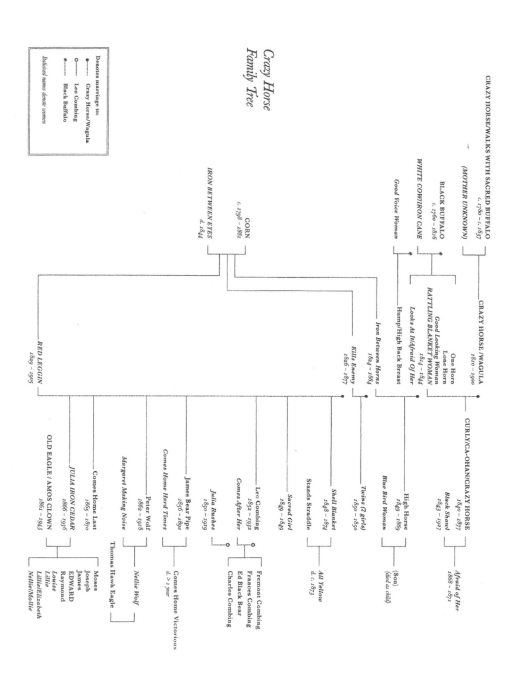

Crazy Horse Family Tree

Denotes marriage to:
● ———— Crazy Horse/Waglula
○ ———— Leo Combing
✳ ———— Black Buffalo

Italicized names denote women

The following pages contain a notarized copy of the male side of the family tree.

Family History Chart

(I) Applicant
Blaine E. Clown Sr.
Tribe: C.R.S.T.
BD: 7-15-34 DOD 4-4-1999

Blaine--Children:
Blaine E. Clown Jr.
Charlene Red Thunder.
Douglas A. War Eagle.
Mary Ellen Clown.deceased.
Donald P. Red Thunder.
Doreen Amy Clown.deceased.
Sheila Red Thunder.

(II) Father
Edward Clown
Tribe: C.R.S.T.
BD: 1-1-08 DOD: 8-14-87

Other Children;
Edwina Bernard.
Beverly Bagola.
Delmar Clown Sr.
Floyd Clown Sr.

(II) Mother
Amy(Talks) Clown
Tribe: C.R.S.T.
BD: 11-17-13 DOD: 2-27-96

(III) Grandfather
Amos Clown
Tribe: C.R.S.T.
BD: --1863 DOD: --1943

Other Children;
Moses.
Joe.
James.
Raymond.
Lillie.
Louise.

(III) Grandmother
Iron Cedar-Julia
Tribe: C.R.S.T.
BD: --1866 DOE: 7-10-1936

(III) Grandfather
Peter/Red Leaf Talks
Tribe: C.R.S.T.
BD: --1889 DOD: 8-14-1966

Other Children; Step-
Douglas Dupris.
Andrew Dupris.
Marcella(Dupris)RedBird.

(III) Grandmother
Mary Traverise-Dupris
Tribe: C.R.S.T.
BD: --1870 DOD: 3-15-1956

(IV) Great-grandfather
Fights The Thunder
Tribe:
BD: 1828 DOD: --1916
2-Wives.

(IV) Great-grandmother
Thin Out And Rail Rotation
Tribe:
BD: DOD:

(IV) Great-grandfather
Crazy Horse/Worm/Kills at Nigh
Woman Breast,
Tribe:
BD: --1810 DOD: --9-7-1900

(IV) Great-grandmother
Red Leg-Leggin Corn
Tribe: Minniconjou.
BD: --1825 DOD: --5-22-1900

(IV) Great-grandfather
James Talks about Him
Tribe: C.R.S.T.
BD: DOD:

(IV) Great-grandmother
Otter/Nancy Knife
Tribe:
BD: --1856 DOD:

(IV) Great-grandfather
Paul Traverise
Tribe: C.R.S.T.
BD: --1845 DOD: 4-11-1900

(IV) Great-grandmother
Mary Bruguier
Tribe:
BD: --1846 DOD: 5-11-1909

Red Thunder and Iron Branch/Melt None.
Parents of Fights The Thunder.
Fights The Thunder and Rail/Rotation.
Their Children;
Cega-Paul Red Bird.
Amos Clown.
Grows In A Day/Lucy Poor Buffalo.

Walks With Sacred Buffalo and Mother Unknown Parents.
Crazy Horse/Worm/Kills at Night/Woman Breast.
1st Wife-Rattle Blanket Woman-- Crazy Horse 2.
2nd Wife--Iron Between Horns--High Horse.
3rd Wife--Kills Enemy--Two Children, both died.
4th Wife--Red Leg-Leggin, her Children;
Leo Combing.
James Bears Pipe.
Peter Wolf.
Coming Home Last.
Shell Blanket.
Iron Cedar/Julia Clown.
Unnamed Infant Girl.

August Traverise and Santee Woman, Parents of Paul.
Paul Traverise and Mary Bruguier,
Their Children;
Andrew Paul.   Elizabeth Lebeau
Whitley.   Edna Frazier
Edward.
Theophile.   MARY Traverise-Dupris-Talks.
Sam.
Thomas.
Alex.
Charles.

Lone Horn and Stiff Leg, Parents of Talks.
James Talks about Him and Otter/NancyKnife
Their Children;
George Talks.
Peter Talks.
Charlie Talks.
Book/Agne(Talks)Widow.
Ellen(Talks)Black Moon,her Mother
is Susie White Weasel.